MONTVALE PUBLIC LIBRARY
062857

THE BOOK OF GNS3

THE BOOK OF GNS3

Build Virtual Network Labs Using Cisco, Juniper, and More

by Jason C. Neumann

San Francisco

THE BOOK OF GNS3. Copyright © 2015 by Jason C. Neumann.

All rights reserved. No part of this work may be reproduced or transmitted in any form or by any means, electronic or mechanical, including photocopying, recording, or by any information storage or retrieval system, without the prior written permission of the copyright owner and the publisher.

Printed in USA

First printing

19 18 17 16 15 1 2 3 4 5 6 7 8 9

ISBN-10: 1-59327-554-4
ISBN-13: 978-1-59327-554-9

Text stock is SFI Certified

Publisher: William Pollock
Production Editor: Serena Yang
Cover Illustration: Tina Salameh
Interior Design: Octopod Studios
Developmental Editor: Jennifer Griffith-Delgado
Technical Reviewer: Jeremy Grossmann
Copyeditors: Gillian McGarvey and Kim Wimpsett
Compositor: Susan Glinert Stevens
Proofreader: James Fraleigh
Indexer: BIM Indexing & Proofreading Services

For information on distribution, translations, or bulk sales, please contact No Starch Press, Inc. directly:

No Starch Press, Inc.
245 8th Street, San Francisco, CA 94103
phone: 415.863.9900; info@nostarch.com
www.nostarch.com

Library of Congress Cataloging-in-Publication Data

Neumann, Jason C.
The book of GNS3 : build virtual network labs using Cisco, Juniper, and more / by Jason C. Neumann.
pages cm
Includes index.
Summary: "Shows readers how to create and manage virtual networks on a PC using the popular open-source platform GNS3, with tutorial-based explanations"-- Provided by publisher.
ISBN 978-1-59327-554-9 -- ISBN 1-59327-554-4
1. Computer networks--Computer simulation. I. Title.
TK5105.5.N4865 2015
004.6'8--dc23

2014040973

No Starch Press and the No Starch Press logo are registered trademarks of No Starch Press, Inc. Other product and company names mentioned herein may be the trademarks of their respective owners. Rather than use a trademark symbol with every occurrence of a trademarked name, we are using the names only in an editorial fashion and to the benefit of the trademark owner, with no intention of infringement of the trademark.

The information in this book is distributed on an "As Is" basis, without warranty. While every precaution has been taken in the preparation of this work, neither the author nor No Starch Press, Inc. shall have any liability to any person or entity with respect to any loss or damage caused or alleged to be caused directly or indirectly by the information contained in it.

BRIEF CONTENTS

MONTVALE PUBLIC LIBRARY

CONTENTS IN DETAIL

3 CONFIGURATION 19

4 CREATING AND MANAGING PROJECTS 31

5 INTEGRATING HOSTS AND USING WIRESHARK 47

FOREWORD

Networks are everywhere. They connect all kinds of businesses, from local bookshops to huge corporations to universities, across multiple cities and continents. Networks are conceptually simple to understand, yet they are becoming more and more complex, with innovation in areas such as Software Defined Networks (SDN), the Internet of Things (IoT), and other technologies just around the corner.

To understand, design, and manage today's complex networks, network professionals must not only master the theory but also practice and validate concepts in these ever-changing environments. This is where GNS3 comes in: it gives users immense flexibility to build their own networking labs, allowing them to experiment with new network features, capture packets to dissect protocols, and verify configurations for later deployment on real devices. All of this is done without the need to invest in expensive hardware.

GNS3 is a powerful and adaptable tool, evolving to now integrate multiple vendors and iterating to meet the growing needs of network professionals. But how do you master GNS3 itself and where do you start?

In *The Book of GNS3,* Jason covers everything that network engineers, administrators, and people studying for certifications need to get started, from walking you through installing and configuring GNS3 to creating and managing your projects. Jason digs deep while showcasing the true breadth of the software, covering topics like how to capture network packets, how to connect to real networks and live switches, and how to include advanced systems such as Juniper's vSRX Firefly and Cisco's IOS-XRv in your labs. He spends significant time explaining concepts and giving tips that will make you an expert user in no time.

Jason's book is ideal to harness GNS3 and make the most out of your network labs. Whether you are a beginner in the networking space or a seasoned professional, I can guarantee that you will walk away learning something new.

Jeremy Grossmann
Co-founder of GNS3
May 2015

ACKNOWLEDGMENTS

It's been said that it takes a village to raise a child, and GNS3 is everyone's baby. I'd like to thank all the people who have helped to create and promote GNS3 and make it the awesome software tool that it is. You're all great!

Special thanks to:

- My wife, Sharon, for her patience and for allowing me to be a GNS3 übergeek
- Jeremy Grossmann, our benevolent GNS3 dictator
- Christophe Follot, the creator of Dynamips, the man who started it all
- Julien Duponchelle, the silent code master
- Stephen Guppy, who answers more email in a day than I do in a year
- Mark Blackwell, GNS3 evangelist extraordinaire
- Flávio J. Saraiva, Dynamips guru
- Chris Welch, the creator of GNS3 Workbench and Jungle crowd control
- Radovan Brezula, who can make any network OS run in GNS3
- Daniel Lintott—we can convert that project, but let's use Debian!
- Rene Molenaar of gns3vault.com, u bent groot. Dank u veel!
- Chris Bryant of the Bryant Advantage, Bulldogs unite!

- Jeremy Cioara, Cisco God extraordinaire (grip #1)
- Keith Barker, Cisco God extraordinaire (grip #2)
- Andrew Coleman, GNS3 Super Moderator, get some sleep!
- The GNS3 Crowd Funders—you know who you are!

I'd also like to extend special thanks to everyone at No Starch Press for all their help with creating *The Book of GNS3*. In particular, I'd like to thank:

- Jennifer Griffith-Delgado—you're the best!
- Serena Yang—you've been very patient with me, and you're awesome!
- Bill Pollock, the NSP overlord

Because I'm a schmuck, I'm sure that I've forgotten loads of important people, but rest assured that I appreciate you too! Let me now say to all you unnamed souls out there: thank you!

INTRODUCTION

I started using GNS3 early in its development and took to it like a duck to water. From the beginning I could see it was going to be an invaluable networking tool. I've used it to get hands-on experience with operating systems such as Cisco IOS, Junos OS, and Arista, as well as to pass quite a few network certification exams. To this day, I use it on a regular basis to test router configurations before deploying real equipment to the field. *The Book of GNS3* is my way of sharing this great resource with other networking professionals, like you.

Who This Book Is For

This book is for anyone involved with networking routers, switches, or firewalls. Whether you use Cisco, Juniper, Arista, Vyatta, or some other network operating system, GNS3 is a great alternative to building physical labs. Unlike labs that use physical equipment, GNS3 virtual labs let you create and save unlimited network configurations, without having to tear apart an existing lab. This book covers all the details to get your projects up and running fast.

What's in This Book

The Book of GNS3 guides you through installing, configuring, and running GNS3 on Windows, OS X, and Linux, and it shows you some geeky and fun tricks along the way. Whether you're just getting started or have used GNS3 before, I think you'll find a new appreciation for how much is possible when you have the right tool. I don't cover TCP/IP networking fundamentals, but I do provide plenty of examples of how to configure GNS3 devices.

My Approach

The most effective way of learning is by doing. That's why I use a tutorial-based approach to creating fully functional multivendor labs using GNS3. The tutorials explain how to build and configure labs using the virtual devices introduced in the chapters. I provide examples of configuring Cisco IOS, Junos OS, and Juniper vSRX Firefly, and more. You don't need to be an expert with network operating systems because I'll guide you step-by-step through the configurations. You could spend days, or even weeks, searching the Web to figure out how to configure features such as connecting to live switches, creating a virtual access server, or connecting your virtual labs to the Internet. But there's no need to do that after you read *The Book of GNS3*.

Book Overview

The Book of GNS3 guides you through the installation and use of GNS3, and each chapter introduces new concepts that build on skills from previous ones. You'll learn how to create and manage simple to complex projects, using only a single computer or sharing the load across multiple computers.

- **Chapter 1, Introducing GNS3**, covers what GNS3 is and how it works, provides an overview of GNS3, and discusses the benefits of virtual networks.
- **Chapter 2, Installing a Basic GNS3 System**, discusses installing GNS3 on Windows, OS X, and Linux, and it explains the benefits of using virtual appliances to run GNS3 as an alternative to installing it directly on your PC.
- **Chapter 3, Configuration**, looks at installing a Cisco IOS image and setting up your first virtual router using Dynamips. You'll also learn the importance of setting an Idle-PC value for Dynamips routers.
- **Chapter 4, Creating and Managing Projects**, teaches you to configure a virtual router. After that, you'll look at all the toolbar options and create a simple two-router network.

- **Chapter 5, Integrating Hosts and Using Wireshark**, shows you how to install VPCS and use it to add simple PC-like hosts to your projects. You'll learn how to add full-blown virtual PCs using VirtualBox and create a lab using a virtual Cisco IOS router and a VirtualBox Linux PC. You'll then learn about capturing packets using Wireshark.
- **Chapter 6, Juniper Olive and vSRX Firefly**, explains how to install QEMU and use it to create your own virtual Juniper router. You'll create a network using Juniper and Cisco, learn how install Juniper vSRX Firefly, and configure a basic vSRX firewall.
- **Chapter 7, Device Nodes, Live Switches, and the Internet**, demonstrates the built-in device nodes in GNS3 and explains how they can be used to conserve resources on your PC. You'll also learn how to connect your GNS3 projects to live switches and the Internet.
- **Chapter 8, Cisco ASA, IDS/IPS, and IOS-XRv**, takes you from setting up GNS3 devices to configuring them. You'll create a Cisco ASA firewall and an IDS/IPS and create a network lab using Cisco IOS-XRv.
- **Chapter 9, Cisco IOS on Unix and NX-OSv**, continues the theme of device creation. You'll learn how to install Cisco IOS on Unix and create a virtual NX OS switch using NX-OSv.
- **Chapter 10, Cool Things to Do on a Rainy Day**, presents some fun things you can do with your new GNS3 knowledge, such as creating a simulated access server to managing your devices and deploying GNS3 virtual device configurations to real Cisco routers.
- **Appendix A, Help! I've Fallen and I Can't Get Up**, discusses some common problems that you may encounter in GNS3 and provides solutions to correct them.
- **Appendix B, Cisco Hardware Compatible with GNS3**, lists Cisco routers that are compatible with GNS3 and what Cisco IOS image files work best.
- **Appendix C, NM-16ESW and IOU L2 Limitations**, provides information about IOS on Unix and NM-16ESW Cisco switches that are used in GNS3.

Now, get ready to dive into GNS3. Before embarking on this journey, be sure to kiss your family goodbye because once you get started, you won't be able to stop!

1

INTRODUCING GNS3

GNS3 is a cross-platform graphical network simulator that runs on Windows, OS X, and Linux, and it's the collaborative effort of some super-talented, industrial-strength nerds—folks such as Christophe Fillot, Jeremy Grossmann, and Julien Duponchelle, just to name a few. Fillot is the creator of the MIPS processor emulation program (Dynamips) that allows you to run Cisco's router operating system, and Grossmann is the creator of GNS3. He took Dynamips and integrated it, along with other open source software, into an easy-to-use graphical user interface. Duponchelle assists with coding GNS3, and his contributions have helped to advance the software.

GNS3 lets you design and test virtual networks on your PC, including (but not limited to) Cisco IOS, Juniper, MikroTik, Arista, and Vyatta networks, and it's commonly used by students who need hands-on experience with Cisco IOS routing and switching while studying for the Cisco Certified Network Associate (CCNA) and Cisco Certified Network Professional

(CCNP) exams. But that merely scratches the surface of what GNS3 can do. In this chapter, I discuss what GNS3 is, as well as the benefits and limitations of the software.

Why Use GNS3?

Before the wonders of virtualization, network engineers, administrators, and students had to build labs with physical hardware or rent time on a rack. Both options can be expensive and inconvenient, and they limit the network designs available to you. Software simulation programs such as RouterSim and Boson NetSim have been around for a long time, too, but these limited applications merely simulate the commands of Cisco IOS. Cisco Education does offer cheaper virtualized rack rental, based on Cisco IOS on Unix (IOU), but it allows you to practice on only specific preconfigured network configurations. It also requires that you have an active Internet connection to access the labs. Cisco also offers a product named Virtual Internet Routing Lab (VIRL) that's similar to GNS3, but it requires an annual fee, limits the number of objects you can use in your labs, and uses only simulated Cisco operating systems.

GNS3, on the other hand, allows you to customize your network labs to exactly meet your needs, create unlimited projects using Cisco and non-Cisco technology, add unlimited objects to your projects, and access those projects anytime, regardless of Internet connectivity. GNS3 provides maximum flexibility for your designs through a combination of emulated hardware devices that run real network operating systems such as Cisco IOS, simulated operating systems such as NX-OSv, and the ability to share resources across multiple computers.

Emulated Hardware

GNS3's graphical interface allows you to create virtualized network labs with a variety of routers, switches, and PCs, but it really shines when it's paired with Cisco IOS. Unlike similar applications, GNS3 doesn't merely mimic Cisco IOS commands or features. Instead, it uses a backend hypervisor application to emulate the hardware that runs Cisco IOS. Because only the hardware is emulated, you run an actual IOS image file on your PC. All the configuration commands and output come from a real IOS, and theoretically, any protocols or features that an IOS version supports are available to use in your network designs. This functionality distinguishes GNS3 from programs such as RouterSim, Boson NetSim, or VIRL, which simulate the entire experience and provide only limited environments, commands, and scenarios for you to work with.

Simulated Operating Systems

In addition to emulated hardware, GNS3 integrates simulated operating systems, and they can be fully networked to other GNS3 devices. One such example is Cisco IOU, which I cover in Chapter 9. IOU consists of a series of Linux binary files that emulate the features of IOS images, and it's fully supported by GNS3.

In addition to Cisco IOS, GNS3 can integrate Quick Emulator (QEMU) and VirtualBox virtual machines running operating systems such as Linux, BSD, or Windows. For example, to practice installing and configuring an Apache web server on Linux, just add a VirtualBox virtual machine (VM) running Linux and Apache to GNS3 and test it by browsing to it from another VirtualBox host. All of this is done within the GNS3 user environment. If you want to throw a firewall in front of your Apache server, you could use a Cisco router, adaptive security appliance (ASA) firewall, or even a Linux-based firewall such as Vyatta.

Scalability with the GNS3 Server

GNS3 leverages client-server technology; much like a web browser connects to a web server to access and display web pages, the GNS3 graphical user interface (GUI) program accesses a GNS3 server, allowing it to start, stop, and otherwise control GNS3 devices. This allows your projects to scale because they're not restricted to running on a single computer. If you work with large or complex topologies, you can also run the GNS3 server program on a different PC than the GNS3 GUI program. If you have access to a high-end server with a lot of memory and processing power, you can install the GNS3 server program on the server hardware but control all the devices from the GNS3 GUI program running on a more modest PC.

Virtual Connectivity

The true beauty of GNS3 lies in its ability to network your virtual devices together, usually using protocols such as Internet Protocol version 4 (IPv4) and Internet Protocol version 6 (IPv6), to create labs that can run on just a single computer. Some of the simplest designs may have only a few components, like the project shown in Figure 1-1.

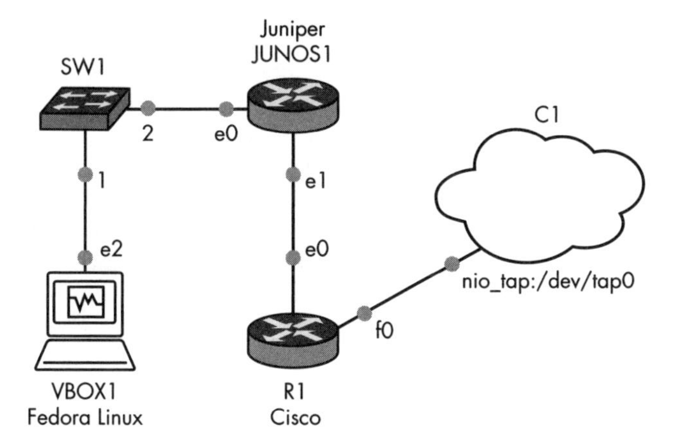

Figure 1-1: A GNS3 topology integrating Fedora Linux, Cisco, and Juniper routers

The project in Figure 1-1 allows a Fedora Linux host to access the live Internet via a switch, a Juniper router, a Cisco router, and finally a GNS3 Cloud node. That's a simple network, but you can create complex networks made up of a dozen or more routers, switches, and PCs, like the design in Figure 1-2.

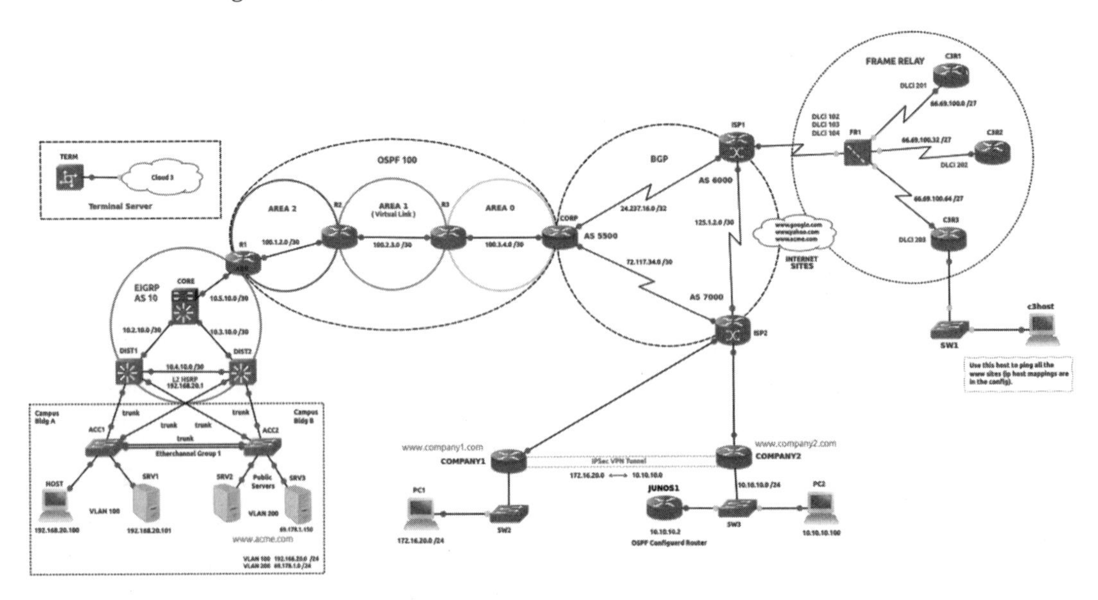

Figure 1-2: A complex, multiprotocol GNS3 topology

The project in Figure 1-2 is configured with more than 25 devices, including redundant switch blocks, EtherChannel, L2 Hot Standby Routing Protocol (HSRP), Frame Relay, Enhanced Interior Gateway Routing Protocol (EIGRP), Open Shortest Path First (OSPF), and Border Gateway Protocol (BGP), but the project can be run on a modestly configured PC. To keep your devices straight, you can also annotate your designs with colored, scalable text, as I've done in this example. If you have a laptop, you can even take projects on the road to present to clients, solve design issues, or study for certification exams. CCNA or CCNP candidates can also create all the training labs necessary to learn Cisco's exam material, practice with real operating systems, and study from anywhere.

GNS3 has the ability to bridge virtual interfaces in your lab devices to one or more physical Ethernet interfaces in your PC. This allows you to connect your virtual networks to real hardware such as routers, switches, and other PCs. For example, you can run two or more GNS3 networks using multiple PCs and connect the PCs together using an Ethernet crossover cable or a physical switch. Doing so gives you the capability to connect all GNS3 devices across all the PCs. (I affectionately refer to this as a GNS3 *ubernet*!)

Open Source Integration

GNS3 performs its magic by leveraging open source technologies, including Dynamips, QEMU, and VirtualBox. It can run Juniper, Arista, and many other network operating systems as easily as Cisco IOS.

The Dynamips Hypervisor

To emulate Cisco hardware, GNS3 comes bundled with Dynamips, a wonderful application created in 2005 by Christophe Fillot of France and kept current by contributions from Flávio J. Saraiva and others. The Dynamips hypervisor program can emulate Cisco 1700, 2600, 3600, 3700, and 7200 series router hardware. Thanks to Dynamips, you can quickly and easily configure these router models with a variety of emulated Cisco network SLOT and WAN interface cards (WICs) in GNS3. Virtual input/output (I/O) cards allow you to add multiple Ethernet interfaces, switch modules, and serial ports to your devices. You can even add or remove memory on a per-device basis, depending on your project requirements and Cisco IOS version.

QEMU and VirtualBox

You can add QEMU and VirtualBox virtual machines to GNS3 and use them in your projects. These devices can be linked to other GNS3 devices to form a complete end-to-end network. For example, you can connect a VirtualBox host to a series of switches and routers and permit it to access resources on another VirtualBox host on that network. In this scenario, you can configure and test all sorts of routing protocols as well as features such as network address translation (NAT), access control lists (ACLs), and virtual private networks (VPNs). Naturally, your physical computer's hardware places restrictions on your resources, but modern computers have many unused resources just waiting to be tapped by GNS3.

A Few Limitations

GNS3 is not without its limitations. Dynamips has been limited in such a way that you cannot use it in a production environment, making it useful only for education. Additionally, switching is limited to a modest command set, unless you integrate one or more physical Catalyst switches into your GNS3 projects. Fortunately, IOU helps bridge some of this gap.

Some Assembly Required

All great things come at a price, and GNS3 is no exception. Most notably, GNS3 requires one or more Cisco IOS images to run on your virtual Dynamips routers, and GNS3 does not provide them. Images can be copied from a router you own or through a Cisco connection online (CCO) account, if you have a contract with Cisco.

Limited Emulation

Dynamips is unable to emulate the application-specific integrated circuit (ASIC) hardware of Cisco's advanced Catalyst switches. This is a minor setback for the aspiring CCNA or even CCNP, but it does hamper aspiring Cisco Certified Internetwork Experts (CCIEs) who need the switches' advanced features. However, the versatility of GNS3 allows you to integrate your GNS3 virtual labs with actual Catalyst switches. This can greatly reduce the cost of creating a CCIE lab, and because most of the lab is virtualized, it allows for greater flexibility in your configurations.

When you don't need those advanced features, you can add a virtual switch module, like the Cisco NM-16ESW, to one of your virtual Cisco routers to create a simple layer 3 switch. This device should satisfy modest switching needs, including virtual local area networks (VLANs), 802.1Q trunking, spanning-tree, EtherChannel, and multiprotocol routing using EIGRP, OSPF, BGP, and other protocols. Lastly, Cisco IOU images can be used to emulate Cisco switches, and they provide more commands than the Dynamips switch module.

Hamstrung Network Performance

Another GNS3 limitation is network performance. Because Dynamips is an emulator that doesn't provide any hardware acceleration, throughput is restricted from 1.5Mb to 800Mb per second, depending on which IOS you use and your configuration. This may seem like a limitation, but it's actually a good thing because it prevents users from virtualizing Cisco hardware and placing it into production environments. Imagine if emulated devices ran at full throughput: every network nerd from here to Timbuktu would install virtual routers on cheap PCs and use them in production networks, effectively stealing Cisco's intellectual property. If that happened, Cisco would have come down on the Dynamips developers like a proverbial ton of bricks, and GNS3 wouldn't exist today. This limitation has little to no effect when using GNS3 for education and testing.

Final Thoughts

Now that I've hit the highlights of GNS3, I hope you're as excited as I am to use it on your own computer. Unlike similar applications or tools, GNS3 gives you complete control, leaving you free to use your imagination to create, learn, and develop elaborate networks that meet your needs. Furthermore, you can do it all without the hassle of spending a ton of money on routers and switches only to end up with a room full of noisy, electricity-sucking hardware.

In the next chapter, I'll show you how to install GNS3. Let's get started!

2

INSTALLING A BASIC GNS3 SYSTEM

Say good-bye to the world of hardware and say hello to GNS3! It's a whole new way to learn networking. In this chapter, I'll guide you through the process of installing a basic GNS3 system on Microsoft Windows, Mac OS X, and Ubuntu Linux.

A basic installation consists of the GNS3 application and a few helper applications. On Windows and OS X, all prerequisite applications come bundled in the GNS3 installer package, which is available from the GNS3 website (*http://www.gns3.com/*).

When installing on Linux, you can download and install GNS3 through a platform-specific package manager or directly from source code. The principles used for installing from source code can be applied to just about any Unix-based system, and it is a great way to ensure that you have the latest software.

General Requirements

The requirements for running GNS3 are largely determined by the operating system you're installing on, the model and number of routers you want to use in your projects, and whether you integrate external programs like QEMU or VirtualBox into your designs. Most computers purchased in the last few years should be able to run this base installation without a hitch.

That said, if you decide to move beyond creating projects using only Cisco routers and incorporate other virtual environments into your GNS3 designs (such as Linux, BSD, ASA, IDS, or Juniper), you'll want as much horsepower as you can get your hands on. The more memory and processing power you have, the better everything will run because programs like QEMU and VirtualBox require RAM to run their guest operating systems, and they compete with your native operating system for CPU time. You'll also need additional disk space to store your guest operating systems.

You can visit the GNS3 website to verify the requirements for your operating system, but a good rule of thumb for a simple base install is the following:

- 1.5 GHz processor
- 4GB RAM
- 250MB free disk space

These are the *minimum* specifications, and a system that has them should be able to run a simple GNS3 topology using a handful of Cisco routers. Of course, as your projects become larger and more complex, GNS3 will benefit greatly from a more powerful system.

NOTE *If the installation instructions look overwhelming right now, never fear! Jump ahead to the "GNS3 Appliances" on page 14 to learn how to download a pre-built GNS3 appliance, and dive right in.*

Installing on Microsoft Windows

Compared to other operating systems, installing GNS3 on top of Windows is a no-brainer. The Windows installer package includes almost all of the applications GNS3 needs, plus a few extras not found on other platforms, and everything installs with little user intervention.

The Windows installer includes a few extra useful applications, including QEMU, used for Juniper and ASA; Wireshark, a popular network monitoring program; PuTTY, a Windows terminal emulation program; and VPCS, a simple DOS-like command simulator for testing connectivity using the `ping` and `traceroute` commands. The installer contains both a 32-bit and a 64-bit version of GNS3, and it should install the correct version automatically.

Follow these steps to install GNS3 on Windows:

1. Download the GNS3 all-in-one installer from the GNS3 website (*http://www.gns3.com/*) and launch it to begin installation.
2. Click **Next** on the Setup Wizard screen, and click **I Agree** on the License Agreement screen.
3. Select the folder where you want the installer to place a shortcut to the application on the Start Menu, and then click **Next**. (The default folder is *GNS3*.)
4. You can then choose the components to include in your installation, as shown in Figure 2-1. The default option installs all components to create a fully functional GNS3 system, including Wireshark, VPCS, and QEMU. To save disk space, or if you don't need these added features, uncheck those options. WinPCAP is required for NIO Ethernet cloud connections, and Dynamips is required to create projects using Cisco routers and switches. Make your selections and then click **Next**.

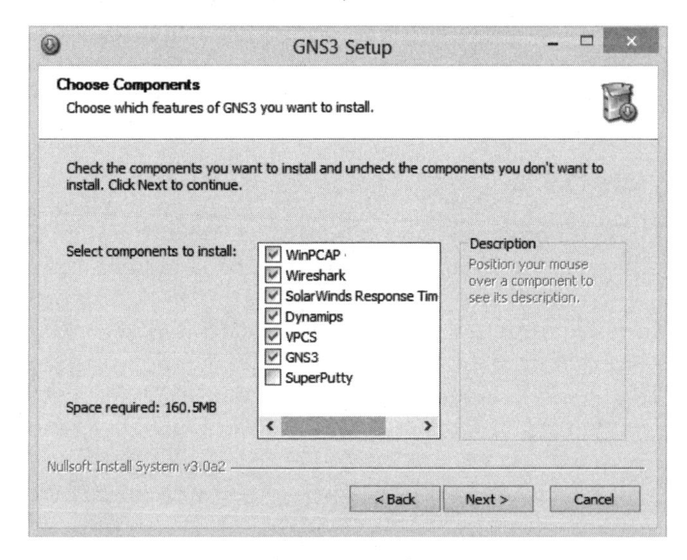

Figure 2-1: Choosing the GNS3 components to install

5. You should see the Choose Install Location screen, as shown in Figure 2-2. To install GNS3 to an alternative location, enter the new location in the Destination Folder field and click **Install**.
6. Continue following all the prompts to complete the installation. I recommend you accept all default settings.

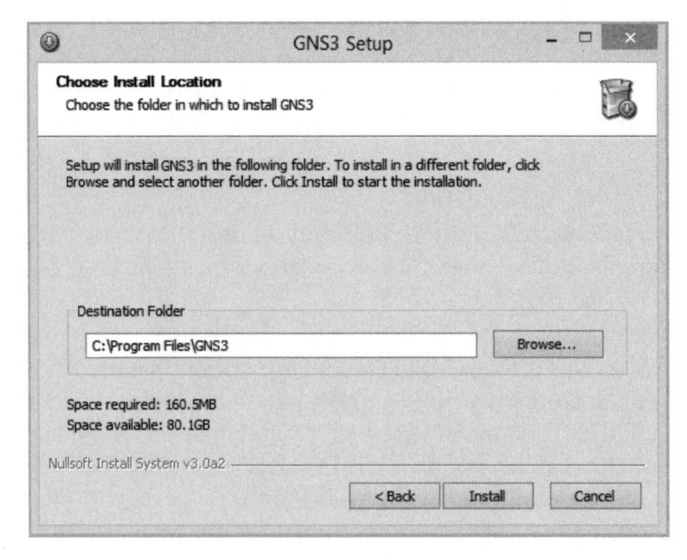

Figure 2-2: Choosing the destination folder location

Upon completion, GNS3 should place an icon on your desktop.

Installing on OS X

GNS3 is supported only on Intel-based Macs running OS X. You should probably make sure you have the latest version of OS X before you run GNS3.

To install the GNS3 application on OS X, download the appropriate installer from the GNS3 website (*http://www.gns3.com/*), and then double-click the installer and a DMG disk image file will appear on your desktop. Double-click the image file to open the *GNS3* folder, and drag the GNS3 icon to your *Applications* folder, as shown in Figure 2-3.

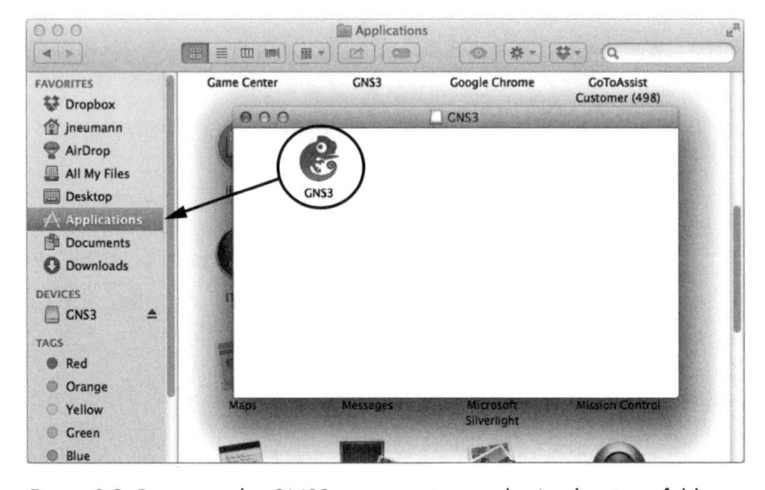

Figure 2-3: Dragging the GNS3 program icon to the Applications *folder*

To run GNS3 on current OS X versions, you might have to right-click the installed application icon and select **Open** the first time you run it. You'll be prompted with a dialog warning you that the package is from an unidentified developer and asking if you're sure you want to open the application. Click the **Open** button to circumvent this OS X Gatekeeper feature. GNS3 will start normally from then on, without any warnings.

Installing on Ubuntu Linux

GNS3 runs well on many different Linux distributions, but there's an unfortunate lack of documentation for most of them. In this section, I'll strip away the mystery and show you how simple it is to get GNS3 running on a Unix-based platform. I've chosen to cover Ubuntu because it's one of the most commonly used distributions.

There are two ways to install GNS3 on Linux. You can install a bundled package through your package manager or you can install from source code. Using a packaged install is quick and easy, but the downside is that you're stuck with whatever version of GNS3 has been ported to your specific platform, which may not be the latest version. This is where a source install comes in handy. Installing from source requires only a few extra steps and provides you with the latest version of GNS3. Even though I highly recommend installing from source code, we'll cover both methods here.

Installing GNS3 from Packages

To install GNS3 using the Advanced Package Tools, open the terminal program and enter the following command:

```
$ sudo apt-get install gns3
```

When prompted, enter your password. The output from this command displays a list of packages that will be installed and shows how much disk space will be used by the installation. The installer prompts you to confirm that this is okay before proceeding. When confirmed, the packages are installed and GNS3 is ready to run.

You can start the application from the terminal program by entering `gns3` or launching GNS3 from your display manager's application menu. You're now ready to configure GNS3.

Installing GNS3 from Source Code

Installing from source code ensures that you get the latest version of GNS3 and is, in my opinion, the best way to install GNS3 on Unix-based systems. No matter which version of Linux you're using, you should be able to use these instructions as a guide to get GNS3 up and running on your system. In the following example, I'll use Ubuntu Linux as a framework, but keep in mind that these instructions can be applied to just about any Unix-based distribution. The primary difference between distributions is the dependencies that are required and how you install them. Be sure to check the GNS3 website for the latest dependency requirements.

I've installed GNS3 on Solaris, FreeBSD, OpenBSD, Ubuntu, Mint, OpenSUSE, Fedora, Fuduntu, Debian, Arch, Gentoo, Kali, Netrunner, and PCLinuxOS, so I'm sure you can run it on your system, too!

Download and unzip the installation files from the GNS3 website (*http://www.gns3.com/*).

Extracting the Source Code

When you download GNS3 for Linux, you're provided a ZIP file that contains the Linux source code. Upon extracting the file you will see individual ZIP files for each program that GNS3 uses. Unzip the GNS3 source file using the following command, replacing *x* with your version of the file:

```
$ cd ~/Download
$ unzip GNS3-x-source.zip

dynamips-x.zip
gns3-gui-x.zip
gns3-server-x.zip
vpcs-x.zip
iouyap-x.zip
```

Next, you will update the Ubuntu package manager.

Updating the Package Manager

Updating your package manager's index files ensures that you install the most current versions of the dependencies. On Ubuntu, open the terminal program and enter:

```
$ sudo apt-get update
```

Installing Dependencies

GNS3 dependencies and package names are specific to each distribution of Linux, so you'll need to download the ones for your operating system. You also might want to check the GNS3 website beforehand as dependencies can change over time. On Ubuntu, enter the following commands:

```
$ sudo apt-get install python3-dev
$ sudo apt-get install python3-setuptools
$ sudo apt-get install python3-pyqt4
$ sudo apt-get install python3-ws4py
$ sudo apt-get install python3-netifaces
```

After installing all the python packages, move on to Dynamips.

Installing Dynamips

You'll need to install a few more packages on your Ubuntu system before compiling Dynamips:

```
$ sudo apt-get install libpcap-dev
$ sudo apt-get install libelf-dev
$ sudo apt-get install uuid-dev
$ sudo apt-get install cmake
```

Next, unzip the source code file, compile, and install Dynamips using the following commands. Replace `x` with your version of the software.

```
$ unzip dynamips-x.zip
$ cd dynamips-x
$ mkdir build
$ cd build
$ cmake ..
$ make
$ sudo make install
```

When you're finished, you should have a file named *dynamips* in your */usr/local/bin/* directory. Change the program's ownership to root and the file permissions to executable. This permits Dynamips devices to connect to the Internet or to live hardware like Cisco switches using your PC's Ethernet adapter.

```
$ sudo chown root /usr/local/bin/dynamips
$ sudo chmod 4755 /usr/local/bin/dynamips
```

For folks who are concerned about security, there is an alternative. You can achieve the same functionality without providing root-level permissions to Dynamips. The following works on Ubuntu and should work on most systems running a Linux kernel 2.2 or greater. This method does not work on BSD-based systems.

```
$ sudo apt-get install libcap2
$ sudo setcap cap_net_raw,cap_net_admin+eip /usr/local/bin/dynamips
```

Next, you'll install the GNS3 server and GUI source files.

Installing the GNS3 Server and GUI

GNS3 consists of two main applications: a server application and a GUI application. The server application runs in the background on your PC and is generally not seen by normal users. It runs and manages all the helper applications, such as Dynamips, QEMU, and VirtualBox. The GUI application provides the frontend user experience, and it's where you interact with GNS3.

```
$ unzip gns3-server-x.zip
$ unzip gns3-gui-x.zip
```

To complete the install, run the GNS3 setup script for each application. This step requires elevated root-level privileges, so have your root password handy. Start with the GNS3 server.

```
$ cd gns3-server-x
$ sudo python3 setup.py install
```

Next, install the GNS3 GUI application.

```
$ cd gns3-gui-x
$ sudo python3 setup.py install
```

When the installation finishes, the application is installed under */usr/local/bin/*.

Next, install the Virtual PC Simulator (VPCS) by unzipping the *vpcs* ZIP file and running the `mk.sh` installer script. This software simulates a simple host PC and can be used to test routers in your projects.

```
$ unzip vpcs-x.zip
$ cd vpcs-x/src
$ ./mk.sh
$ sudo cp vpcs /usr/local/bin
```

The final step is specific to Ubuntu and a few other Linux distributions, and it is necessary due to their implementation of the Gnome Desktop. Without this command, the program will run fine, but some of the menu icons won't display in GNS3.

```
$ gconftool-2 --type Boolean --set /desktop/gnome/interface/menus_have_icons True
```

To start the program, enter the following terminal command:

```
$ gns3
```

That's it! You're now ready to move on to configuring GNS3 and creating projects.

GNS3 Appliances

An alternative to installing GNS3 on your PC is to use a preconfigured *GNS3 appliance*. A GNS3 appliance is simply a virtual machine that comes with GNS3 already installed. GNS3 appliances are extremely flexible because they run using an application like VirtualBox. VirtualBox is free and runs on most operating systems (including Windows, OS X, Linux, and FreeBSD).

A Few Pros and Cons

There are several advantages to running GNS3 in a virtual environment. The primary ones are ease and portability. Most of the setup work has been done for you and you'll have a portable GNS3 installation that can be moved from one PC to another. If you buy a new computer, you can copy the appliance to the new PC and everything should run exactly as before, regardless of the hardware or operating system your new computer is running.

On the other hand, your host machine needs to have a fast processor and plenty of RAM if you want your guest OS and GNS3 to run well, especially if you create large or complex projects. And because you're emulating the guest OS's hardware, your project might take a slight performance hit depending on the underlying hardware.

GNS3 WorkBench

There are several GNS3 appliances to choose from, but I recommend GNS3 WorkBench (*http://rednectar.net/gns3-workbench/*), shown in Figure 2-4. The developer has done a good job making the interface clean, and configuration is fairly straightforward. Built on top of Linux, GNS3 WorkBench comes with GNS3, Wireshark, and VPCS preinstalled. It also comes with a bunch of exercises and preconfigured labs to help you prepare for Cisco's CCNA certification exams. Many of the labs contain problems to troubleshoot, with the objectives clearly spelled out.

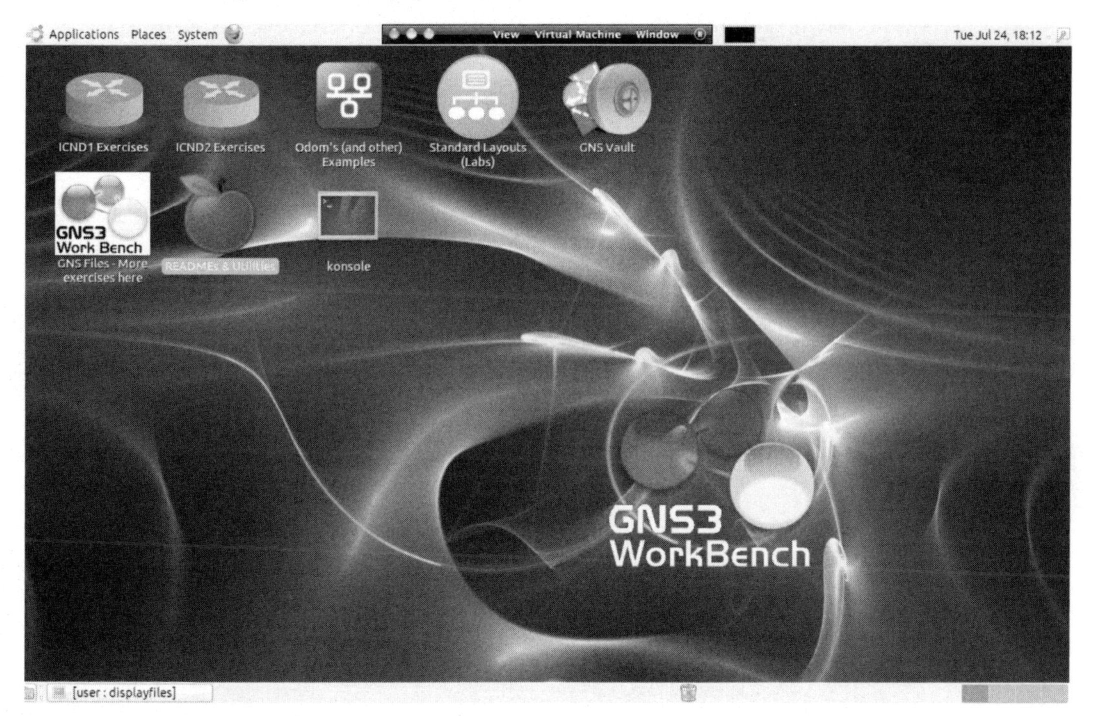

Figure 2-4: GNS3 WorkBench

GNS3 WorkBench assumes the user has a minimal level of Linux experience, but some previous Linux experience is helpful. Linux shell scripts are included to assist you with installing Cisco IOS, and the labs are designed so that they only need a couple of IOS images to work. As a bonus, the developer has included a bunch of exercises from the GNS3 Vault. The GNS3 Vault website (*http://www.gns3vault.com/*) is dedicated to all things GNS3, has a strong focus on Cisco education, and provides practice exercises for anyone preparing for Cisco CCNA or CCNP certification.

Installing GNS3 WorkBench

GNS3 WorkBench is free and available only as a VMware virtual machine. However, you can import the virtual Disk Image and run the appliance using VirtualBox. If you have a desire to natively run the appliance using VMware, visit their website (*http://www.vmware.com/*) and verify that your platform is supported. Otherwise, I recommend using VirtualBox (*http://www.virtualbox.org/*) because it supports more platforms—specifically, Windows, Linux, FreeBSD, and OS X—and is free for all of them.

Before you begin, make sure your workstation has 10GB of hard disk space free and that you've installed VirtualBox. To install GNS3 WorkBench under VirtualBox, download the GNS3 WorkBench appliance from the GNS3 website (*http://www.gns3.com/*), and follow these steps:

1. Launch VirtualBox and create a new virtual machine by clicking **New** from the startup screen. After the wizard opens, click **Continue** to begin.
2. Name your virtual machine, choose **Linux** as the Operating System and **Ubuntu** as the Version (as shown in Figure 2-5), and then click **Continue**.

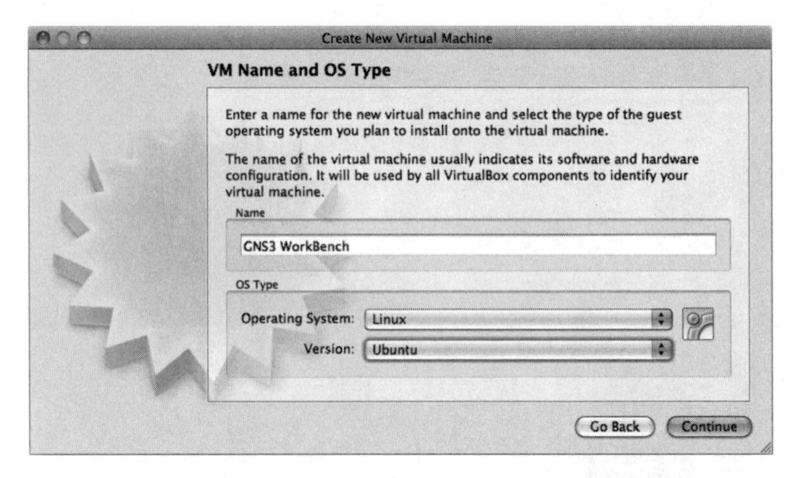

Figure 2-5: Creating a new Ubuntu Linux virtual machine for GNS3 WorkBench

3. Adjust the memory settings as required and click **Continue** to advance to the Virtual Hard Disk dialog. Then, check the **Use existing hard disk** radio button, click the yellow folder icon, and browse to the location where you saved your GNS3 Workbench files. Select the file named *GNS3 WorkBench.vmdk*, be sure there's a check next to **Start-up Disk**, and click **Continue**, as shown in Figure 2-6. This is the virtual equivalent of removing a hard drive from one PC and installing it in another.

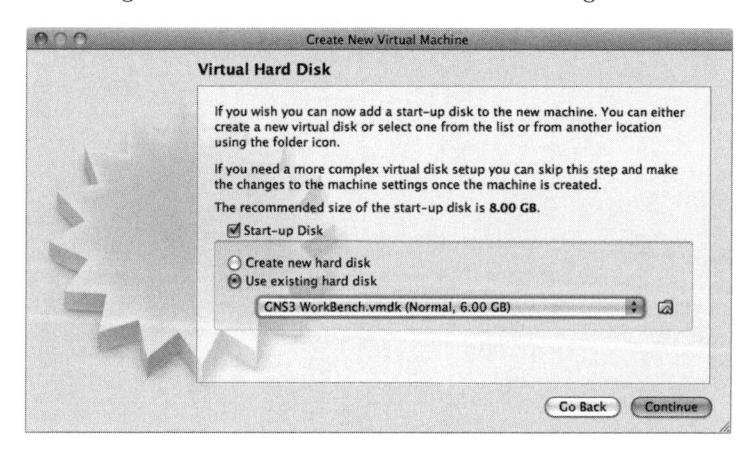

Figure 2-6: Selecting the VMware Disk Image to use with VirtualBox

4. Click **Next** and **Complete** to finish the Install.
5. Finally, launch GNS3 WorkBench and install the guest additions. Guest additions software provides the hardware drivers for your new virtual machine. Click **Devices ▸ Install Guest Additions** and follow the onscreen instructions. On FreeBSD, guest additions are installed via the *virtualbox-ose-additions* package.

NOTE *If your host PC has extra RAM, you may want to give GNS3 WorkBench 2GB of RAM (or more), instead of the 1GB default. 1GB of RAM is minimal for GNS3. Increasing the available memory will improve performance.*

After you complete the install, click **Start** to boot up Ubuntu. Instructions on how to configure and use GNS3 WorkBench should appear.

Final Thoughts

In this chapter, you've learned that GNS3 can be installed on just about any operating system and that you don't need a PhD in Computer Science to do it. That's not to say it installs as easily on every system. Some Linux distributions, for example, may not have a GNS3 package at all (or the available package may be too outdated to meet your needs), but that's the beauty of open source software: you can install directly from the source code. Another potential pitfall is that all the necessary dependencies—or the proper version of those dependencies—might not be available for your operating system version, and that's a guaranteed showstopper. In that case, I recommend you use an appliance like GNS3 WorkBench, or use VirtualBox and install a guest operating system that, like Ubuntu, fully supports GNS3.

With GNS3 installed, you're ready to move on to the next chapter where you'll learn how to configure GNS3 and create projects.

3

CONFIGURATION

Installing GNS3 is only the first step on the road to creating projects; the second step is configuration. Fortunately, GNS3 has never been easier to configure, and you need to perform only a few tasks. In this chapter, I'll cover the basic GNS3 configuration options you need to get IOS routers up and running using Dynamips.

Acquiring an IOS Image

The virtual Dynamips routers provided by GNS3 are emulated hardware devices. Like a freshly formatted PC hard drive, your virtual routers are patiently waiting for you to install an operating system so they can do something useful. What they need is Cisco IOS!

Before you can boot up a router, you'll need to install and configure at least one Cisco IOS image file in GNS3, though you're on your own when it comes to acquiring one. IOS is the intellectual property of Cisco Systems and not ordinarily available to the public. Additionally, because the GNS3 developers have no affiliation with Cisco, they can't legally supply you with an IOS image either (so please don't ask).

The simplest way to acquire an IOS image file is to copy an image from a Cisco router that you own. The upside to this approach is that you're not stealing an image; you already have an IOS image that's licensed for your router. The downside is that GNS3 supports only a few models out of the hundreds that Cisco manufactures, and your router may not be one of them. (See Appendix B for a complete list of compatible Cisco routers and hardware configurations.)

To copy an IOS image file from a router to a workstation, log on to your router and use the Cisco `copy` command to copy the image file from your router's flash memory to an FTP server. If you don't know the name of your IOS image file, you can use the `show flash` command on your router. In the following example, the IOS image filename is *c7200-ios-version.bin*; my FTP server is running on a PC with the IP address 192.168.1.25, and my FTP username and password are *jason* and *mypass*, respectively.

```
# copy flash:c7200-ios-version.bin ftp://jason:mypass@192.168.1.25
```

When the command is executed from the router, the image file will be copied from the router's flash memory to an FTP server running on 192.168.1.25 using the supplied credentials.

If you want to use TFTP instead, download a free TFTP server from the Jounin website (*http://tftpd32.jounin.net/*). When the server is installed and running, use the following `tftp` command to copy the file from your router to your TFTP server:

```
# copy flash:c7200-ios-version.bin tftp
Address or name of remote host []? 192.168.1.25
Destination filename [c7200-ios-version.bin]? <enter>
```

Press ENTER after `Destination filename [c7200-ios-version.bin]` to complete the copy.

If, on the other hand, you don't own a Cisco router, there are more unsavory ways to find IOS image files, as you'll surely find with a simple Internet search. While companies like Cisco and Juniper have turned a blind eye to this sort of thing in the past (as long as the software is used only for educational purposes), you may not want to use a bootleg version of Cisco IOS. Such images may work just fine, but there's always the possibility that they contain malware or have been tampered with in unexpected ways.

Lastly, if you work for a large company that happens to be a Cisco partner, you should be able to log on to the Cisco website using your partner credentials and get any IOS image you desire. Be aware that this sort of activity could be grounds for marching you to the corporate gallows, so get permission before using your company account.

However you obtain an IOS image, you can use only image files that are designed for router models supported by GNS3, and some IOS versions for a given model may work better than others. If you find that a Dynamips router is acting persnickety, try swapping the IOS for a different version because this often corrects the problem.

NOTE *In general, stay away from c26xx images because they seem to be the least stable!*

Choosing the right router and IOS image is critical to creating stable projects. Recommended IOS versions are c36xx, c37xx, and c7200 (but not the c7200p) because these are the most stable versions for Dynamips and GNS3. Consider the IOS version number, as well. While new IOS versions provide the latest bells and whistles, older versions tend to use fewer PC resources, such as processor power and memory. If you're creating simple projects for CCNA study, you might want to use an older IOS from the 12.2 or 12.3 train to conserve resources, but if you're studying for your CCIE, you might need to install the newest IOS available.

Setting Up Your First IOS Router

Once you have an IOS image, you need to do a few things before you can start using your virtual routers. First, verify the path to Dynamips (this is specific to Linux). Next, copy your IOS images to a folder and then add the images to GNS3. Finally, set an Idle-PC value for each IOS image that you've added to GNS3. I'll walk you through these steps now.

Configuring Dynamips

On Windows and OS X, the preferences should be set up for you, but on Linux you should verify that the path to the Dynamips application is correct. Go to **Edit ▸ Preferences**, select **Dynamips**, and click the **General settings** tab, as shown in Figure 3-1.

Verify that the Path to Dynamips field points to */usr/local/bin/dynamips*. If you've installed the Dynamips application in some other directory, set the path to that directory instead.

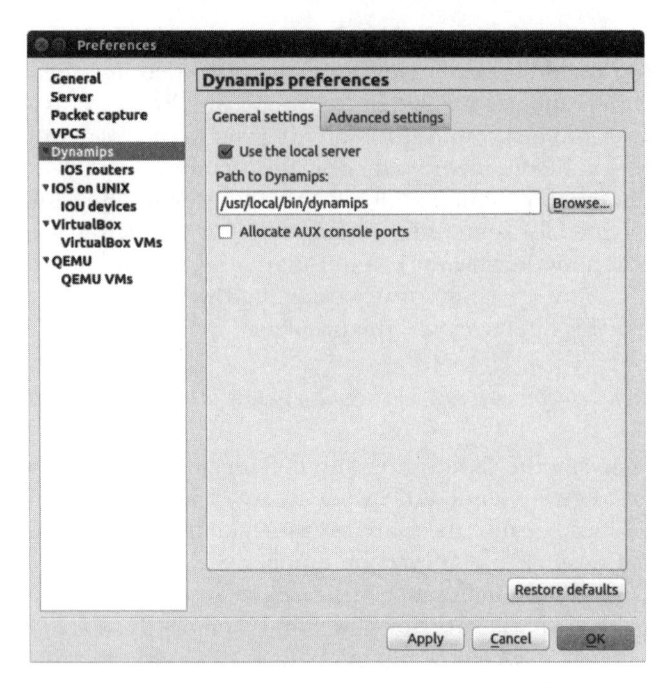

Figure 3-1: Dynamips preferences, General settings tab

Next, click the **Advanced settings** tab to display the settings in Figure 3-2.

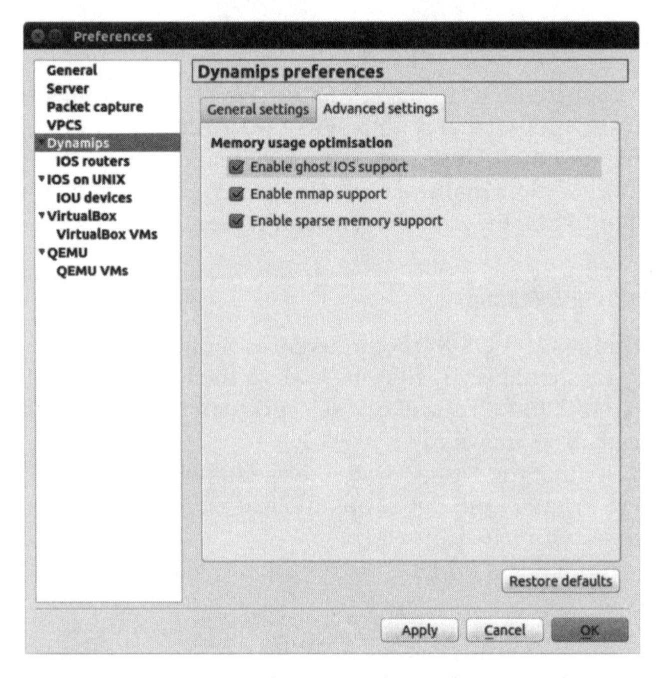

Figure 3-2: Dynamips preferences, Advanced settings tab

The Dynamips Advanced settings options mostly relate to Dynamips stability and memory usage. As a rule you shouldn't change them, but I'll discuss the options so you can decide for yourself.

The Memory usage optimisation settings are all about conserving memory in your PC. The less memory Dynamips uses per router, the more routers you can add to your projects. The Enable ghost IOS support option reduces memory consumption in your PC by allocating one shared region of memory that multiple routers can use, as long as they're running the same IOS image. This is a good reason to use the same router model multiple times in a project; using several different models, with different IOS versions, will eat up more of your PC's memory. The Enable mmap support option allows the contents of router memory to be written to a file on your hard drive, similar to a cache or swap file. The Enable sparse memory support option reduces the amount of virtual memory used by your routers so you can run more router instances per Dynamips process.

Adding IOS Images to GNS3

Before you start creating projects using IOS routers, add at least one IOS image to GNS3. To add an IOS image, select **Edit ▸ Preferences** on Windows and Linux, or select **GNS3 ▸ Preferences** on OS X. Expand **Dynamips** from the pane on the left and click **IOS routers**, as shown in Figure 3-3.

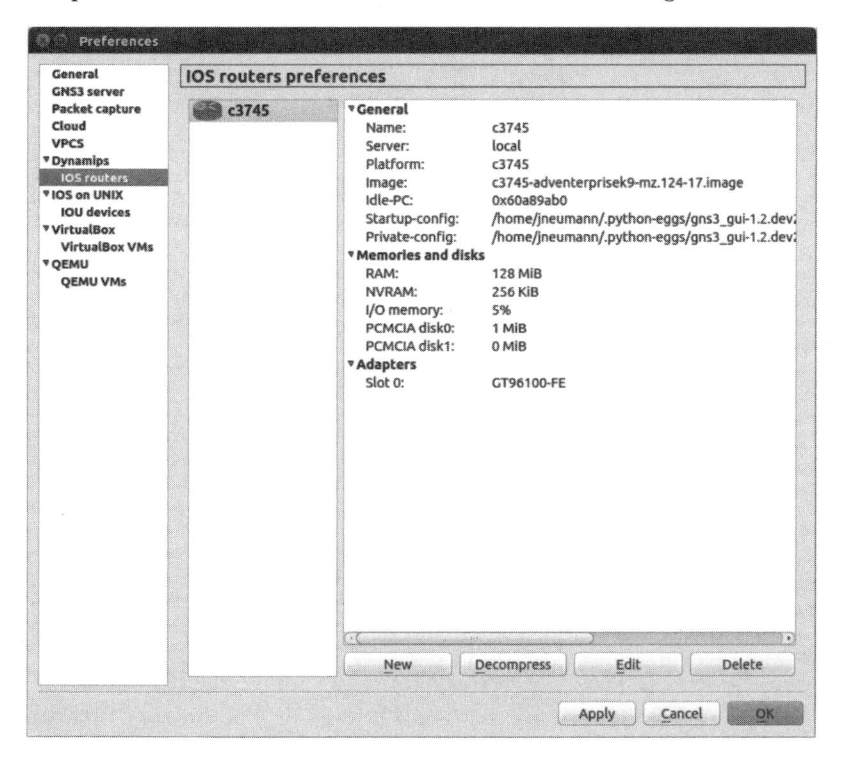

Figure 3-3: IOS routers preferences

Click **New** to start the wizard and then click the **Browse** button to locate your image file. After selecting your image file, you'll be asked whether you would like to decompress the IOS image, as shown in Figure 3-4.

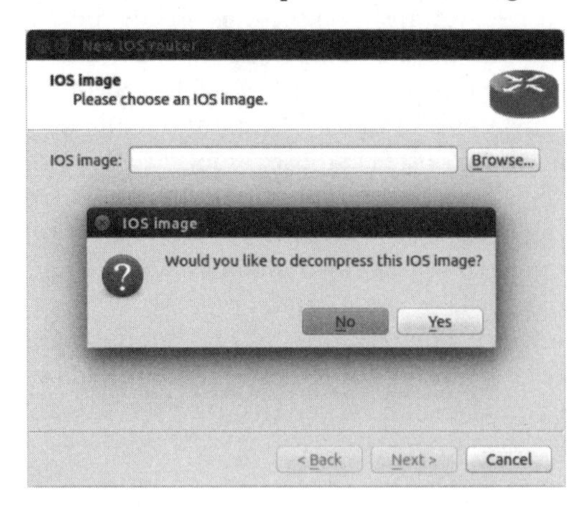

Figure 3-4: Deciding whether to decompress the IOS image

It's a good idea to let GNS3 decompress your image files; otherwise, your routers will have to decompress the images every time a router loads. Decompressing the images ahead of time will make your routers boot much faster. After decompressing your image, click **Next**, and GNS3 will attempt to recognize the router platform that your IOS belongs to, as shown in Figure 3-5.

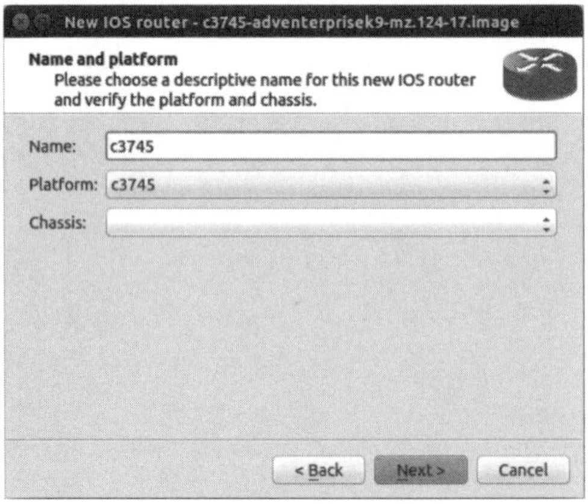

Figure 3-5: Name and platform screen

GNS3 has determined that my image file belongs to a c3745 router platform and has automatically named it *c3745*. If you think this is incorrect, you can use the Platform drop-down menu to choose another platform, but in my experience, GNS3 does a good job of getting this correct. You can change the name of your router to anything you like by entering a name in the Name field.

In general, from here, you can just click through all the configuration settings to configure a basic router model, but the wizard provides opportunities for you to customize router memory and other features during this process. For now, click **Next** to continue. You should be presented with the Memory screen, shown in Figure 3-6.

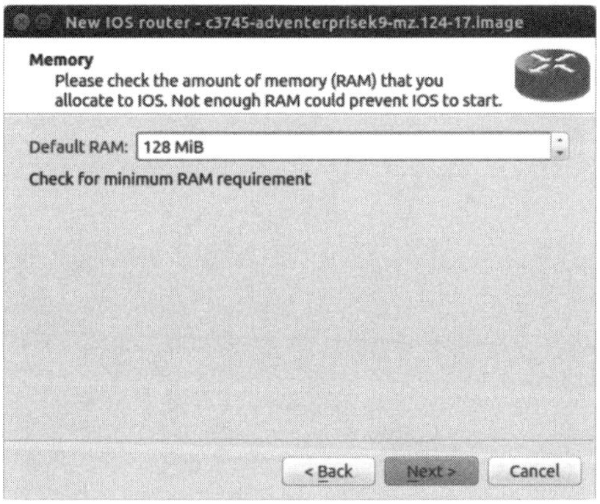

Figure 3-6: IOS Memory screen

Your routers should run fine with the default memory setting. But if you're unsure, click **Check for minimum RAM requirements**, and GNS3 will launch a web browser and take you to the Cisco Feature Navigator web page at *http://www.cisco.com/*. From here, you can search for your IOS image's specific memory requirements. Enter that value in the Default RAM field. When you're done, click **Next**, and you will be presented with the Network adapters screen, as shown in Figure 3-7.

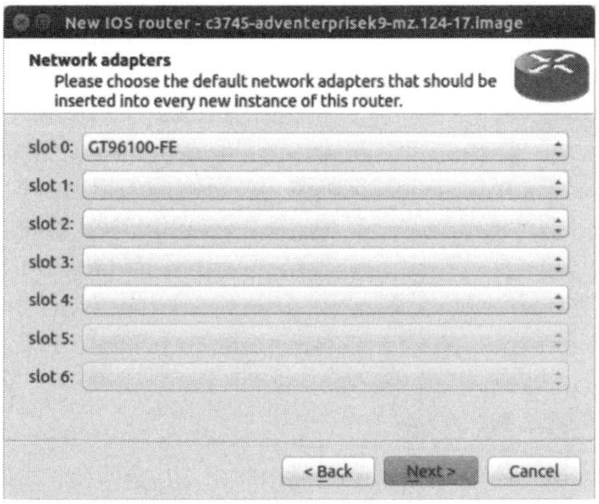

Figure 3-7: Network adapters screen

The default setting configures your router with the same standard options that are provided with a real model of the same Cisco router. If you would like to add more interfaces, use the drop-down menu next to the available slots and choose the desired network modules. The slot options will be limited to actual options that are available in the real version of the Cisco router. When you're done, click **Next** and choose any WIC modules that you would like to install. Then click **Next** again to display the Idle-PC screen, shown in Figure 3-8.

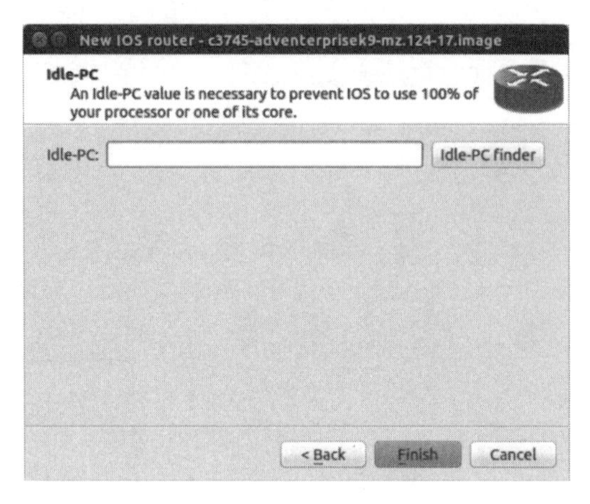

Figure 3-8: Idle-PC screen

If you start a router in GNS3 without an Idle-PC setting, your computer's CPU usage will quickly spike to 100 percent and remain there. This happens because Dynamips doesn't yet know whether your virtual router is doing something that requires system resources, so it overcompensates by giving it all the resources it can. GNS3 will run sluggishly until this is corrected, and if CPU usage is left at 100 percent for a long time, your PC's processor could overheat.

You can easily fix this by having GNS3 look for places in the IOS program code where an idle loop exists (idle loops cause the CPU to spike); the result of this calculation is called an *Idle-PC value*. When the proper Idle-PC value is applied, Dynamips should periodically *sleep* the router when these idle loops are executed, which greatly reduces CPU usage. If you don't care about all the details, just remember that the Idle-PC value is what keeps Dynamips from eating your processor for lunch.

To have GNS3 automatically find a value, click the **Idle-PC finder** button, and GNS3 will attempt to search for a value. If GNS3 finds a suitable value, then you're done; click **Finish**. If it's unsuccessful, leave the field blank and click **Next** to save the router without an Idle-PC configuration.

Setting a Manual Idle-PC Value

If GNS3 is unable to find an Idle-PC value automatically, you'll need to find one manually. You need to calculate an Idle-PC value only once per IOS image. GNS3 applies this setting to *all* virtual routers using that image file. Close the Preferences window, and drag a router from the Devices toolbar to your GNS3 workspace, as shown in Figure 3-9.

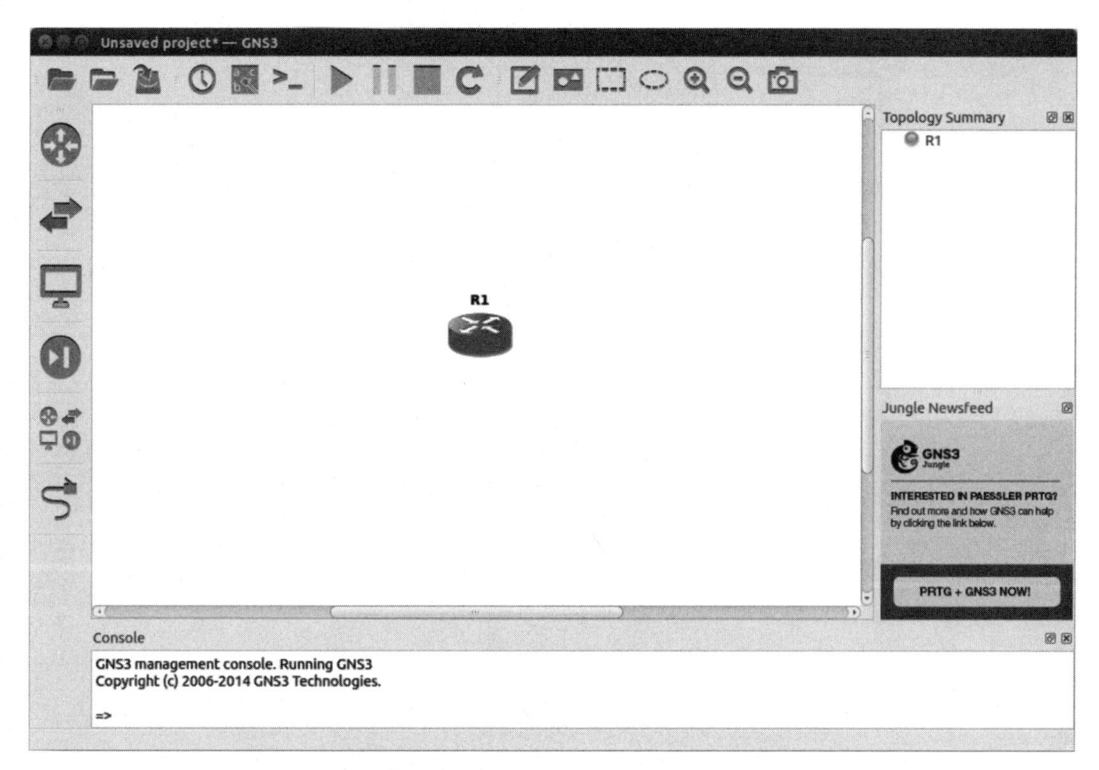

Figure 3-9: Adding a router to a blank workspace

Next, boot the router by right-clicking the router icon and selecting **Start**; then verify that the IOS loads correctly by immediately right-clicking the router again and selecting **Console**. A Cisco console window should open and display the router's boot messages. If the router boots correctly, you're ready to begin the Idle-PC calculation; if not, make sure that the model and default RAM settings assigned to the router are correct, or try a different IOS image.

If you're running Linux and a Cisco console does not appear after selecting Console, check your GNS3 Console Settings. Go to **Edit ▸ Preferences**, click **General**, and select the **Console applications** tab, as shown in Figure 3-10.

Using the Preconfigured commands drop-down menu, select your Linux terminal type and then click **Set**, **Apply**, and **OK**.

When the router boots, your computer's CPU usage will quickly surge to 100 percent. Monitor your CPU usage so that after you've set an Idle-PC value, you can verify that your CPU usage has settled down. On Windows, press CTRL-ALT-DEL and click **Task Manager** to display CPU usage. On OS X, open the Activity Monitor program from the Applications/Utilities folder and click **CPU**. On Linux systems, use System Monitor or enter **`top`** at the terminal.

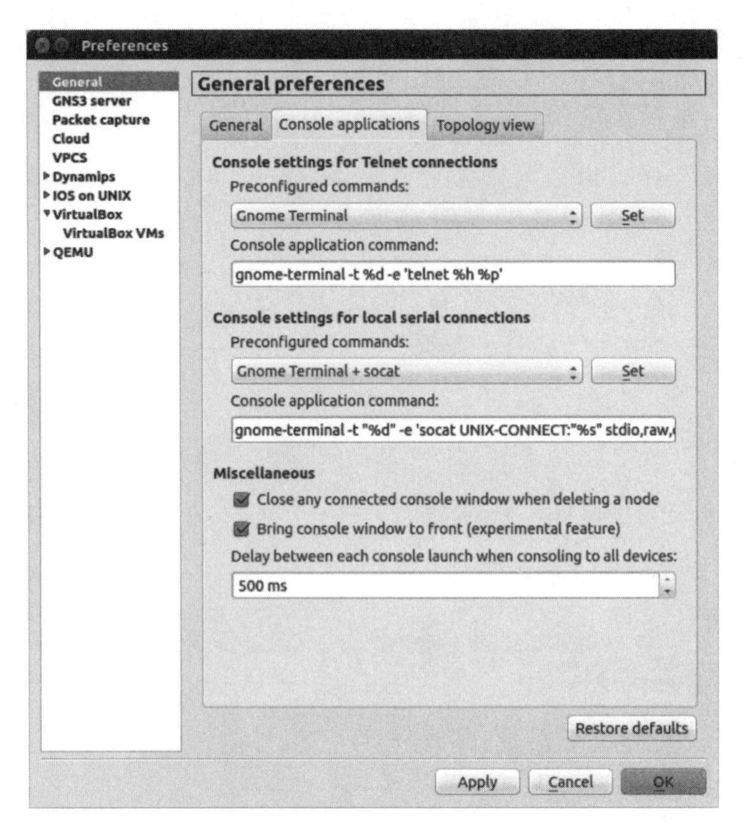

Figure 3-10: Choosing a Console application using Ubuntu Linux

To begin calculating a value, right-click your router and select **Idle-PC** from the menu, as shown in Figure 3-11.

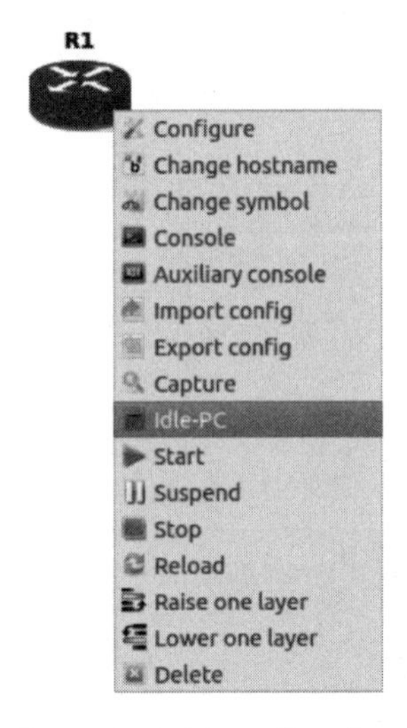

Figure 3-11: Manually calculating Idle-PC values

GNS3 should now calculate Idle-PC values and provide one or more values to choose from. This can take a minute, so give it time to display the results in the Idle-PC values window, shown in Figure 3-12.

If there is an asterisk (*) next to a given value, then GNS3 has determined that value to be the best, and you should choose it. Click **Apply** to choose the value, and recheck your CPU usage.

Occasionally, GNS3 miscalculates the value, and processor usage remains high. If this happens, try again using a different value from the drop-down menu, and click **Apply** again to choose the new value. If no asterisk is displayed, you'll need to find a value that works using a simple trial-and-error method. When you're done, click **OK** to save the value.

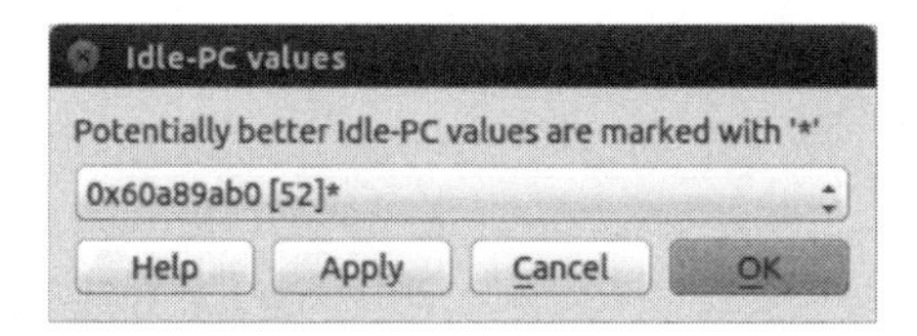

Figure 3-12: Idle-PC values

After a working Idle-PC value has been applied, you're ready to create some projects!

Final Thoughts

Now that you've assigned one or more IOS image files to your routers and configured basic options in GNS3, you're ready to begin working with your routers. You can select any virtual router displayed on the Routers Device toolbar. Give it a try. Drag a couple of routers to the workspace, start them up, and enter a few IOS commands.

Just like real Cisco routers, the limitations of your Dynamips virtual routers are determined by the IOS version they're running. If you find that your router is missing an IOS command or that the syntax for a given command is not what you expected, you may need to try a different IOS version. If you're studying for the CCNA or CCNP exam, this shouldn't be an issue because those certifications require a fairly straightforward set of commands and features. If you're studying for a CCIE or other advanced Cisco certification, you might need the latest IOS that supports a more robust set of features. When in doubt, visit the Cisco website to find out what features and capabilities are supported by a specific router model or IOS. Cisco's Feature Navigator web page is an awesome tool that allows you to search for IOS information by features, technology, software, image, or product code, and it also allows you to compare software versions.

Now that you've assigned an IOS image and configured basic options in GNS3, let's move on to creating projects!

4

CREATING AND MANAGING PROJECTS

Now that you can configure and start a single IOS router, roll up your sleeves and I'll show you how to create a project by networking two or more routers together. Compared to working with real lab equipment, creating virtual networks and managing devices in GNS3 is a breeze. The user interface acts like a master control room, allowing you to manipulate your network designs and devices with just a few clicks. This chapter will show you how to use GNS3 to centrally manage your network, including the virtual hardware.

Project Management Overview

A strong feature of GNS3 is project management. You can create an unlimited number of network designs to save and use whenever you need them. That means you'll never have to waste time tearing apart an existing project to create a new one, which often happens when you use physical equipment.

Not only can you save multiple projects, but you can save multiple snapshots of an entire project configuration. A *snapshot* preserves your project's network layout and the state of all your router configurations at a particular moment in time. You can restore a snapshot whenever you'd like to roll your entire project back to the state it was in when the snapshot was taken.

NOTE *Snapshots are useful for practicing CCNA or CCNP configuration drills. You can create a lab, apply the basic router configurations required for a drill (such as network addresses, routing protocols, and so on), and then take a snapshot. Once you have a snapshot of the basic setup, you can practice applying the scenario's objectives to the network. If you want to practice the same tasks again later, you can revert to the basic snapshot, and your routers should be ready without additional configuration.*

GNS3 also gives you the ability to manage your virtual hardware. Just like with real routers, you can use Cisco expansion modules to upgrade your virtual routers. You can add a wide range of functionality, such as additional random access memory (RAM), Ethernet interfaces, serial ports, Asynchronous Transfer Mode (ATM), and Packet over SONET (POS) ports.

Terminology

Before beginning, let's explore some important terminology. You need to know the difference between a topology and a project. A *topology* file is a text file that ends in *.gns3* and primarily refers to devices and the links between them. A *project* is a user-defined project folder (*MyLab*, for example) stored inside the *GNS3/projects* folder. A user project folder contains a topology file named *<project_name>.gns3*, router configurations, the contents of nonvolatile random access memory (NVRAM), and other saved information. In other words, it represents an entire network, including the topology and all device configurations.

Another term you should be familiar with is *node*. In computer networking, a node is any device connected to your network. In GNS3, a node is any device found on the Devices toolbar.

To be effective at managing devices and projects, you'll need more than just vocabulary; you'll also need to be familiar with GNS3's screen layout.

Screen Layout

Let's take a look at the standard GNS3 layout (shown in Figure 4-1) and define a few concepts used by the program.

❶ **GNS3 toolbar**
A series of icons to easily perform common tasks.

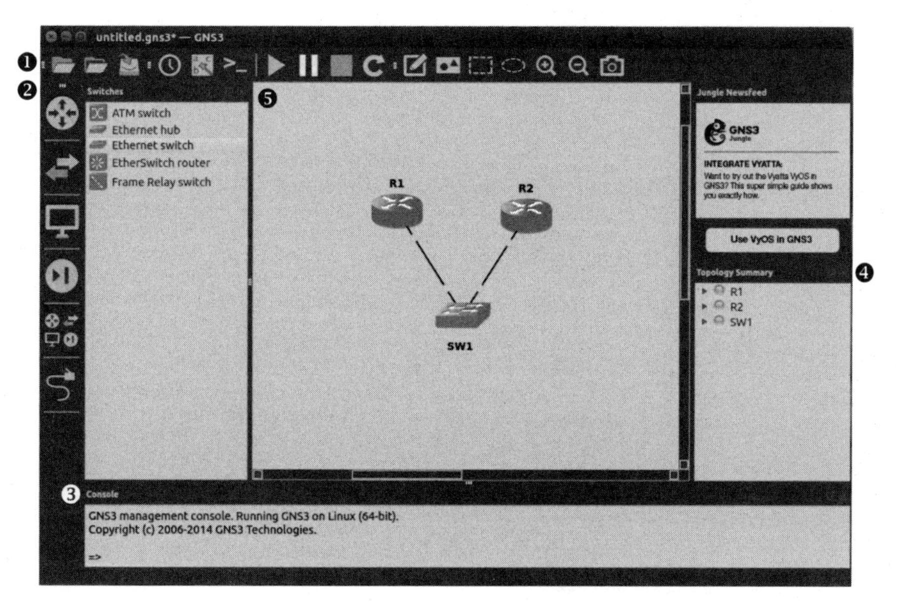

Figure 4-1: Screen layout showing two routers and a switch in the GNS3 workspace

❷ **Devices toolbar**
Used to add routers, switches, end devices, and security devices, as well as to create links between devices. To create topologies, select a device type from the toolbar and drag devices from the device window to your workspace. There are two types of devices: simulated and emulated. A *simulated* device mimics all the characteristics of an actual device (like an Ethernet switch node) and does not run an operating system. An *emulated* device emulates the hardware of an actual device and requires an operating system to function (like virtual Dynamips routers running Cisco IOS).

❸ **Console**
A command line interface where you can manage aspects of your devices.

❹ **Topology Summary**
Displays the state of devices in your project. A green circle by a device indicates that it has started, a red circle indicates that a device is stopped, and a yellow circle indicates that a device is suspended. Simulated devices (like the Ethernet switch node) are always green. To see the links in use on a given device, click the triangle next to the device name.

❺ **Workspace**
The area in which you'll design your network. Drag devices from the Devices toolbar to the workspace and link them together.

Now that you know what the main GNS3 screen looks like, let's look more closely at the options you'll find there.

Using the GNS3 Toolbar

The GNS3 toolbar contains several groups of icons that are roughly organized by function and offer a simple way to get things done. The first group deals with projects, the second with links, the third with devices and snapshots, and the fourth with additional ways to visually organize your projects.

First Toolbar Group

The first group of toolbar icons, shown in Figure 4-2, deals with actions that affect entire projects.

Figure 4-2: First toolbar group

From left to right, these icons are as follows:

New blank project Creates a new project folder and allows you to choose what to name your project.

Open project Opens a previously saved project. To open a project, choose the project folder name and select the file named *<project_name>.gns3*.

Save project Saves a complete project to the GNS3 *projects* folder. By default, a PNG image file of your workspace is saved with your project.

Second Toolbar Group

The buttons in the second group of toolbar icons, shown in Figure 4-3, allow you to create project snapshots, show or hide interface labels, and connect to your devices using the virtual console port on your devices.

Figure 4-3: Second toolbar group

From left to right, these icons are as follows:

Snapshot Creates a snapshot of your devices, links, and IOS configurations to record the state of your workspace at that time. You can save more than one snapshot and revert to a saved snapshot at any time. Options are Create, Delete, Restore, and Close.

Show interface labels Shows or hides interface names used by a link. These labels are abbreviated and displayed with devices in your workspace (for example, f0/0 is displayed for FastEthernet0/0).

Console connect to all devices Opens a console connection to all running routers in your workspace.

NOTE *When you open a console connection to all devices, your screen might become cluttered with open console windows unless your terminal supports tabbed sessions. When dealing with large topologies, you might find it easier to open and close single sessions as needed by right-clicking a device node and choosing Console.*

Third Toolbar Group

The third group of toolbar icons, shown in Figure 4-4, primarily deals with controlling devices.

Figure 4-4: Third toolbar group

From left to right, these four icons are as follows:

Start/Resume all devices Starts all stopped devices or resumes all suspended devices in your workspace.

Suspend all devices Places all suspend-capable devices in a suspended state.

Stop all devices Stops all devices.

Reload all devices Reloads all devices. Be sure to save your router configurations and project before reloading or else you might lose your configurations!

Fourth Toolbar Group

The final group of toolbar icons, shown in Figure 4-5, provides tools to present your network layouts more clearly. You can add objects such as rectangles and ellipses to your project, and even generate a screenshot of your workspace.

Figure 4-5: Fourth toolbar group

From left to right, the icons in the last toolbar group are as follows:

Add a note Creates text annotations in your workspace. Double-click text to modify it, and right-click the text object to change the Style attributes (such as font size and color). You can also rotate text objects from 0 to 360 degrees.

Insert a picture Adds images and logos to your projects. GNS3 supports PNG, JPG, BMP, XPM, PPM, and TIFF file formats.

Draw a rectangle Draws dynamically sizable rectangles. You can right-click a rectangle object to change the Style attributes for border and border color. Rectangle objects can be rotated from 0 to 360 degrees.

Draw an ellipse Draws dynamically sizable ellipses. You can right-click an ellipse object to change the border style and color.

Zoom in Zooms in your workspace to see details.

Zoom out Zooms out of your workspace for a bigger bird's-eye view.

Screenshot Generates a screenshot of your workspace. The image can be saved as a PNG, JPG, BMP, XPM, PPM, or TIFF file and by default is saved in your *GNS3/projects* folder.

> **WINDOW STYLES AND DOCKS**
>
> GNS3 provides several window styles to choose from. To change the default style, select **Edit ▸ Preferences** on Linux and Windows, or select **GNS3 ▸ Preferences** on OS X. Select the **General** category, select the **General** tab, and use the drop-down menu under Style to choose your new default style. Click **Apply** and **Okay** to activate your change. GNS3 will remember your selection between program restarts.
>
> Window docks, on the other hand, are the windows that surround the GNS3 workspace. GNS3 displays the Console and Topology Summary docks by default.
>
> To view or hide a window dock, select **View ▸ Window Docks** and select the dock you want to display; any dock with a check mark next to its name should appear onscreen. To resize a dock, click the border of the dock window where it connects to the workspace and drag the border until you achieve the desired size.

Objects (notes, pictures, and shapes) that you add to your workspace can be grouped into layers. To raise or lower an object, right-click the object and select **Raise one layer** or **Lower one layer**. This feature allows you to manipulate objects in a layer without affecting other layers. You can display layer positions for your objects by choosing **View ▸ Show Layers** from the menu, which is useful during advanced layer manipulation.

By adding shapes and colors with this toolbar, you can divide network components into logical groups. With text, you can add notes and reminders about how your project is configured. Figure 4-6 shows how you can present information more clearly using shapes, colors, and annotated text messages.

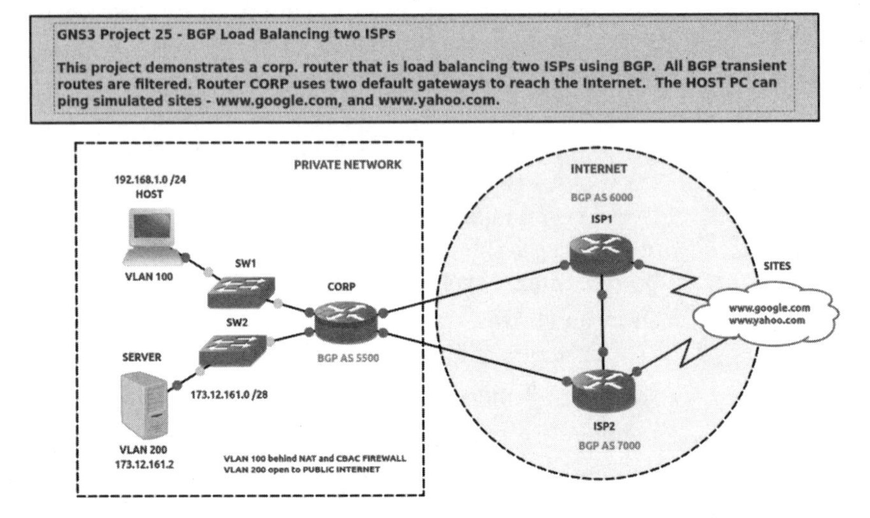

Figure 4-6: Sample project with annotations

Once you've created several projects, it's easy to forget how you configured them or what your objectives were. Adding notes (like the helpful one in Figure 4-6) is a simple way to quickly remind yourself of that information, especially after a few weeks or months have gone by. Notes are awesome—use them!

Using the Devices Toolbar

The Devices toolbar (shown in Figure 4-7) organizes devices by function. Click an icon on the Devices toolbar to see all the devices in that device group.

Figure 4-7: Devices toolbar

To add a device node to your project, click an icon from the Devices toolbar to display a list of configured devices and then drag a device to your workspace. You can press SHIFT to add multiple identical devices. From left to right, the device types in the toolbar are as follows:

Routers Displays all available Dynamips router nodes that have been configured with a valid IOS image file, as well as IOU L3 routers.

Switches Displays all available switch nodes, including Ethernet switch, Ethernet hub, ATM switch, Frame Relay switch, EtherSwitch router, and IOU L2 switches.

End Devices Displays all available end devices, including QEMU guests, VirtualBox guests, host, and cloud.

Security Devices Displays all available security devices, including ASA firewall, IDS/IPS, and any custom nodes you've created.

All Devices Displays all available devices from the Devices toolbar.

Add a Link When this is selected, your mouse pointer changes to a crosshair, indicating that you can link two devices together using their virtual interfaces. To link devices, click the first device and select an interface; then repeat for the second device to complete the connection.

Click the **All Devices** icon now, and you should see a window containing every configured device in GNS3. You can drag any of the devices to your workspace and use them in your project.

Creating Your First Project

Now that you know your way around the GNS3 interface, let's dig into some project management details. I'll cover the easiest way to get things done, but keep in mind that GNS3 often provides more than one way to do things.

When you launch GNS3, a New project window appears, as shown in Figure 4-8. From here, you can either open an existing project or create a new one.

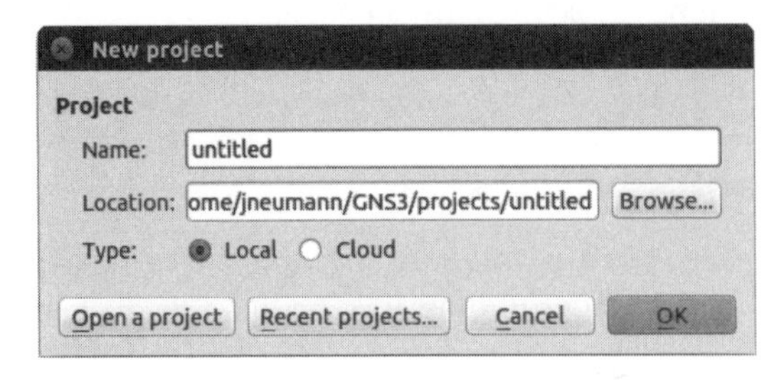

Figure 4-8: New project window

To create a new project, replace *untitled* with your project name, and click **OK**. If you're already in GNS3, select **File ▸ New** to create a new project.

Once you've created a new GNS3 project, it's time to build a topology, starting with some Dynamips routers.

Working with Routers

Begin a project by dragging a couple of routers from the Devices toolbar to the GNS3 workspace. If you press SHIFT when adding devices, you should see a dialog that allows you to add multiple identical devices. Try adding the first pair of routers this way. If you don't see any routers on the Devices toolbar, please refer to "Setting Up Your First IOS Router" on page 21 to learn how to add devices to GNS3.

After adding the routers to your workspace, they should be named R1 and R2 automatically. The routers got their names from the command `hostname %h` found in the GNS3 file *ios_base_startup-config.txt*. This file contains default IOS settings that are applied to all your routers and are assigned to a device when it's configured with an IOS image file. To locate the Dynamips configuration files, go to **Preferences**, choose **Dynamips** from the pane on the left, and choose **IOS Routers**. Select a configured router and click **Edit** to display the Dynamips IOS Router configuration options, shown in Figure 4-9.

From here, you can verify the path to your device's startup-config and private-config files. When a router is placed in your workspace, the contents of the startup-config file *ios_base_startup-config.txt* are applied to the router startup configuration and loaded to the router's running configuration when the router is started. If you would like to create custom parameters that are globally applied to your routers (for example, to bring up an interface automatically or use a preassigned username and password), use a text editor to modify and save the *ios_base_startup-config.txt* file. You can apply any valid Cisco IOS commands to the file, provided your IOS supports them, of course. You shouldn't need to modify the *ios_base_private-config.txt* file. This file was installed by GNS3 so that you can use Secure Shell (SSH) between router restarts, without having to generate new crypto keys on your routers.

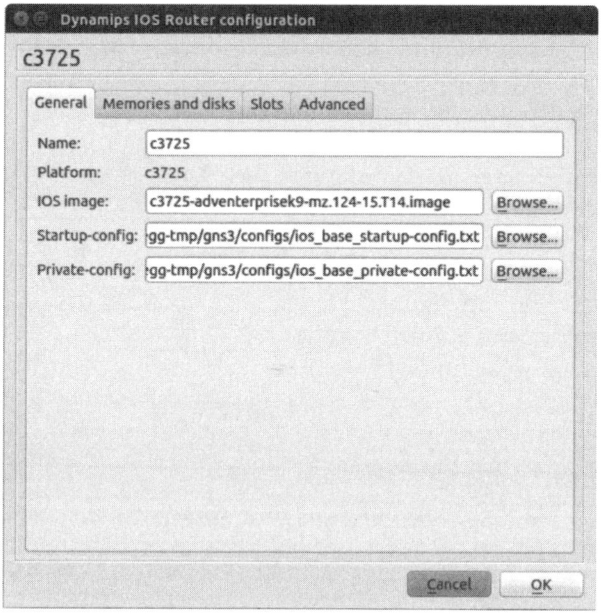

Figure 4-9: Dynamips IOS Router configuration dialog

It's important to note that the changes you make are applied only to routers you add to new projects and can't be applied retroactively to routers in your previously saved projects.

WARNING *Before modifying your* ios_base_startup-config.txt *file, you may want to save a backup copy. If you enter invalid commands, your routers may produce errors and misbehave.*

Creating Links Between Your Routers

After you've placed devices in your workspace, you'll need to add links between them to create a fully functional network. This is equivalent to cabling up a real network, except that you're using virtual cables rather than physical ones. To add links to your devices, click the **Add a link** icon in the Devices toolbar. Your cursor should change to a crosshair, indicating that you can select devices. To create a link, click a device. You'll be presented with a drop-down menu of available interfaces, as shown in Figure 4-10.

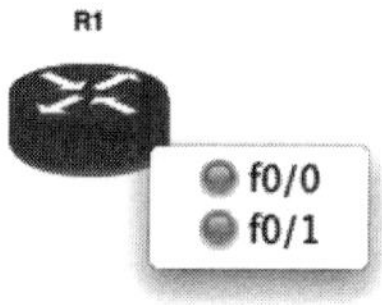

Figure 4-10: A router with two FastEthernet interfaces

A red circle next to an interface indicates that it's available to use; a green circle indicates the interface is already being used by an existing link. Select any available interface to establish the link, and then select an interface on another device to complete the connection. You can create connections only between two compatible interface types. In other words, just like with physical hardware, you can't plug a serial cable into an Ethernet interface.

At some point, you may want to break a link between two devices to simulate an outage, to reconfigure your network, or for some other reason. To break a link between two devices, right-click the link and select **Delete**, as shown in Figure 4-11.

Figure 4-11: Deleting links between devices

To reestablish a link, click the **Add a link** icon again and choose the same devices.

Configuring Virtual Hardware

When you place virtual routers in your workspace, they have the same configuration options that were applied when you configured the device's IOS image. But that doesn't mean your routers are stuck with this configuration. Like PCs, Cisco routers have expansion ports to provide additional functionality, and GNS3 Dynamips routers provide the same expansion options as their physical counterparts. To modify a router's hardware configuration, right-click the router and select **Configure**; then click the node name (R1, for example), as shown in Figure 4-12.

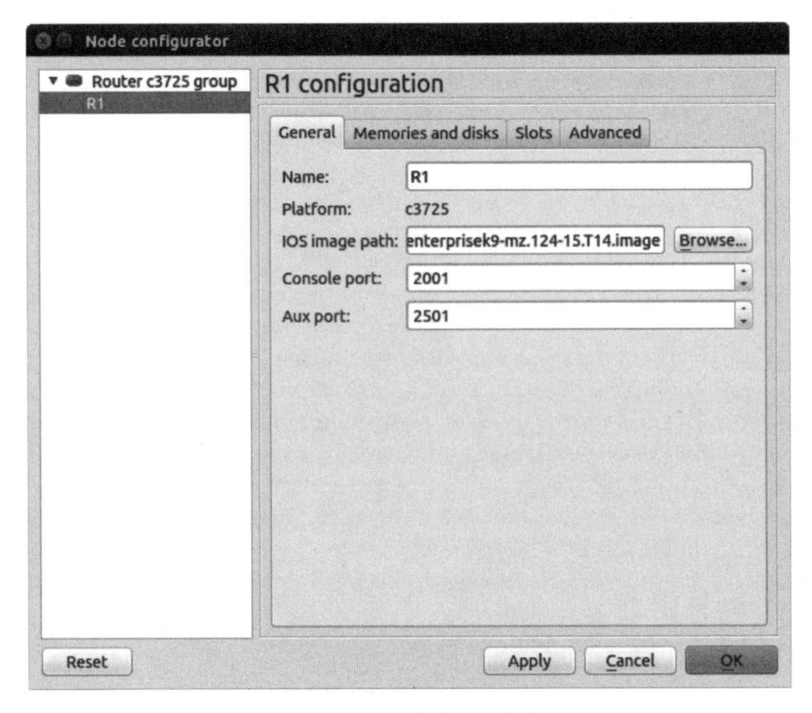

Figure 4-12: Cisco IOS router Node configurator dialog

In the Node configurator dialog, you should see the available configuration options for that model of router. Basic models only allow you to add simple options, such as Cisco SLOT, WIC, or RAM cards, while more advanced models allow you to define features such as the chassis type or a Network Processing Engine (NPE) type that can be found in Cisco 7200 series routers.

You can configure and apply the same device options for memory and slots that were covered in Chapter 3, but the changes you make here will be applied only to the devices or device group you chose in your project. All other devices will remain unaffected.

Starting, Stopping, and Pausing Routers

I've shown you how to start and stop routers by right-clicking a router and choosing either Start or Stop, but you can also suspend your router by right-clicking it and choosing Suspend. Suspending a router is handy when you want to simulate a failure without having to go through the process of saving your configuration, stopping the router, and restarting it. In fact, repeatedly stopping and restarting GNS3 routers can cause Dynamips to crash with some IOS versions, so I recommend suspending and resuming instead.

The suspend feature really shines in network convergence tests. You can quickly simulate failures and recoveries to test routing protocols such as the Routing Information Protocol (RIP), EIGRP, and OSPF, as well as redundancy protocols such as the HSRP, Virtual Router Redundancy Protocol (VRRP), and Gateway Load Balancing Protocol (GLBP). To simulate a failure, click **Suspend** and monitor your other routers to verify that failover or convergence has occurred.

To simulate a recovery, resume the router by right-clicking the device and choosing **Start**. Due to throughput limitations placed on Dynamips because of the emulation, failover or convergence may take a little longer than you're used to when using real hardware. Don't worry—this is totally normal.

Of course, even if you can start and stop your routers, you won't be able to do too much with them until you've logged on to a console.

Logging On to Routers

You log on to your routers using the simulated console port. If this sounds familiar, it's because that's also how you log on to actual Cisco equipment. On a physical piece of hardware, the console port is where you plug in Cisco's little blue serial console cable. Be sure the router is started before you open a console connection; otherwise, you won't get a console screen.

CONFIGURING TERMINAL SETTINGS

Whether you're running Windows, OS X, or Linux, there are a number of terminal types available to use with GNS3. But why would you prefer one over the other? One reason might be that it's what you have installed on your system. On Linux, for example, you may be using the Gnome Desktop, which has gnome-terminal installed by default. If that's the case, you may want to modify the GNS3 terminal setting to use gnome-terminal. Another reason is that some terminal programs provide more features than others. You may want to choose a terminal type that allows you to use tabbed windows, for example, so you can open more than one console at a time without a bunch of open windows cluttering the screen.

To modify the terminal settings, go to **Preferences**, click **General**, and then click the **Console applications** tab to display the window shown in Figure 4-13.

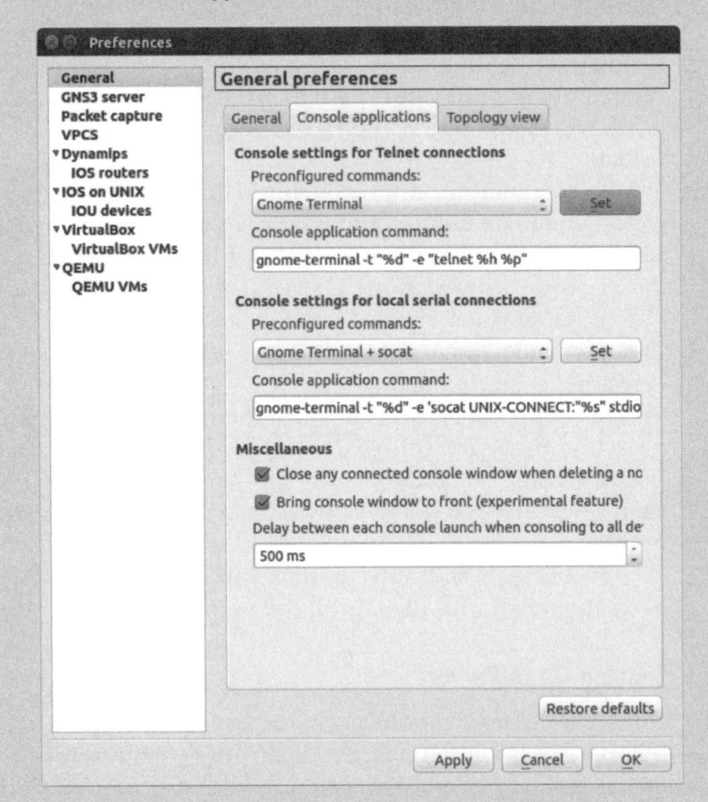

Figure 4-13: Terminal settings

From here, you can choose a predefined terminal type and customize the command settings under Console application command. (Check your terminal application documentation to find out what options are available on your system.) When you're done, click **Set** and then **Apply** and **OK**.

To log on to all your routers at once, click the **Console connect to all devices** icon in the second toolbar group (see Figure 4-3 on page 34). To log on to a single router, right-click the router node in your workspace and select **Console** or **Auxiliary console** from the menu (see Figure 4-14).

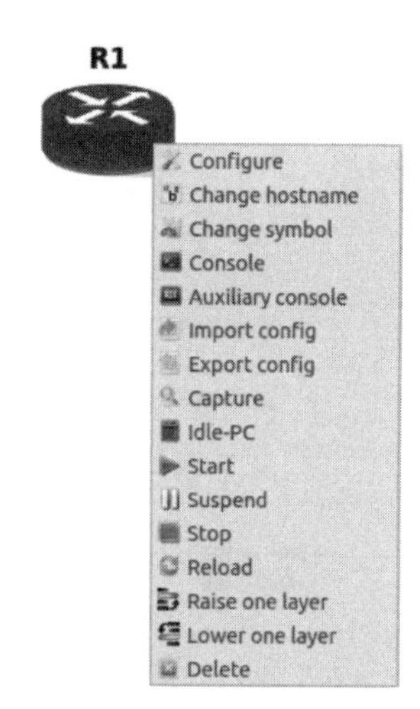

Figure 4-14: Choose Console or Auxiliary console to connect to a router

To change the Transmission Control Protocol (TCP) port number on which a router's console or AUX port listens, right-click a device in your workspace, click **Configure**, and select the **General** tab. The port number you choose must be unique for every device in GNS3 and on your PC. As a rule, I try not to mess with port numbers unless I must. GNS3 does a pretty good job of keeping them all straight, and mucking with them can lead to headaches. But if some other TCP/IP application running on your PC happens to conflict with GNS3, you may have to make some changes before you can log on to your router.

NOTE *Use the `netstat` command on your PC to verify what TCP/IP ports are already in use.*

Once you've established a console connection to the router, you should see a familiar Cisco console window.

```
Trying 127.0.0.1...
Connected to 127.0.0.1.
Escape character is '^]'.
Connected to Dynamips VM "R1" (ID 1, type c3725) - Console port
Press ENTER to get the prompt.
ROMMON emulation microcode.

Cisco 1720 (MPC860) processor (revision 0x202) with 55206K/9830K bytes of memory.
Processor board ID FTX0945WOMY (4279256517), with hardware revision 000
M860 processor: part number 0, mask 0
Bridging software.
X.25 software, Version 3.0.0.
1 FastEthernet/IEEE 802.3 interface(s)
32K bytes of non-volatile configuration memory.
4096K bytes of processor board System flash (Read/Write)

SETUP: new interface FastEthernet0 placed in "shutdown" state

Press RETURN to get started!
00:00:02: %LINK-5-CHANGED: Interface FastEthernet0, changed state to administratively down
00:00:03: %LINEPROTO-5-UPDOWN: Line protocol on Interface FastEthernet0, changed state to down
R1#
```

At this point, you can begin using standard IOS commands to configure the router. One command that might look odd is the `show flash` command. Normally this command displays files saved in flash memory, such as the router's IOS image file and other default files from Cisco. In GNS3, however, you'll notice there are no files saved here by default. What's more, the flash drive may be *unformatted*; if that's the case, you'll need to issue the `erase flash:` command before you can save files to flash memory. Otherwise, you may receive an error similar to the following:

```
%Error opening slot0:router-confg (Bad device info block)
```

NOTE *If you use an NM-16ESW switch module, you may have to erase your router's flash memory before you create VLANs; otherwise, the VLAN database* (vlan.dat) *will not be able to be saved.*

This section has been all about Dynamips routers so far, but you can also use switches in your GNS3 projects, which I'll cover next.

Ethernet Switch Nodes

The Ethernet switch node is an emulated virtual switch that allows you to create VLAN access and trunk ports. The Ethernet switch node supports access ports, industry-standard 802.1Q trunk ports, and QinQ tagging. It does not, however, support Cisco's proprietary Inter-Switch Link (ISL) trunking protocol.

To use an Ethernet switch node, drag the node to your workspace. You never have to start an Ethernet switch node; they're always ready to use.

To configure the switch, right-click the **Ethernet switch node** icon and select **Configure**. Using the Node configurator window shown in Figure 4-15, click the switch name (SW1, for example) to modify the default switch ports or add new ports.

By default, there are eight access ports assigned to VLAN 1. To change a port, click the port number and modify the settings as needed. When you're done, click **Apply** and **OK**. To add a new port, define the port settings and click the **Add** button; then click **Apply**. When you're finished adding ports, click **OK** to complete the setup.

One alternative to the Ethernet switch node is to configure a Dynamips router with a network switch module. The advantage of using a switch module is that it supports more features (such as the Spanning Tree Protocol); the downside is that using a network switch module uses more PC resources. If you need the functions of only a simple switch, I recommend you stick with the Ethernet switch node. If you need full IOS switching capability, use a router with a switch module installed like the EtherSwitch router, or use an IOU L2 switch image (discussed in Chapter 9).

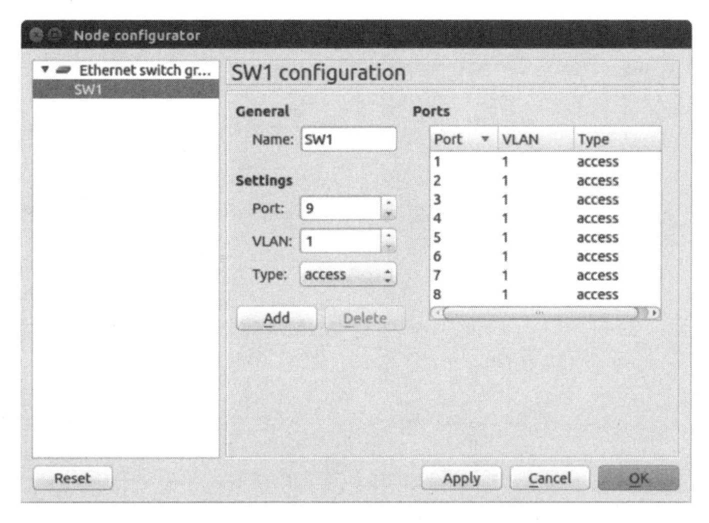

Figure 4-15: Ethernet switch Node configurator window

Changing Symbols and Organizing Your Devices

You can change the symbols that are used to represent devices in your workspace and choose where your devices are located in the Devices toolbar. Let's say you want to change an IOS router's symbol. To change the symbol of the device, select **Edit ▸ Preferences** on Linux and Windows or select **GNS3 ▸ Preferences** on OS X. Next, go under the device you want to change, right-click the device icon, and select **Change symbol**, as shown in Figure 4-16.

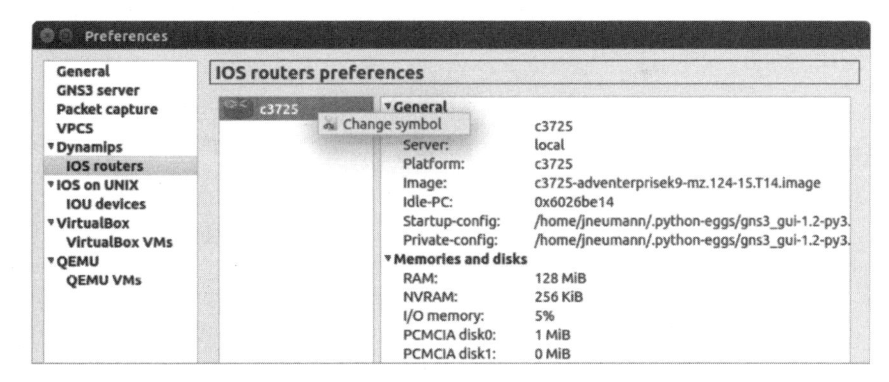

Figure 4-16: Changing the symbol

You can change the symbol for IOU devices, VirtualBox virtual machines, and QEMU virtual machines in the same way. The Symbol selection window, as shown in Figure 4-17, should appear after you click **Change symbol**.

Figure 4-17: Symbol selection and device category

To change a device symbol, scroll down in the Symbol selection window and select the symbol you want to use. Next, use the drop-down menu to choose a category. This is the category where the device will be placed in the Devices toolbar. The categories include Switches, Routers, End Devices, and Security Devices. When you're finished, click **OK** to complete the change.

Final Thoughts

In this chapter, you learned the basics of setting up a GNS3 network, so now is a good time to create a few labs and practice what you've learned. If you're studying for a Cisco certification, spending as much hands-on time as possible with Cisco gear is the only way to gain enough experience to pass the exams. (They're tough!)

Start by creating the network in Figure 4-1. After creating the topology, log on to the routers, configure their interfaces, and try pinging between them. Simulate a failure and recovery by using the suspend and resume feature or by starting and stopping a device. Once you've explored some IOS commands and GNS3 features, try creating a simple CCNA lab with three or more routers; there are plenty of CCNA and CCNP example labs online.

One last word of caution: if you create large topologies that use multiprotocol routing, you might find that you have to increase your router's protocol timers to prevent your interfaces from repeatedly going up and down. (It's rare, but it does happen sometimes.) The problem is caused by the inherent effects of latency within Dynamips. Serial connections are another common problem area; some router images can be flaky when running on emulated serial ports. If you find a router's serial port is acting up by either crashing your router or flapping the connection, try another router model or different IOS image. In general, c36xx, c37xx, and 7200 IOS images are the most stable with Dynamips and should be used whenever possible.

In Chapter 5, you'll explore the basics of capturing network packets with Wireshark and expanding your networks by adding hosts using VPCS, VirtualBox, and Linux.

5

INTEGRATING HOSTS AND USING WIRESHARK

Up to this point, you've learned how to create networks using Cisco devices, but GNS3 can do so much more! It uses a robust set of network tools that allow you to integrate external applications into your GNS3 projects. In this chapter, you'll explore some of these tools by learning how to integrate PC hosts into projects using Virtual PC Simulator and VirtualBox. The chapter will also cover basic packet sniffing using Wireshark.

Virtual PC Simulator

One way to add hosts to your projects is with VPCS, a small application that simulates up to nine DOS-like PCs. VPCS hosts have a limited set of commands but are well suited for testing end-to-end connectivity across your GNS3 networks. VPCS uses very few PC resources, which allows you to add numerous hosts to projects without bogging down your PC.

Installing VPCS

If you're running Windows or OS X, VPCS should have been included when you installed GNS3. If you're using a Linux system, VPCS source code should have been included in your GNS3 for Linux download, but it will need to be compiled before you can use it. Compile and install it using the following commands, replacing *x* with the version number of your VPCS source file:

```
$ unzip vpcs-x.zip
$ cd vpcs-x/src
$ sh mk.sh
$ sudo cp vpcs /usr/local/bin/
```

To use VPCS, drag a VPCS host node from End Devices on the Devices toolbar to your workspace. Before you can start a VPCS host, it must be connected to another device in your project. After starting a VPCS host and opening a console, you'll be presented with a window similar to Figure 5-1.

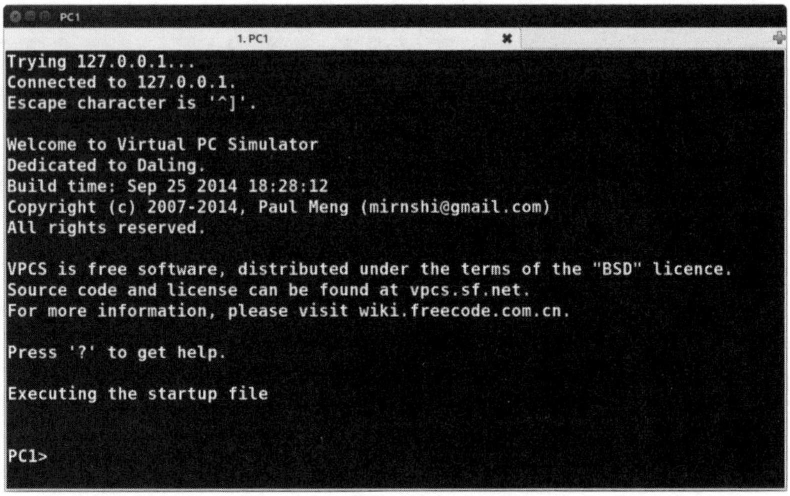

```
PC1
1. PC1
Trying 127.0.0.1...
Connected to 127.0.0.1.
Escape character is '^]'.

Welcome to Virtual PC Simulator
Dedicated to Daling.
Build time: Sep 25 2014 18:28:12
Copyright (c) 2007-2014, Paul Meng (mirnshi@gmail.com)
All rights reserved.

VPCS is free software, distributed under the terms of the "BSD" licence.
Source code and license can be found at vpcs.sf.net.
For more information, please visit wiki.freecode.com.cn.

Press '?' to get help.

Executing the startup file


PC1>
```

Figure 5-1: The VPCS console

If you don't see the VPCS console or if your application displays errors, verify that the program resides in */usr/local/bin/* (on Linux) and that the path has been set correctly in the GNS3 preferences. The developer provides very little in the way of support or documentation, so if you continue to have problems, you may want to visit the GNS3 forums (*http://community.gns3.com/*) for a possible solution.

VPCS Commands

The commands in VPCS are mostly self-explanatory, but I'll cover a couple of them here to get you started. To see a full list of supported commands, you can enter a question mark, ?. To display the configuration of your hosts, you can enter the `show` command. To display the parameters for a specific command, enter the command name followed by a question mark. For example, entering `ping ?` would display all the options of the `ping` command.

NOTE *Like Cisco IOS, VPCS supports abbreviated command syntax. For example, the* `ping` *command can be entered as* `p`. *You can abbreviate any VPCS command, but you must enter enough letters of the command so that it's unique from other commands that begin with the same letters.*

VPCS IP Addressing

After launching VPCS, you need to configure the host for use with GNS3. Typically, this only requires setting the IP address, subnet mask, and gateway address.

VPCS supports IPv4 and IPv6 addressing. You can manually configure an IP address or acquire one automatically if a Dynamic Host Configuration Protocol (DHCP) server is running in your GNS3 project. To manually configure an IPv4 address, you would enter *`ip-address mask gateway`*. The following example sets an IPv4 address to 192.168.1.50 using a subnet mask of 255.255.255.0 and sets the default gateway to 192.168.1.1:

```
PC1> ip 192.168.1.50 255.255.255.0 192.168.1.1
```

You can enter the same IPv4 address using Classless Inter-Domain Routing (CIDR) notation in place of a standard subnet mask, as shown here:

```
PC1> ip 192.168.1.50 /24 192.168.1.1
```

To manually configure an IPv6 address, enter the `ip` command followed by a valid IPv6 address and mask. The following example sets the IPv6 address to 2014:12:1a::50 using a 64-bit subnet mask:

```
PC1> ip 2014:12:1a::50 /64
```

To configure a host automatically using DHCP, enter the `dhcp` command for each host that requires an address, as in this example:

```
PC1> dhcp
```

Use the `save` command to save your VPCS settings with your GNS3 project.

```
PC1> save
. done
```

The settings will be saved in the GNS3 projects folder under *GNS3/projects/<project_name>/project-files/vpcs/<vpcs_uuid>*. Later, when you load your GNS3 project, the configuration settings will automatically be applied to the host.

To test VPCS, create a project using a VPCS host node and link it to some other device, like a router. Assign an IP address to your VPCS host and the other device, and then use `ping` or `trace` to test connectivity. If all goes well, you should receive a reply like the one in this example:

```
PC1> ping 192.168.1.1
192.168.1.1 icmp_seq=1 ttl=255 time=35.821 ms
```

After successfully pinging devices, you can examine the ARP cache (MAC address to IP table) using the `arp` command, as in the following:

```
PC1> arp
cc:00:05:a9:00:00  192.168.1.1 expires in 114 seconds
```

If a ping is unsuccessful, VPCS displays a "host not reachable" message:

```
PC1> ping 192.168.1.1
host (192.168.1.1) not reachable
```

You can troubleshoot this by verifying that your router interfaces are up in GNS3 and checking that all the IP addresses and subnet masks have been correctly assigned.

Another cause may be your PC's firewall settings, especially if you're using a Windows PC. In general, disabling your firewall entirely while working with GNS3 is a good idea and might resolve this and other issues.

VirtualBox

VPCS is a great tool for adding simple hosts to GNS3 and testing connectivity, but sometimes you need a host that's running a real operating system rather than a simulated one. This is where VirtualBox comes in. VirtualBox can run most PC-based operating systems, including Windows, Linux, FreeBSD, and others. It's also useful for running network operating systems such as Arista vEOS, Juniper Firefly, and NX-OSv.

The upside to using VirtualBox is that it provides you with hosts running actual operating systems; the downside is that those operating systems may need substantial resources from your PC. If all you need to do is test connectivity, then stick with VPCS, but if you need a host that provides a robust set of network utilities (to test the security of your GNS3 network, for example) or to run some other router or switch OS, then you might want to use VirtualBox.

Installing on Windows

To install VirtualBox on Windows, download the appropriate installer from the VirtualBox website (*http://www.virtualbox.org/*). Launch the installer and click **Next** when you see the Welcome screen to bring up a customization window. Make any desired customizations here and follow the onscreen instructions to complete the installation. I recommend accepting the default values to ensure that VirtualBox runs correctly with GNS3.

After the installation completes, you can launch the application by using the Windows Start menu or by clicking the VirtualBox icon.

Installing on OS X

To install VirtualBox on OS X, download the appropriate installer from the VirtualBox website (*http://www.virtualbox.org/*) and launch it. When the VirtualBox installation screen appears, double-click the **VirtualBox.pkg** icon and follow the onscreen instructions. The installation requires elevated privileges, so have your administrator password handy. Once the package is installed, you can launch it from your *Applications* folder by double-clicking the VirtualBox icon.

Installing on Linux

VirtualBox is supported on most Linux distributions, but check your Linux package manager to verify that it's supported on your specific platform. On Ubuntu and most other Debian-based Linux systems, use the `apt-get` utility to update your package manager and install the latest version of VirtualBox. Be sure that you have Internet access and enter the following from a terminal window:

```
$ sudo apt-get update
$ sudo apt-get install virtualbox
```

Once the utility is installed, you can launch it either by opening a terminal window and entering `virtualbox` or by launching it from your Linux window manager.

Importing Appliances

A VirtualBox *appliance* is a preconfigured virtual machine, often running a custom Linux distribution, that you can use in your GNS3 projects. Using a real operating system gives you more commands and greater flexibility than using a simulator like VPCS. You can download preconfigured VirtualBox appliances from the GNS3 website under the Download section.

Appliances need to be imported into VirtualBox before you can use them. Appliance package names end in *.ova*, which stands for *Open Virtual Appliance*, and are often referred to as *OVA* files. To import an appliance, launch VirtualBox, and you'll be presented with the VirtualBox Manager window. From the VirtualBox Manager, you can import or create new virtual machine guests and manage all of your installed guest operating systems. Importing an appliance is a fast and easy way to add a guest because the configuration and installation of the operating system has already been done for you.

The appliances found on the GNS3 website are often optimized to use fewer PC resources than a standard installation of the same operating system. Unfortunately, this means your appliance might not have all the commands or tools you need, but you should be able to update or install additional software through its software package manager.

In Figure 5-2, you can see that VirtualBox has been configured with one guest (Linux Microcore).

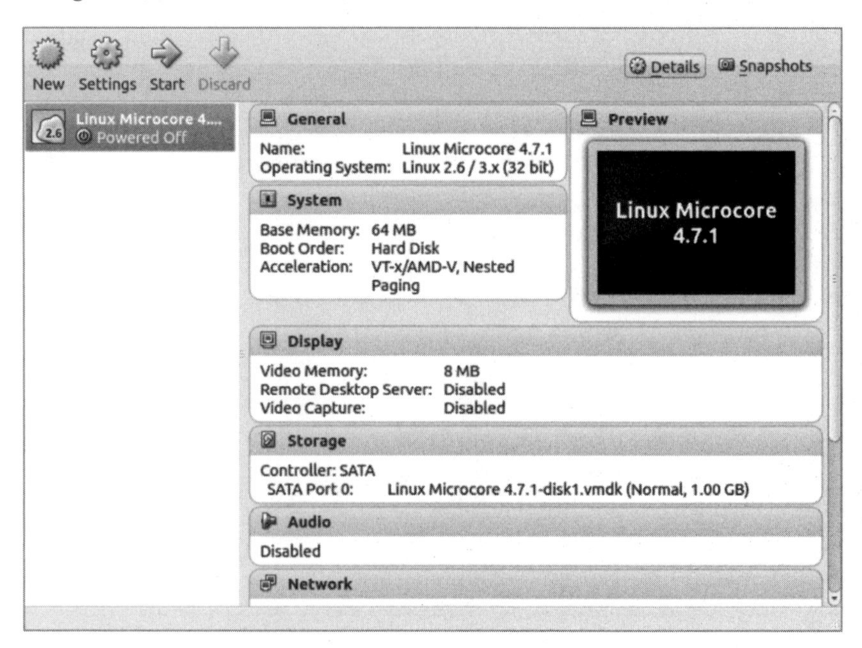

Figure 5-2: VirtualBox Manager showing an imported Linux guest OS

Selecting the guest OS displays basic information about the guest's configuration, such as the base memory and how much disk space has been assigned to the virtual machine. To modify the settings of a virtual machine, highlight the guest and click **Settings** in the toolbar. Just like real PCs, virtual PC guests often run better when given more resources, such as memory or additional CPU cores.

To import a VirtualBox guest appliance, download an image file and copy it to a folder in your user directory. Launch VirtualBox and select **File ▸ Import Appliance**; then click **Open Appliance** and browse to the location where you saved the file. Select the image file and click **Continue** followed by **Import** to complete the process. To test your VirtualBox guest, click **Start**, and your OS should boot up and run like a normal PC.

After testing your newly imported OS, you're ready to configure the GNS3 VirtualBox preferences.

VirtualBox Preferences

To manage VirtualBox guests, GNS3 uses the VBoxManage application. This program is automatically installed when you install VirtualBox. Before adding a VirtualBox guest to GNS3, verify the path to VBoxManage. Launch GNS3, select **GNS3 ▸ Preferences** on OS X or **Edit ▸ Preferences** on Windows and Linux, and then click **VirtualBox** to reach the window shown in Figure 5-3.

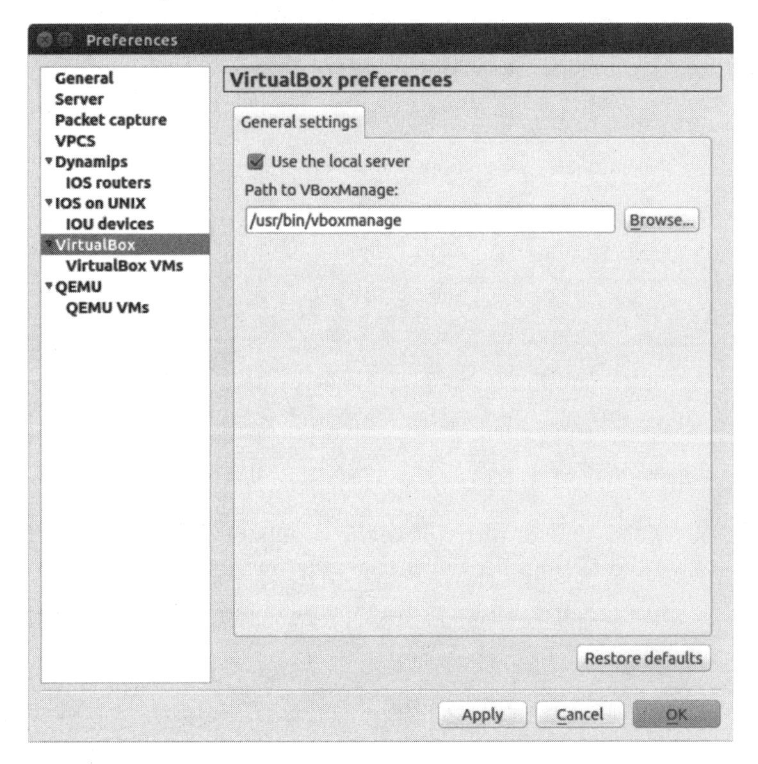

Figure 5-3: VirtualBox General Settings tab

On Ubuntu Linux, the path on the General Settings tab should be set to */usr/bin/vboxmanage*. Adjust the path as necessary and then click **Apply** and **OK**. On Windows and OS X, the VBoxManage path shouldn't need to be changed.

Unchecking **Use the local server** will allow you to choose a local or remote GNS3 server when creating a VirtualBox host. Leaving the box checked ensures that VirtualBox guest will always run locally on your PC.

If you experience problems while starting a VirtualBox host or opening a console connection to a host, one or more of the default console port numbers may already be in use by another application running on your PC. To fix this, try closing the offending application or disabling your PC firewall. Another possible cause might be that the VirtualBox guest you're using isn't configured to accept console connections.

VirtualBox Virtual Machine Settings

After configuring (or at least reviewing) the VirtualBox preferences in GNS3, you need to set up one or more VirtualBox hosts to use in your projects.

Begin by selecting **VirtualBox VM** from the left pane. Click **New** and select your VirtualBox virtual machine from the VM list drop-down menu, as shown in Figure 5-4.

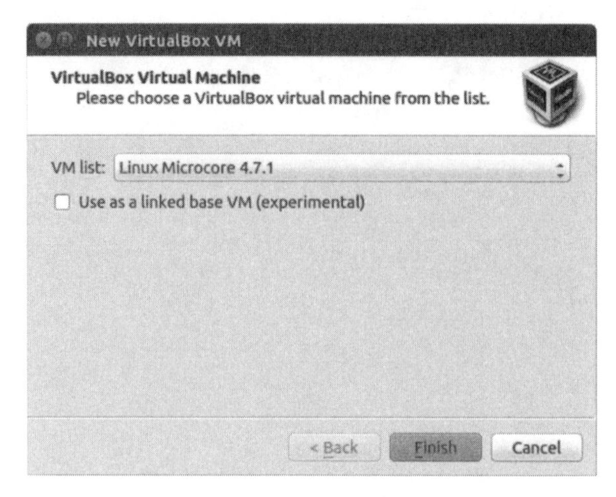

Figure 5-4: New VirtualBox VM screen

Click **Finish** to complete the installation. You should see the currently assigned settings for the virtual machine, as shown in Figure 5-5.

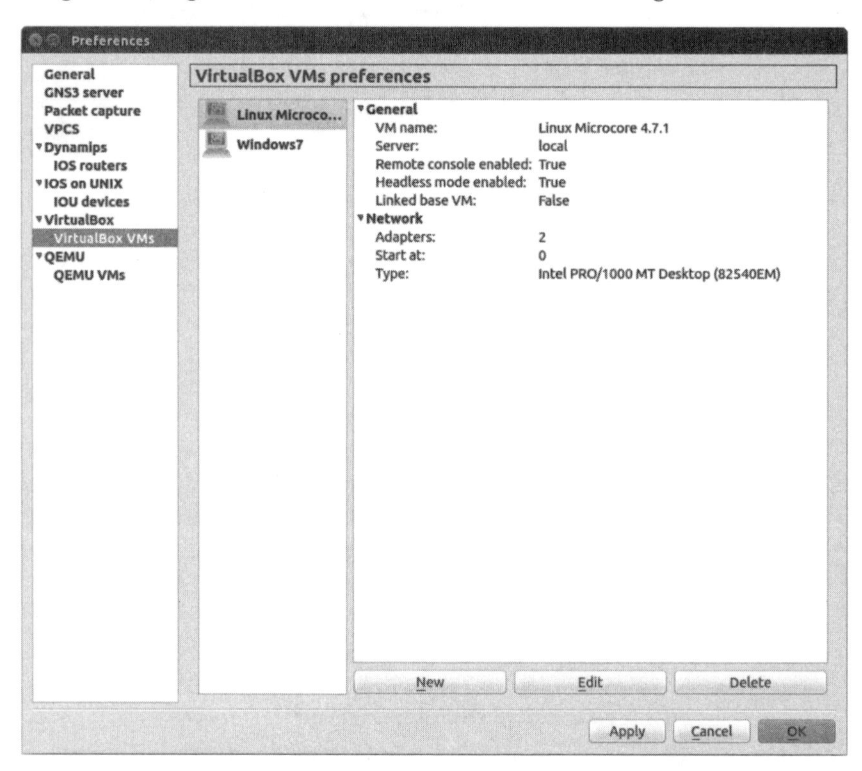

Figure 5-5: VirtualBox VMs preferences

By default your virtual machine device can be found under End Devices in the Devices toolbar. By right-clicking the virtual machine icon in the Preferences window (Linux Microcore in this example), you can assign a different icon to the virtual machine and choose where it will reside in the Devices toolbar. This allows you to better organize all your GNS3 devices.

To modify the settings of a virtual machine, select the virtual machine and click **Edit**. In most cases you'll want to go to the General settings tab and select the **Enable remote console** and **Start VM in headless mode** boxes, as shown in Figure 5-6. The first option allows you to access the console of a running virtual machine from GNS3's assigned terminal application; the second option suppresses VirtualBox from opening a console window when you start a virtual machine in GNS3.

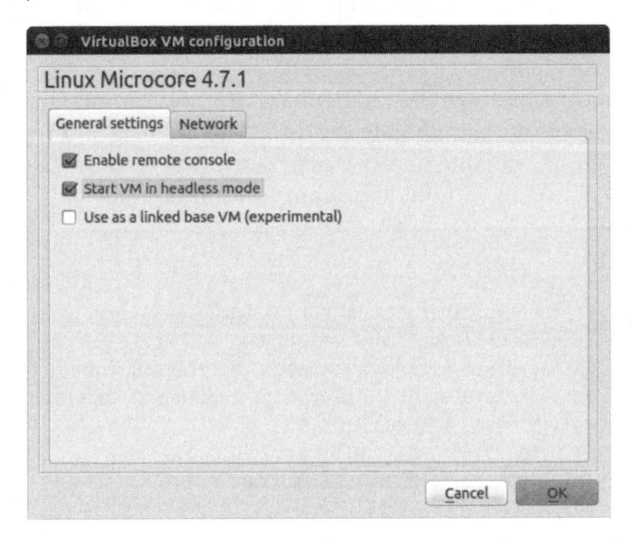

Figure 5-6: VirtualBox VM configuration's General settings tab

To modify network settings, click the **Network** tab. You can change the number of adapters installed in the virtual machine, the starting adapter number (usually 0 or 1), and the type of adapter installed in the virtual machine. When you're finished, click **Apply** and **OK** to save the modifications.

After you have configured a virtual machine guest operating system, you can use it in your GNS3 projects.

Using VirtualBox Hosts in a Project

To add a VirtualBox host to a project, drag a VirtualBox host node icon from the End Devices window to your GNS3 workspace.

A VirtualBox host can be used only one time per GNS3 project. If you want to use a particular VirtualBox host more than once, launch VirtualBox and use the Clone feature to create a cloned copy of the virtual machine.

Then, launch GNS3 and follow the same steps outlined earlier to configure the cloned host under VirtualBox Preferences. The next time you add a VirtualBox host node to your workspace, the cloned OS will be available.

After a VirtualBox host node has been added to your workspace, you're ready to link it to other GNS3 devices.

Linking VirtualBox Host Nodes to Other Devices

To add a link between a VirtualBox host node and another device, click the **Add a Link** toolbar icon; then click your VirtualBox host node and choose an interface to use for the link. Select another device and choose an interface to complete the connection.

To boot the host, right-click the VirtualBox host node icon and select **Start**. Test the connection by configuring an IP address on your VirtualBox host and the device to which it's linked; then use the `ping` command to verify connectivity.

On most Linux systems, like Microcore, you can manually configure an IP address and default gateway using the `ifconfig` and `route` commands. To see a list of available network interface cards (NICs) in Linux, use the `ifconfig` command without any configuration options.

```
$ ifconfig

eth0      Link encap:Ethernet  HWaddr 08:00:27:7F:91:0A
          UP BROADCAST MULTICAST  MTU:1500  Metric:1
          RX packets:0 errors:0 dropped:0 overruns:0 frame:0
          TX packets:0 errors:0 dropped:0 overruns:0 carrier:0
          collisions:0 txqueuelen:1000
          RX bytes:0 (0.0 B)  TX bytes:0 (0.0 B)
          Interrupt:10 Base address:0xd020

eth1      Link encap:Ethernet  HWaddr 08:00:27:C5:FC:66
          UP BROADCAST MULTICAST  MTU:1500  Metric:1
          RX packets:0 errors:0 dropped:0 overruns:0 frame:0
          TX packets:0 errors:0 dropped:0 overruns:0 carrier:0
          collisions:0 txqueuelen:1000
          RX bytes:0 (0.0 B)  TX bytes:0 (0.0 B)
          Interrupt:9 Base address:0xd060
```

NOTE *Not all Linux systems use the `ifconfig` or `route` command to configure TCP/IP, but most do. If these commands aren't available with your distribution, check your Linux documentation to see how to configure an interface.*

If you're using a Windows PC virtual machine, you can manually configure an IP address by opening the Network and Sharing Center and clicking **Change Adapter Settings**. Right-click the adapter you want to configure and select **Properties** to modify the TCP/IP settings, as shown in Figure 5-7.

Internet Protocol Version 4 (TCP/IPv4) Properties

General

You can get IP settings assigned automatically if your network supports this capability. Otherwise, you need to ask your network administrator for the appropriate IP settings.

Obtain an IP address automatically

Use the following IP address:

IP address: 192 . 168 . 1 . 50

Subnet mask: 255 . 255 . 255 . 0

Default gateway: 192 . 168 . 1 . 1

Obtain DNS server address automatically

Use the following DNS server addresses:

Preferred DNS server: . . .

Alternate DNS server: . . .

Validate settings upon exit

Advanced...

OK Cancel

Figure 5-7: Windows TCP/IP interface properties

Enter your IP address information and click **OK** when finished. If you have a DHCP server configured in your GNS3 project, you can leave the fields blank and choose **Obtain an IP address automatically** instead.

Simple VirtualBox Project Using a Linux Virtual Machine

Now that you've added a Linux VirtualBox virtual machine to GNS3, let's create a simple project that networks the host to a Cisco IOS router. Begin by creating the project in Figure 5-8. Drag a VirtualBox Linux host and Dynamips router to your workspace and link them together using an Ethernet switch node.

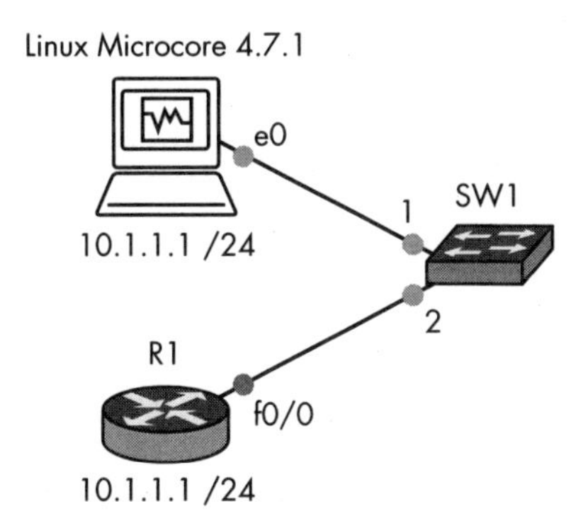

Figure 5-8: VirtualBox host and Cisco IOS router project

Start the devices and begin configuring your project by assigning an IP address to interface eth0 of the VirtualBox Linux host. Right-click the Linux Microcore node and select **Console** to open the terminal. From the Linux terminal shell, enter the following command to assign the IP address:

```
$ sudo ifconfig eth0 10.1.1.1 netmask 255.255.255.0 up
```

Next, open a console to router R1, assign an IP address to interface f0/0, and bring up the interface.

```
R1# configure-terminal
R1(config)# interface f0/0
R1(config-if)# ip address 10.1.1.2 255.255.255.0
R1(config-if)# no shutdown
R1(config-if)# exit
R1(config)# exit
R1#
```

Finally, test connectivity by pinging your Linux host's IP address from router R1.

```
R1# ping 10.1.1.1

Type escape sequence to abort.
Sending 5, 100-byte ICMP Echos to 10.1.1.1, timeout is 2 seconds:
!!!!!
Success rate is 100 percent (5/5), round-trip min/avg/max = 8/16/32 ms
```

Now let's take a look at how you can use Wireshark to analyze packets on your GNS3 networks.

Wireshark

Wireshark is one of the most robust packet analysis tools available to network engineers, and it's free! A *packet analyzer*, sometimes called a *packet sniffer*, is software that allows you to capture IP packets as they traverse your network. You can then open the packets to reveal and analyze their contents. Packet sniffers like Wireshark are used to troubleshoot networking protocols, thwart hackers, and even identify viruses, but they are often overlooked by beginners. If you're an aspiring networking engineer, using GNS3 and Wireshark together is an excellent way to learn the ins and outs of networking and how network protocols work.

Installing on Windows

If you installed GNS3 using the Windows all-in-one installer, then Wireshark should already be installed. If you're using OS X or Linux, then you need to download and install Wireshark manually.

Installing on OS X

Before installing Wireshark on OS X, you need to install XQuartz, an OS X version of the X Window System that's similar to X.Org on Linux systems.

Download the appropriate version of XQuartz from the Mac OS Forge website (*http://xquartz.macosforge.org/*). Double-click the installer and then click the *XQuartz.dmg* installer package. Click **Continue** until you reach the welcome screen, and then click **I Agree** and **Install** to complete the installation.

Next, download and install Wireshark from the developer website (*http://www.wireshark.org/*). Double-click the downloaded file, followed by the *wireshark.dmg* installer package. At the welcome screen, click **Continue**, **I Agree**, and **Install** to complete the installation.

The first time you launch Wireshark, OS X will ask for the location of the X Window program. From the File window, click **Browse**, navigate to the *Applications/Utilities* folder, and then select **XQuartz**.

NOTE *The first time you launch Wireshark, XQuartz opens an Xterm window but not Wireshark. This strange quirk is easily corrected by closing XQuartz and relaunching Wireshark. It may take a moment to open, but this is normal. When the application starts, you should see the Wireshark welcome screen.*

Now that Wireshark is installed, let's look at how to capture packets from devices in your projects.

Installing on Linux

To install the latest version of Wireshark using the Advanced Package Tools on Ubuntu Linux, open a terminal program and enter the following commands:

```
$ sudo apt-get update
$ sudo apt-get install wireshark
```

Confirm the installation when prompted, and the package will be installed. After the process has completed, Wireshark should be ready to use.

Capturing Packets in GNS3

To begin capturing packets, right-click a link between two devices and select **Start Capture**, as shown in Figure 5-9. (To stop a capture, right-click the same link and select **Stop Capture**.)

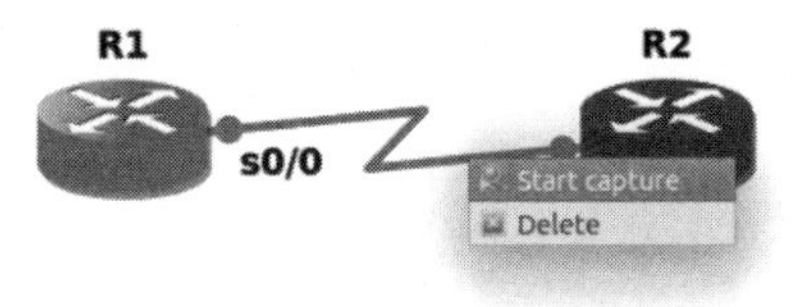

Figure 5-9: Start capturing packets.

GNS3 prompts you for the source device, the interface name, and the encapsulation type to use for capturing data. You can capture data on Ethernet and serial interfaces. On Ethernet connections, you can choose only Ethernet encapsulation: DLT_EN10MB, but on serial connections, you can choose Cisco HDLC encapsulation: DLT_C_HDLC, Cisco PPP encapsulation: DLT PPP_SERIAL, or Frame Relay encapsulation: DLT_FRELAY.

To capture standard Cisco serial data (High-Level DataLink Control), choose **HDLC**; to capture serial Point-to-Point Protocol data, choose **PPP**; and to capture Frame-Relay data, select **FRELAY**. Use the drop-down menu to make your selection, as shown in Figure 5-10.

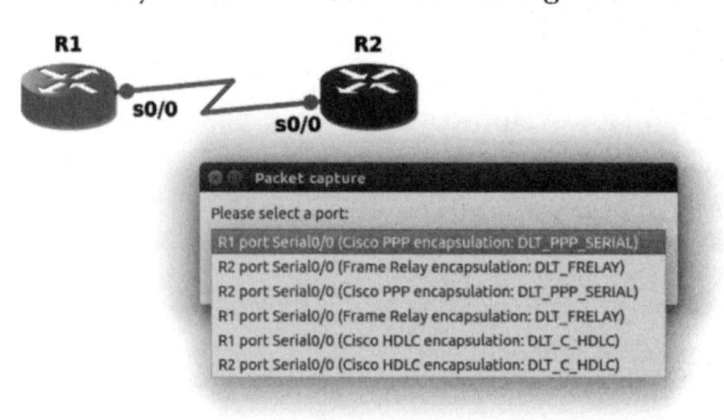

Figure 5-10: Source selection for capturing serial packets

After making a selection and clicking **OK**, GNS3 will open Wireshark and begin capturing packets, as shown in Figure 5-11. Notice that the Wireshark window is divided into three distinct panes.

❶ **Packet List pane**
The top pane of the window is dedicated to displaying individual packets as they're being captured. Packet fields are displayed across the top and include the packet sequence number (No.), timestamp (Time), source IP address (Source), destination IP address (Destination), protocol name (Protocol), frame length size (Length), and information field (Info). Packets containing different protocol types are displayed in different colors to help identify them.

❷ **Packet Details pane**
After a packet is selected from the packet list, details about the protocols and protocol fields of the packet are displayed in the middle pane. You can expand and collapse the fields to show or hide their details. The displayed field names are specific to the type of packet being captured and will change from one packet type to another.

❸ **Packet Bytes pane**
The lower pane of the main window displays the raw data in hexadecimal format, with ASCII characters displayed to the right. This is what the data looks like natively as it crosses the network. Wireshark allows you to view this information in either hexadecimal or binary.

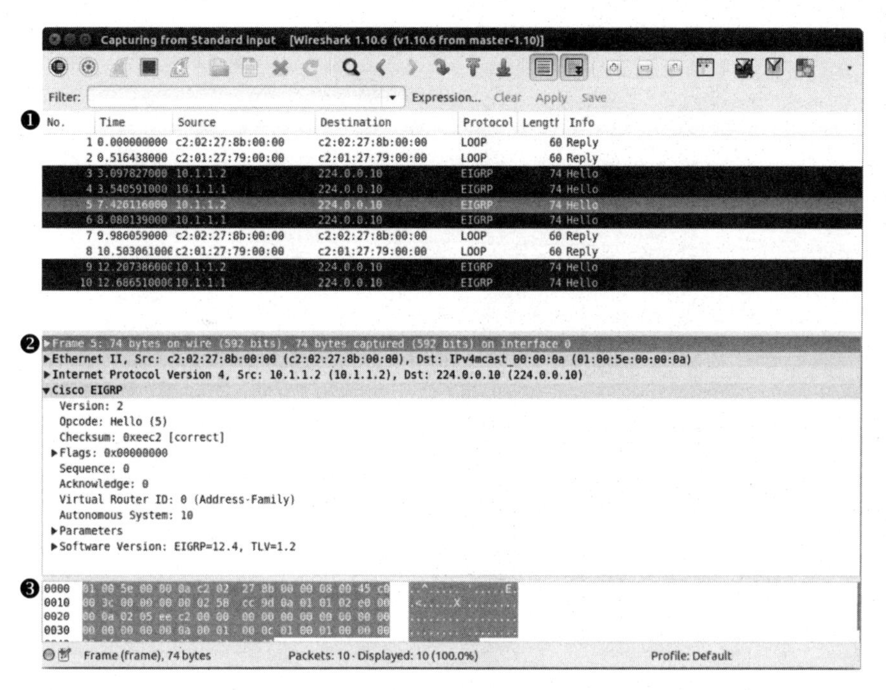

Figure 5-11: Simple Wireshark capture from GNS3

If you don't see any packets displayed in the packet list, close Wireshark and stop the capture. Be sure your router interfaces are up and have been assigned IP addresses and then restart a capture and start Wireshark again.

NOTE *To learn more about using Wireshark, I highly recommend reading* Practical Packet Analysis, 2nd Edition *by Chris Sanders (No Starch Press, 2011). You could even become a Wireshark Certified Network Analyst (WCNA).*

To change the default behavior of Wireshark in GNS3, go to **Preferences** and select **Packet Capture**. To prevent GNS3 from automatically starting Wireshark when you capture packets, uncheck **Automatically start the packet capture application**, as shown in Figure 5-12.

You have the option to save packet captures and analyze them later. To do so, select **Wireshark Traditional Capture** from the drop-down menu (under Preconfigured packet capture reader commands) and then click **Set**, **Apply**, and **OK**. Now when GNS3 captures data, it will automatically save the captured files in a directory named *captures* within your project folder, as in *GNS3/projects/<project_name>/project-files/captures/*.

To review saved packet captures, launch Wireshark on your PC, select **File ▸ Open**, browse to the *captures* folder, and select a capture file. The *.pcap* capture files will be named after the GNS3 devices involved in the capture, as in *R1_FastEthernet0-0_to_R2_FastEthernet0-0.pcap*.

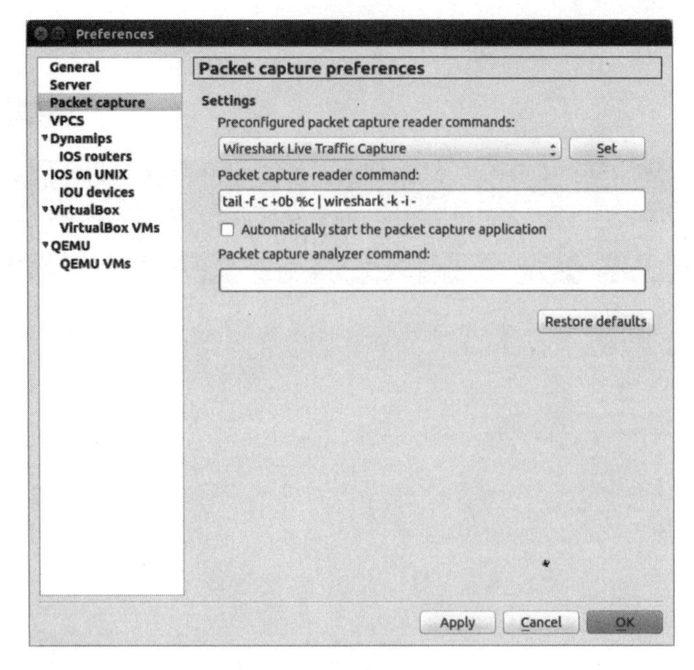

Figure 5-12: Wireshark capture preferences

To learn more about Wireshark, check out the online User's Guide (*http://www.wireshark.org/docs/wsug_html_chunked/*). It's well organized and provides a lot of information about using the software.

Final Thoughts

One key aspect of GNS3 is its modular design and ability to expand projects using other open source software. Using VPCS, you can add a large number of simple PC hosts, and with VirtualBox you can run hosts using full-blown operating systems such as Linux. This feature makes GNS3 very expandable because any network operating system that runs in VirtualBox can be added to your GNS3 projects.

Wireshark is one of the most underutilized tools around, but it's also one of the most powerful. With Wireshark, you can dig deep and really see what's happening on your networks. Whether you're new to networking or already network certified, breaking out Wireshark and examining packets is a great way to hone your skills and increase your understanding of network protocols.

In Chapter 6, you'll look at Quick Emulator, another open source PC emulator, and use it to create a special PC version of Juniper's Junos OS known as Juniper Olive. Juniper Olive allows you to add fully functional Juniper routers to your GNS3 projects.

6

JUNIPER OLIVE AND VSRX FIREFLY

You can install and run Juniper routers with GNS3 in several ways. In this chapter, I show you how to use VirtualBox and Quick Emulator (QEMU) to create GNS3-ready Juniper devices and then install Juniper's vSRX Firefly firewall.

QEMU is an open source PC emulator similar to VirtualBox. It's less polished but has many powerful features and is fully integrated into GNS3. Using QEMU, you can run many network operating systems including Cisco ASA, IDS, IOS-XR, NX-OSv, and a special version of Juniper's Junos OS known as Juniper Olive. In this chapter, I focus only on Juniper.

Installing QEMU on Windows and OS X

If you installed GNS3 on Windows or OS X, then QEMU should have been installed for you already. The GNS3 installer may have installed two versions of QEMU: a stable version that was configured automatically during the

GNS3 installation and a newer version that contains additional, untested features. If you need your projects to be completely stable, I recommend using only the preconfigured version.

If you installed GNS3 using the defaults outlined in Chapter 2, you should find the QEMU applications under *C:\Program Files\GNS3\qemu-0.13.0* on both 32-bit and 64-bit Windows systems, but keep in mind that this directory will change as new versions of QEMU are introduced and added to GNS3. On OS X, you should find QEMU under */Applications/GNS3.app/Contents/Resources/qemu/bin/*.

Installing QEMU on Linux

QEMU on Ubuntu can be installed using a package or compiled from source code. To install from a package, update your package manager and install QEMU from the command line.

```
$ sudo apt-get update
$ sudo apt-get install qemu
```

Alternatively, you can install the `qemu-system-x86` package. This is a much smaller installation that should be capable of running any operating system that you want to use with GNS3. To install the x86 architecture–only version of QEMU, use the following commands:

```
$ sudo apt-get install qemu-system-x86
$ sudo apt-get install qemu-utils
```

You may want to compile QEMU from source code, depending on what version of QEMU is available for your system. Although precompiled packages of QEMU exist on many Linux distributions, they may not be the newest version available and may not include the GTK toolkit that provides the QEMU graphical user interface. In that case, you can access the QEMU interface by installing a VNC viewer program, like GNC Viewer.

When you install from source code, you also have to install other packages required by QEMU before compiling the source. Update your package manager and install these packages now:

```
$ sudo apt-get update
$ sudo apt-get install flex
$ sudo apt-get install bison
$ sudo apt-get install zlib1g-dev
$ sudo apt-get install libglib2.0-dev
$ sudo apt-get install libgtk2.0-dev
$ sudo apt-get install libncurses5-dev
$ sudo apt-get install libpcap-dev
$ sudo apt-get install dh-autoreconf
```

Next, download the QEMU source code from the QEMU website (*http://www.qemu-project.org/*) and unzip the file, as shown here:

```
$ wget http://www.qemu-project.org/download/qemu-2.1.2.tar.bz2
$ bunzip2 qemu-2.1.2.tar.bz2
$ tar xvf qemu-2.1.2.tar
```

After unzipping the files, move to the QEMU installation directory and enter the `configure` and `make` commands to compile the source code.

```
$ cd qemu-2.1.2
$ ./configure
$ make
```

Finally, complete the process by installing the compiled files on your system. This must be done using elevated root privileges.

```
$ sudo make install
```

When the installation is complete, you should find QEMU binaries under */usr/local/bin/*, and the QEMU support files should be in the */usr/local/share/qemu/* directory.

With QEMU installed, you're ready to start creating and using QEMU devices in GNS3.

Introducing Juniper

Most people have heard of Cisco, but relatively few have heard of Juniper Networks. Like Cisco, Juniper produces a wide range of networking hardware, and Internet service providers use its extremely high-throughput devices to efficiently route billions of packets for their customers.

All Juniper devices are designed around a common FreeBSD code base, though not every Juniper device runs the FreeBSD operating system. Instead, they use its kernel only as a framework for another operating system known as Junos OS. However, because Junos OS is designed around FreeBSD, you can run a special version of the software on your PC called Juniper Olive.

Juniper Olive is a functional version of Junos OS. Because it runs on a regular PC and not an actual Juniper chassis, it lacks the proprietary ASIC hardware to achieve the high throughput of a real Juniper device. Otherwise, it's the real deal and not a simulation of the operating system. This makes it well suited for studying for the Juniper Networks Certified Associate (JNCIA) certification and other entry-level certifications.

NOTE *Juniper provides another virtual router called vMX that runs on bare-metal x86 hardware or as a virtual machine using QEMU, VirtualBox, or VMware, which allows it to be integrated into GNS3. It's what Juniper calls a scalable "pay as you grow" solution.*

JUNIPER EXTENDS AN OLIVE BRANCH

Juniper Olive is rumored to be an in-house version of Junos OS that's meant to be used only by Juniper developers and not intended for public consumption, but only Juniper knows for sure. If you contact the company, you'll be told it's an "unsupported version." Juniper won't provide you with the software, and Juniper certainly won't give you any support. However, GNS3 fully supports Juniper Olive integration, allowing you to add Juniper routers to your GNS3 projects.

Installing Juniper

It's been said that if you give a person a fish, you feed them for a day, but if you teach a person to fish, you feed them for a lifetime. This adage holds true when creating a Juniper Olive, so let's go fishing! Although there are many ways to configure and install Olive (including scripts that automate the process or preconfigured virtual machines that can be found on the Internet), learning to do it manually allows you to adjust the parameters as necessary when new Olive versions become available.

When used with GNS3, the Juniper Olive software is often installed using VirtualBox or QEMU. In this section, you'll work with QEMU, but before you can create an Olive, your system must meet the following requirements:

- 8GB available disk space
- 1024MB available memory for QEMU/Juniper
- QEMU installed on your system
- FreeBSD-4.11 mini ISO
- Juniper Olive software

Let's look at how to create an Olive and where to get the software to do it.

Process Overview

The Juniper Olive installation software works a lot like a common parasite, with FreeBSD as its unsuspecting host. To create an Olive, you'll install a copy of FreeBSD using QEMU or VirtualBox. Next, you'll copy a gzipped tarball of the Juniper Olive software to your FreeBSD virtual machine.

There, you'll unzip the package and make a small modification, and then you'll zip the files back into a FreeBSD installable package. Finally, you'll install the package and reboot the FreeBSD system.

This is where things get interesting. The first time you boot your system, the Juniper Olive software invades its FreeBSD host. It will repartition the FreeBSD hard disk, copy new files to the system, and keep any FreeBSD files that it needs. When it's finished, you should have a functional Juniper router.

Acquiring FreeBSD

A FreeBSD CD image is required to install FreeBSD with QEMU. Several versions are available that are suitable for creating Juniper Olive, but I recommend a mini ISO. It contains all the necessary files, and it's the fastest to download. Download the *4.11-RELEASE-i386-miniinst.iso* file from the FreeBSD archive (*ftp://ftp-archive.freebsd.org/*). I recommend this FreeBSD version instead of more recent ones because it seems to work well with almost any Olive version.

NOTE *You can find a ready-to-use QEMU (and VirtualBox) image with FreeBSD already installed at the GNS3 website* (http://www.gns3.com/) *in the Download section, under QEMU appliances.*

Acquiring Juniper Olive Software

Next, you need to acquire the Juniper Olive software. The software is available as a FreeBSD installable package and should have a name like *jinstall-12.1R1.9-domestic-olive.tgz*. Because Juniper Olive is not supported by Juniper, you cannot get a copy of the software directly from Juniper.

Creating a Juniper Olive CD Image File

After you have the Juniper Olive software, you need a way to copy the package to your FreeBSD virtual machine to install it. There's more than one way to do this, but the simplest way is to mount an ISO image file on your FreeBSD virtual machine, just as you would a regular CD. Before you can do that, you have to create your own ISO image of the Olive software.

Creating an ISO in Windows

To create an ISO image file using Windows, you first need to install ISO image creation software. I recommend ISO Recorder (*http://isorecorder.alexfeinman.com/isorecorder.htm*). It's free, easy to install, and works well. Download the software and launch the installer. Then click **Next** and follow the prompts to complete the installation.

After installing ISO Recorder, you should be able to create an ISO image of the Juniper Olive software. Create a folder and copy your gzipped Olive file into the folder (named *juniper-olive*, for example). Then, right-click the folder and select **Create ISO image file**.

The ISO Recorder Creation Wizard appears, as shown in Figure 6-1.

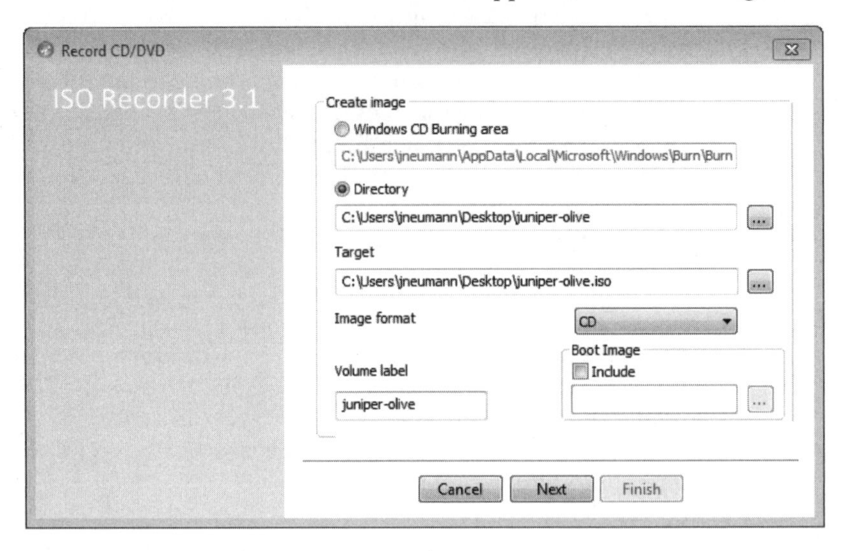

Figure 6-1: ISO Recorder Creation Wizard

Under Create image, select the **Directory** radio button, change the Image format to **CD**, click **Next**, and follow the prompts to create your ISO image. After you have a Juniper ISO, you're ready to install Juniper Olive on Windows.

Creating an ISO in OS X

On computers running OS X, copy your Juniper image file to a folder and use `hdiutil` to create an ISO image of the folder's contents. In the following listing, I've created an ISO image file named *juniper-olive.iso* using a folder named *JUNOS*:

```
$ mkdir JUNOS
$ cp jinstall-12.1R1.9-domestic.tgz JUNOS
$ hdiutil makehybrid -iso -joliet -o juniper-olive.iso JUNOS
```

Now that you have a suitable ISO of the Olive software, you're ready to install Juniper Olive on OS X.

Creating an ISO in Linux

Creating an ISO image on Ubuntu Linux is almost the same as on OS X, except you use the `mkisofs` application. Copy your Juniper image file to a folder (*JUNOS*, for example) and enter the following commands to create the ISO:

```
$ mkdir JUNOS
$ cp jinstall-12.1R1.9-domestic.tgz JUNOS
$ mkisofs -o juniper-olive.iso JUNOS
```

Now that you have your ISO, there are only a few things left to do before you create a Juniper Olive.

Installing and Configuring FreeBSD Using QEMU

The first step in creating a Juniper Olive is to create a QEMU virtual machine of FreeBSD. QEMU doesn't have a graphical user interface, so you'll do everything from the command line. You will use the `qemu-img` program to create a virtual disk image file and the `qemu` program to install and test your virtual machine.

NOTE *Not all QEMU installations are alike. On some installations, the QEMU application file might be named* qemu-system-i386 *or* qemu-system-x86_64*, or you may have both installed. If you're unsure, check your QEMU installation directory.*

Preparing Your Build Directory

Start by creating a build directory and then copy the FreeBSD installation ISO and the Juniper Olive ISO files to the directory, as in the following example:

```
$ mkdir Juniper
$ cp 4.11-RELEASE-i386-miniinst.iso Juniper
$ cp juniper-olive.iso Juniper
```

If you're using Windows, open a command prompt window and enter the following commands instead:

```
c: mkdir Juniper
c: copy 4.11-RELEASE-i386-miniinst.iso Juniper
c: copy juniper-olive.iso Juniper
```

Now that everything is prepped in your build directory, you can begin installing the system.

Installing a Junos-Friendly FreeBSD System

In this section, you'll create a virtual hard disk using `qemu-img` and install FreeBSD on the virtual disk. I'll only cover the basics of preparing FreeBSD for Olive and won't go into a lot of detail about FreeBSD itself.

Preliminary Checks for Windows and OS X

If you're a Windows user, install the Telnet Client application from the Programs and Features Control Panel before you begin.

If you're a OS X user, you'll want to add the QEMU file directory to your OS X search path. Verify the installation path to your QEMU files. If you installed QEMU manually, you should look for the *qemu-img* file in */opt/local/bin* or */usr/local/bin*. If you're using QEMU that was installed with GNS3, you should find the file under */Applications/GNS3.app/Contents/Resources/qemu/bin/*. Enter the following commands to add the QEMU binaries to your OS X search path. Make a backup copy of your .bash_profile file before you begin.

```
$ cd ~
$ cp .bash_profile .bash_profile-backup
$ sudo echo 'export PATH=/Applications/GNS3.app/Contents/Resources/qemu/
bin:$PATH' >> .bash_profile
```

After entering the commands, close and reopen a terminal window to enable the new search path. To verify your path is correct, enter the following command:

```
$ echo $PATH
```

The previous command will display your path configuration. If it's not correct, you may need to restore your *.bash_profile-backup* file and try again. If it is correct, then you're ready to move on.

Getting Started

Begin the installation by creating an 8GB virtual disk image file named *juniper.img* in your build directory. The *qemu-img* command options used here should work on all Unix-like systems.

```
$ cd Juniper
$ qemu-img create juniper.img 8G
```

Next, boot QEMU from the FreeBSD mini ISO using the following command:

```
$ qemu-system-i386 -m 512 -hda juniper.img -localtime -cdrom 4.11-RELEASE-
i386-miniinst.iso
```

Windows users should open a command prompt window and use the following commands instead. Be sure to enter the path command if QEMU isn't already in your Windows path.

```
c: cd Juniper
c: path="c:\program files\GNS3\qemu-0.13.0"
c: qemu-img create juniper.img 8G
c: qemu-system-i386w -m 512 -hda juniper.img -localtime -cdrom 4.11-RELEASE-
i386-miniinst.iso
```

When FreeBSD boots, the Kernel Configuration Menu appears, as shown in Figure 6-2.

```
QEMU
Kernel Configuration Menu

Skip kernel configuration and continue with installation
Start kernel configuration in full-screen visual mode
Start kernel configuration in CLI mode

Here you have the chance to go into kernel configuration mode, making
any changes which may be necessary to properly adjust the kernel to
match your hardware configuration.

If you are installing FreeBSD for the first time, select Visual Mode
(press Down-Arrow then ENTER).

If you need to do more specialized kernel configuration and are an
experienced FreeBSD user, select CLI mode.

If you are certain that you do not need to configure your kernel
then simply press ENTER or Q now.
```

Figure 6-2: FreeBSD Kernel Configuration Menu

Press ENTER to skip the kernel configuration and continue with the installation.

Next, the FreeBSD sysinstall Main Menu appears, shown in Figure 6-3.

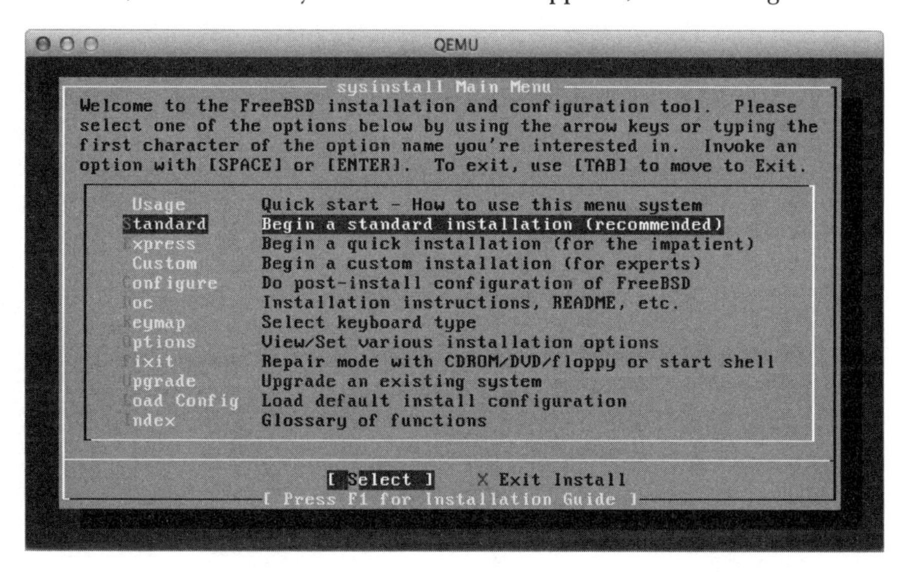

Figure 6-3: sysinstall Main Menu

Use the arrow to move down, select **Standard** to begin a standard installation, and then press ENTER to continue.

Partitioning the Filesystem

The next screen, shown in Figure 6-4, displays basic information about using the FDISK Partition Editor.

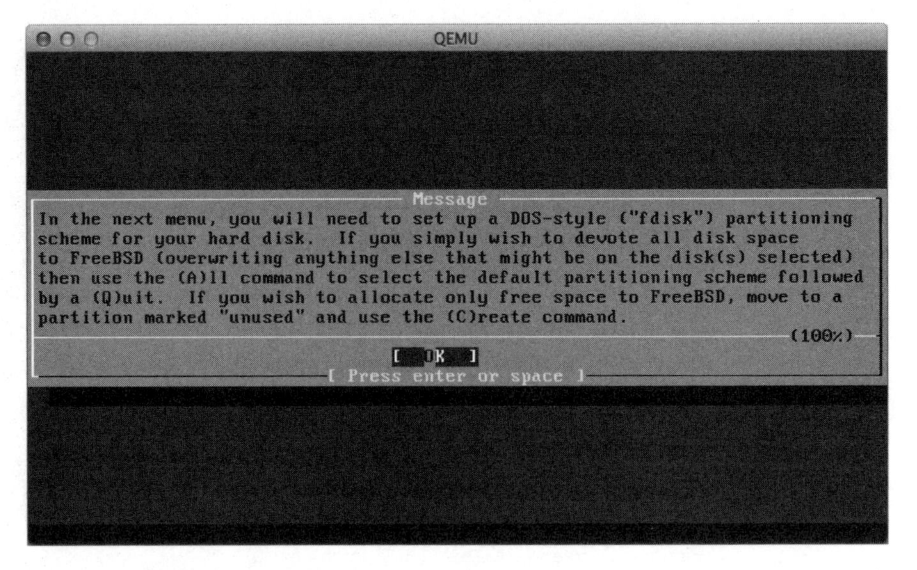

Figure 6-4: FDISK partitioning message screen

Read the instructions and press ENTER to continue to the FDISK Partition Editor menu, shown in Figure 6-5.

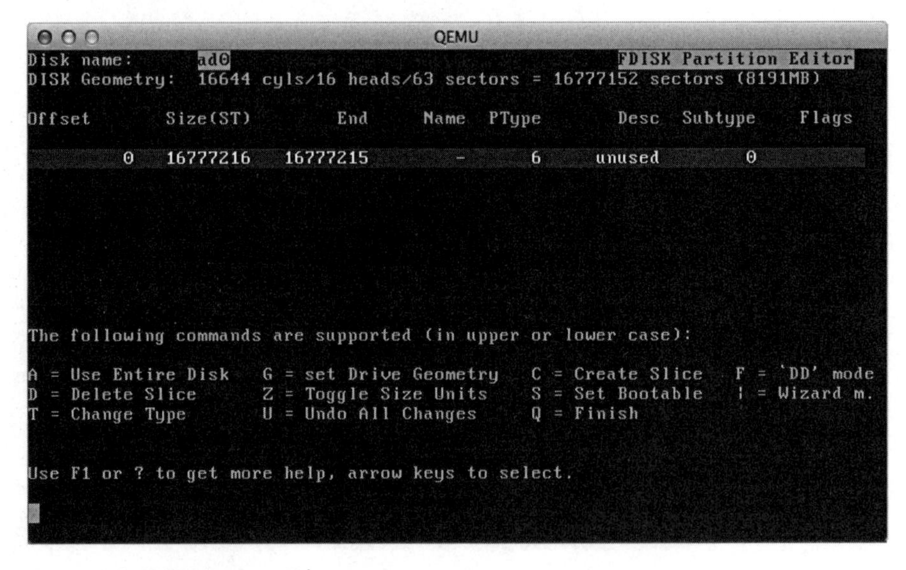

Figure 6-5: FDISK Partition Editor menu

The FDISK Partition Editor allows you to choose how much disk space you want to allocate to FreeBSD. Choose **A** to use the entire disk and then select **Q** to finish.

The Install Boot Manager menu should appear next, as shown in Figure 6-6.

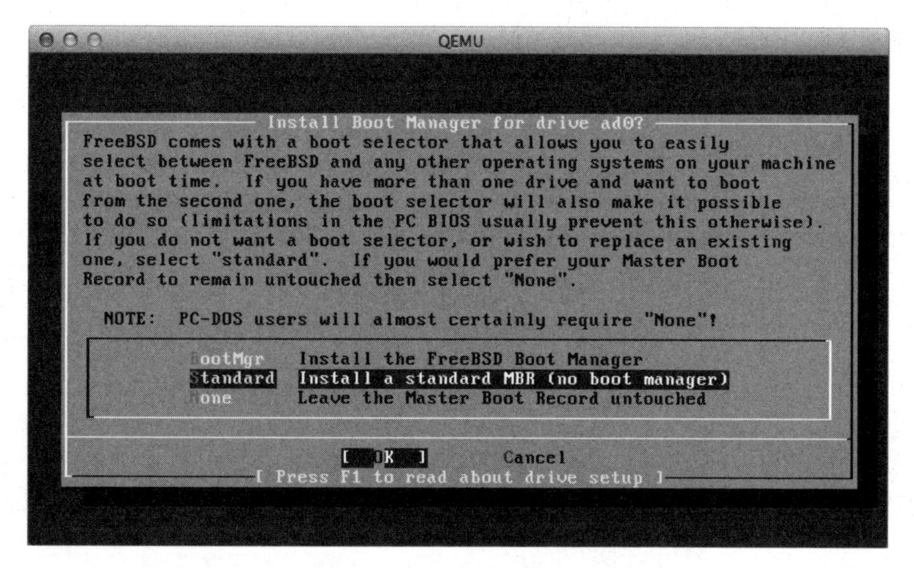

Figure 6-6: Install Boot Manager menu

Use the arrow to move down, select **Standard** to install a standard master boot record (MBR), and press ENTER to continue.

FreeBSD then displays a message about creating BSD partitions inside your newly created FDISK partition, as shown in Figure 6-7.

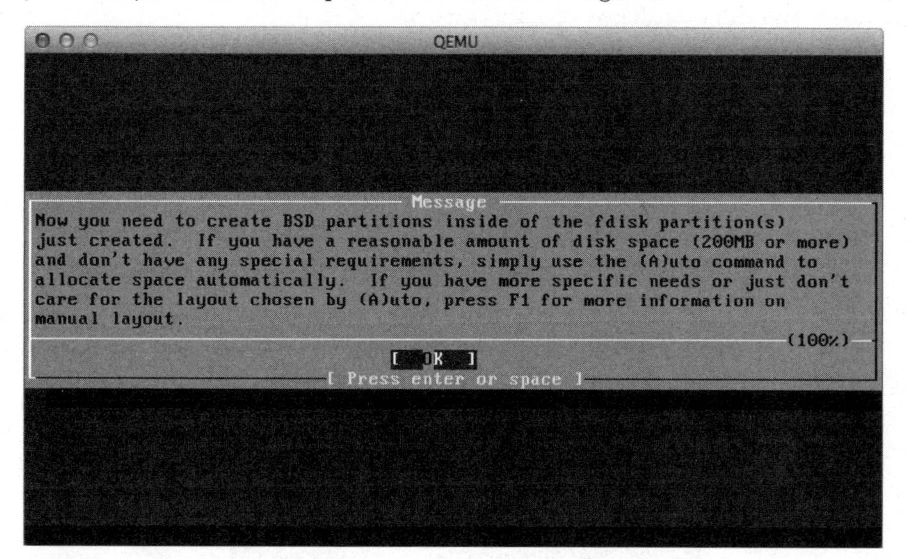

Figure 6-7: BSD partition message

After reading the message, press ENTER to continue to the FreeBSD Disklabel Editor.

The next step is to create *Juniper-compatible partitions.* It's important to pay close attention to how you partition the virtual hard disk because the Juniper Olive package must see the correct FreeBSD partitions or the installation will fail. You also must create your partitions in a specific order.

To create your first partition, select **C** and type the partition size in the field provided, as shown in Figure 6-8.

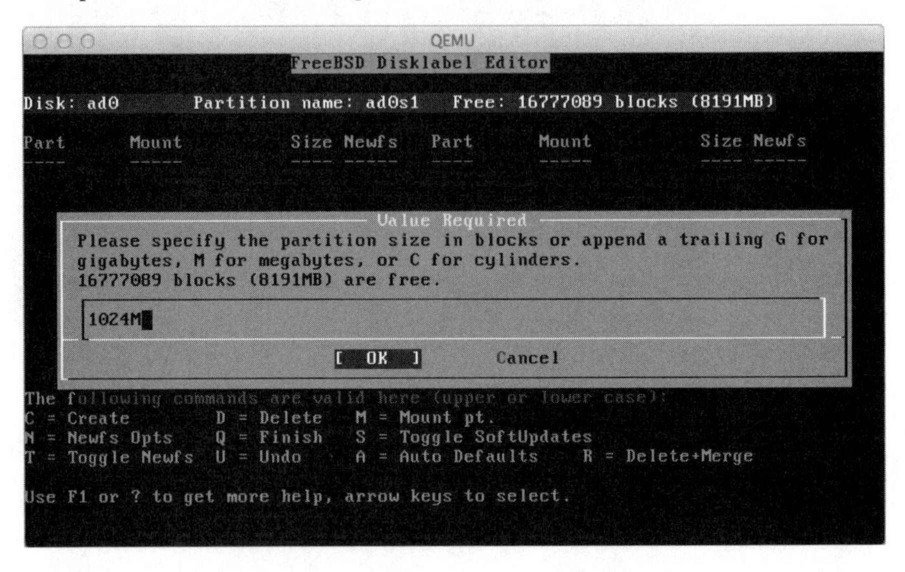

Figure 6-8: Specify a partition size.

I entered 1024M to create a 1GB partition. Press ENTER to accept this value, and you'll see the partition type option screen, shown in Figure 6-9.

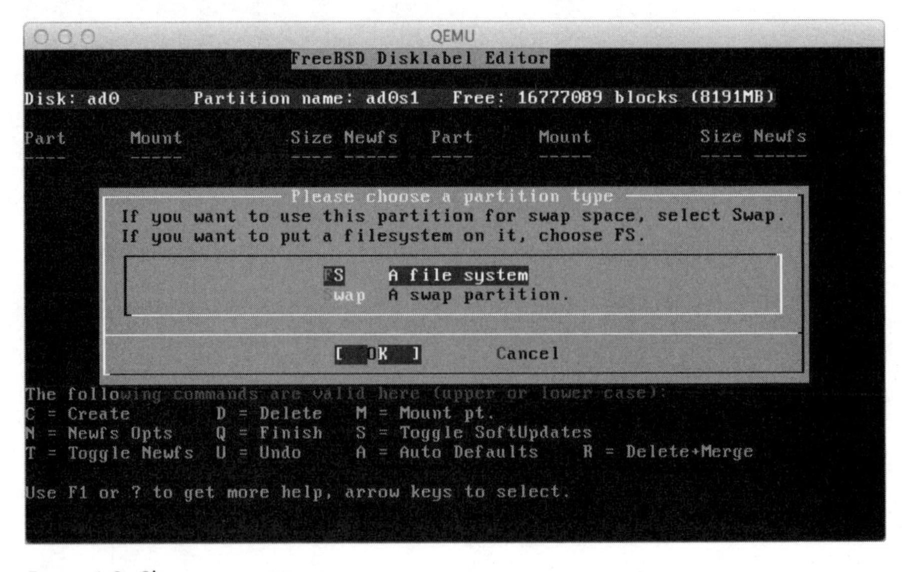

Figure 6-9: Choose a partition type.

Press ENTER to create a filesystem (FS) partition type, and you'll be given the option to choose the mount point for the partition, as shown in Figure 6-10.

Figure 6-10: Choose a mount point for the partition.

To create a mount point for your root partition, type a forward slash (/) and press ENTER to complete the configuration of your first partition.

Using Table 6-1, follow the same procedure to create the complete filesystem layout. The order is important! After creating your root partition (/), work your way down the list, finishing with the /var partition. When you get to the swap partition, make sure you choose swap and not FS as your partition type. The /var partition is last, so when you create it, accept the default partition block size. This value uses the remaining free space on your partition. Remember, if the partitions are not created in sequential order, the partition names won't match the mount points, and Juniper Olive won't install properly.

Table 6-1: FreeBSD Partitioning for Juniper Olive

Part	Mount	Size
ad0s1a	/	1024 MB
ad0s1b	swap	1024 MB
ad0s1e	/config	1024 MB
ad0s1f	/var	remaining space

There are many ways to partition FreeBSD in preparation for the Olive install, but I've found this method to be the most reliable across different versions of Juniper Olive. When you're done, the filesystem should look exactly like the one in Figure 6-11.

```
QEMU
FreeBSD Disklabel Editor

Disk: ad0       Partition name: ad0s1    Free: 0 blocks (0MB)

Part       Mount            Size Newfs   Part       Mount           Size Newfs
----       -----            ---- -----   ----       -----           ---- -----
ad0s1a     /              1024MB UFS    Y
ad0s1b     swap           1024MB SWAP
ad0s1e     /config        1024MB UFS+S Y
ad0s1f     /var           5119MB UFS+S Y

The following commands are valid here (upper or lower case):
C = Create        D = Delete    M = Mount pt.
N = Newfs Opts    Q = Finish    S = Toggle SoftUpdates
T = Toggle Newfs  U = Undo      A = Auto Defaults     R = Delete+Merge

Use F1 or ? to get more help, arrow keys to select.
```

Figure 6-11: Fully configured partition layout suitable for Juniper Olive

Once you've configured all the partitions, choose **Q** to complete the partitioning process and then choose your distribution set, as shown in Figure 6-12.

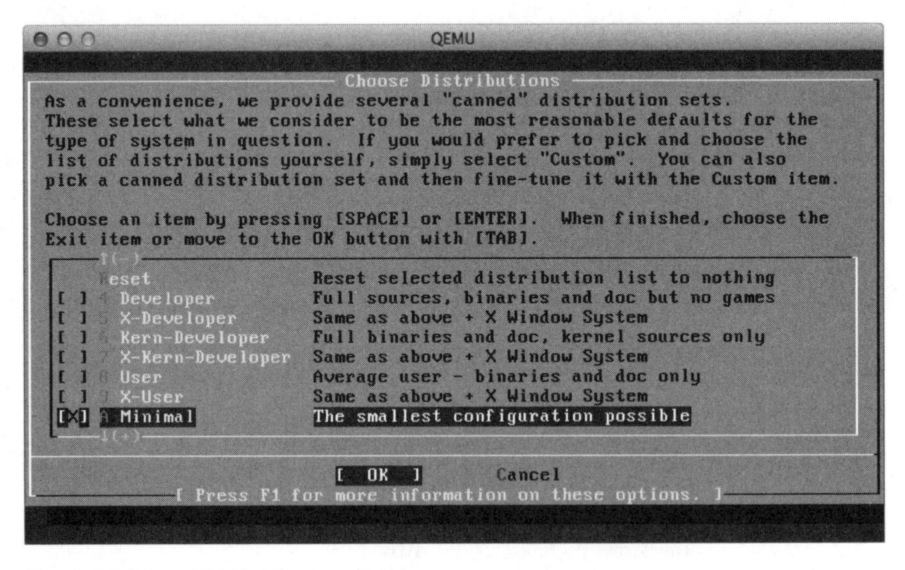

Figure 6-12: FreeBSD distribution choices

Use the arrow keys to scroll down, select **Minimal**, and then press the spacebar to make the selection. Now press TAB to select **OK** and press ENTER to finish.

Finishing Installation of FreeBSD

Next, choose your installation media, as shown in Figure 6-13.

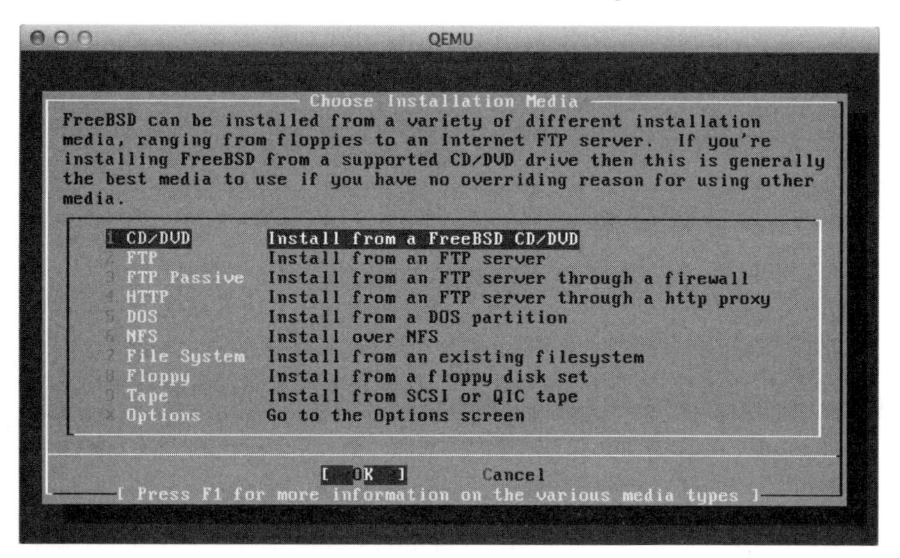

Figure 6-13: Choosing an installation media

Press ENTER to choose **CD/DVD** as your installation media, and the installation will begin. When it's finished, the message shown in Figure 6-14 appears.

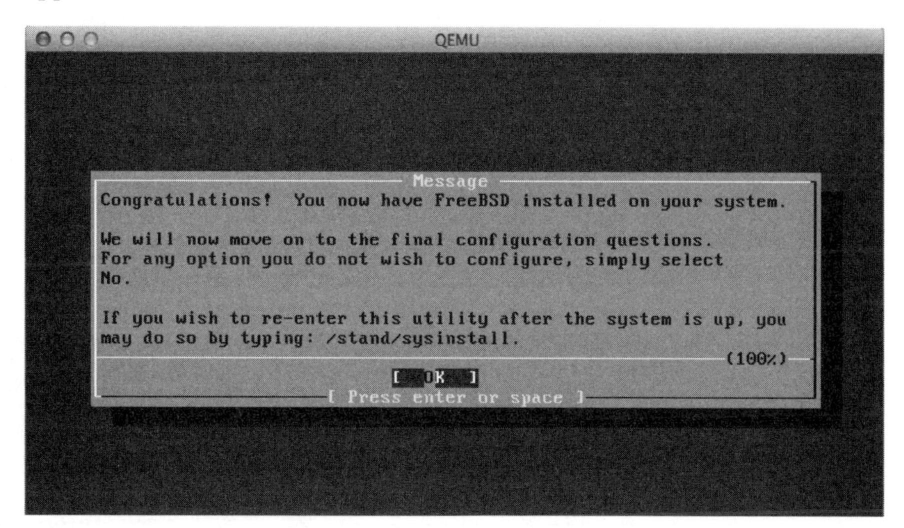

Figure 6-14: File installation complete message

Because you're using FreeBSD as a host for Junos OS, you don't need to concern yourself with any of the FreeBSD configuration questions that follow this screen. Answer "no" to all remaining questions, and when asked to create a password for the root account, press ENTER to leave it blank. When you're finished answering questions, allow the system to reboot, log on as *root*, and shut down FreeBSD using the `halt` command. Then close the window and quit the QEMU program.

Installing the Juniper Olive Package in FreeBSD

Now that the FreeBSD installation is complete, you can install the Juniper Olive package.

Getting Your Olive Up and Running

Boot FreeBSD using QEMU with the following command to ensure that you can mount the *juniper-olive.iso* CD image file you created earlier. (On Windows, replace `qemu-system-i386` with `qemu-system-i386w`.)

```
qemu-system-i386 -m 512 -hda juniper.img -localtime -cdrom juniper-olive.iso
```

If FreeBSD loads correctly, a login prompt should appear. Log in as *root* at the prompt; you shouldn't need to enter a password, so just press ENTER. Then use the `mount` command to mount the *juniper-olive.iso* CD image.

```
# mount /cdrom
```

Create a temporary directory named *olive* on the `/var` partition and extract the Juniper Olive package into the temporary directory.

```
# mkdir /var/tmp/olive
# cd /var/tmp/olive
# tar zxvf /cdrom/jinstall-12.1R1.9-domestic.tgz
```

Next, modify Junos OS to allow you to install the software on your QEMU virtual machine.

```
# mkdir temp
# cd temp
# tar zxvf ../pkgtools.tgz
# cp /usr/bin/true bin/checkpic
```

Extract the *pkgtools* directory from *pkgtools.tgz* to another *temp* directory within the *olive* directory, and replace the *checkpic* file with the FreeBSD *true* file. This removes the Junos OS checkpic protection.

After the modification, gzip the *temp* directory contents back into a tarball named *pkgtools.tgz* and remove the *temp* directory you created.

```
# tar zcvf ../pkgtools.tgz *
# cd ..
# rm -rf temp
```

Next, create a new Olive installation package and install it on your FreeBSD system. In the following listing, I've named the installation package *olive.tgz*:

```
# tar zcvf ../olive.tgz *
# pkg_add -f ../olive.tgz
```

After you install the Olive package, you should see an error message followed by some warning messages, which tell you that the package will erase any files that aren't Junos configuration files and that you need to reboot to load the Junos OS software.

Any other onscreen instructions displayed can be ignored because they apply to an actual Juniper router, not an Olive installation on a PC. However, before continuing, you need to shut down the FreeBSD system using the `halt` command and quit QEMU.

```
# halt
```

The final step in installing Olive is to reboot the system and give the package time to complete its takeover of FreeBSD. At this point, you must provide the installer with extra memory, or the install will fail. Although Junos OS runs comfortably with 512MB of RAM, the installer needs 1024MB of RAM to create the RAM disk that it uses during installation.

In Linux and OS X, boot Juniper Olive with 1024MB of RAM to complete the installation, as follows:

```
$ sudo qemu-system-i386 -m 1024 -hda juniper.img -serial telnet:127.0.0.1:1001,
server,nowait,nodelay -localtime
```

Windows users should enter the following command instead:

```
c: qemu-system-i386w -m 1024 -hda juniper.img -serial telnet:127.0.0.1:1001,
server,nowait,nodelay -localtime
```

After you boot the system, you can watch the Olive software being installed by using telnet to connect to port 1001 of your localhost. (On Windows you may have to install the Telnet Client program from the Programs and Features Control Panel first.) Open a second Windows command prompt or terminal window, and enter the following command to see the installation output displayed on the console:

```
telnet localhost 1001
```

I highly recommend monitoring your install. It's a great way to troubleshoot whether something goes wrong. Otherwise, you won't know why an installation failed. A common problem is that not enough memory has been allocated to your virtual machine; another is that your partition sizes are too small or were created incorrectly.

The Juniper Olive installation can take 15 minutes or longer, depending on your hardware, because the installer performs a lot of tasks, such as repartitioning your FreeBSD hard drive and extracting various packages. When everything is complete, the system should automatically reboot, load Junos OS, and present you with what appears to be a FreeBSD login prompt, shown in Figure 6-15.

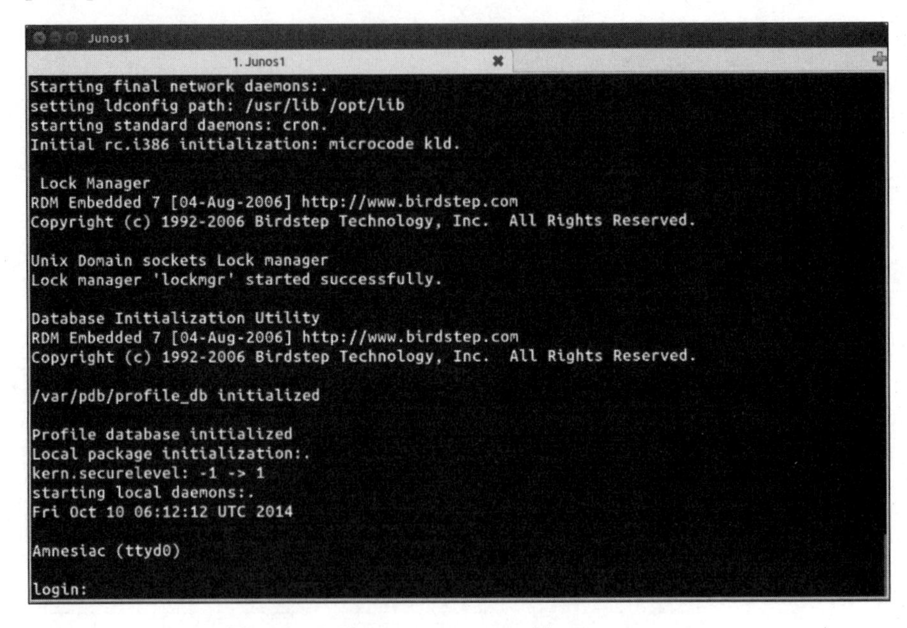

Figure 6-15: Successful Junos OS boot messages and login

This prompt is where you'll log in to Junos OS. If you see the previous messages and the login prompt, then your Juniper router is ready to use.

Backing Up Juniper Olive

After you create a working Olive, make a backup copy of the image for safekeeping. After all, who wants to go through all that work again? Not me!

First, properly shut down Junos OS to prevent triggering a dirty filesystem. A dirty filesystem occurs when files have not been properly closed. This condition can cause file corruption and can even break the Junos operating system. If the filesystem is marked as dirty, a filesystem check is triggered the next time you start Junos OS, and it may take longer than usual to boot until the system is checked and marked clean again (meaning no errors were found, or all errors were fixed).

To shut down Junos OS, log in as *root* (no password necessary) and enter the following commands:

```
Login: root
root@% cli
root> request system halt
Halt the system ? [yes,no] (no) yes
```

It's safe to quit QEMU after you see a message indicating that the operating system has halted, as shown here:

```
The operating system has halted.
Please press any key to reboot.
```

To make a backup copy of your Juniper image, enter the following command from the directory where your image file is saved:

```
$ cp juniper.img backup-juniper.img
```

Windows users can use this command instead:

```
c: copy juniper.img backup-juniper.img
```

Now that you have a Juniper router, you need to configure GNS3 so it can be used in your projects.

Configuring a Juniper Router in GNS3

To configure a Juniper router in GNS3, select **Edit ▸ Preferences** on Windows and Linux or **GNS3 ▸ Preferences** on OS X. Double-click **QEMU** from the sidebar and select **QEMU VMs** to open the QEMU VMs preferences window, shown in Figure 6-16.

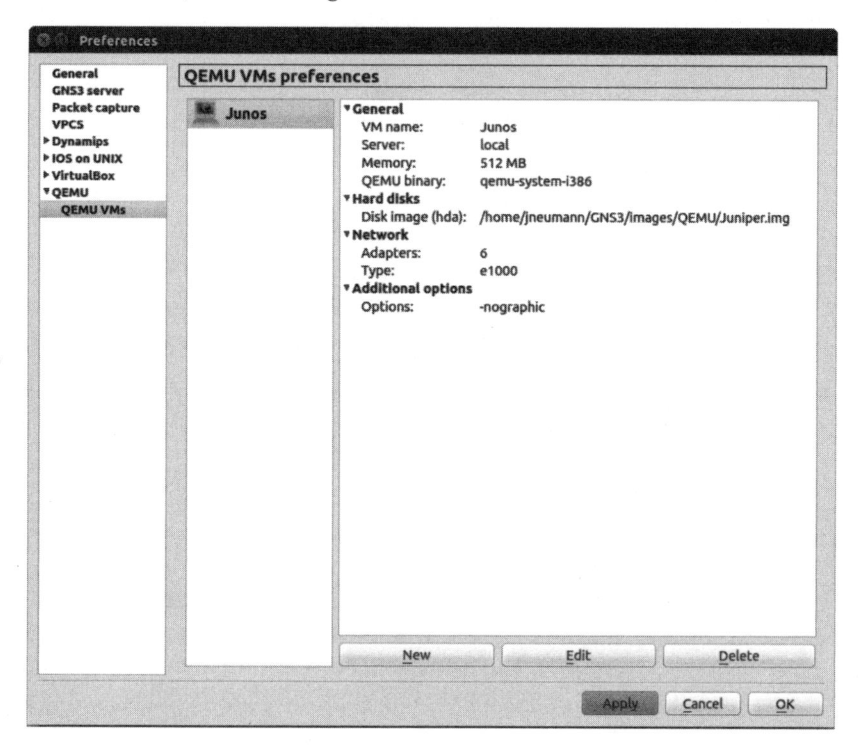

Figure 6-16: QEMU VMs preferences window

From here you can create, edit, and delete QEMU virtual machines, allowing you to bring your Juniper virtual machine into GNS3.

Adding the Juniper Virtual Machine to GNS3

To add your Juniper virtual machine to GNS3, click **New** to start the New QEMU VM wizard. Enter a name for your virtual machine and leave Type set to **Default**. Click **Next** to set the QEMU binary and memory options, shown in Figure 6-17.

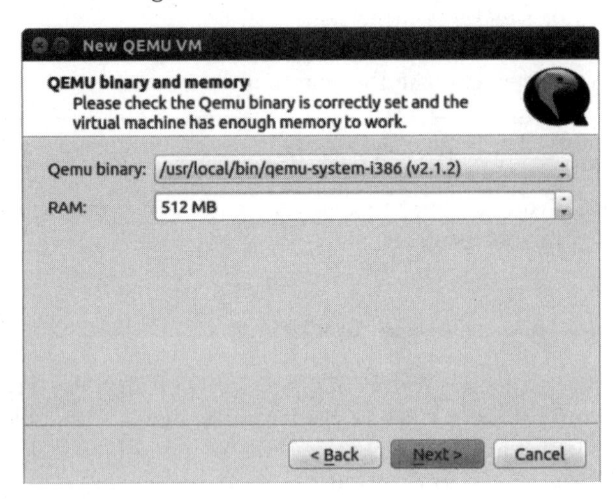

Figure 6-17: Setting QEMU binary and memory

Select **qemu-system-i386** from the Qemu binary drop-down menu. You're choosing this QEMU program because Juniper Olive runs on a 32-bit version of FreeBSD. Give your Olive 512MB of RAM and then click **Next**. Click **Browse** to locate and select the *juniper.img* file that you created previously, and then click **Finish**.

NOTE *Two QEMU binary applications are often used in GNS3:* `qemu-system-i386` *and* `qemu-system-x86_64`*. The difference between them is that* `qemu-system-i386` *is designed to emulate 32-bit architecture, and* `qemu-system-x86_64` *is designed to emulate 64-bit architecture. The* `qemu-system-x86_64` *application is supposed to be 32-bit backward compatible, but it is not compatible with all 32-bit virtual machines (including IOS-XRv, for example).*

Adding Ethernet Interfaces

After creating your virtual machine, go back and add more Ethernet interfaces. I recommend using six interfaces. Highlight your virtual machine and select **Edit**. Click the **Network** tab and change the number of interfaces to 6. Now select the **Advanced settings** tab and enter the **-nographic** option under Additional settings, as shown in Figure 6-18.

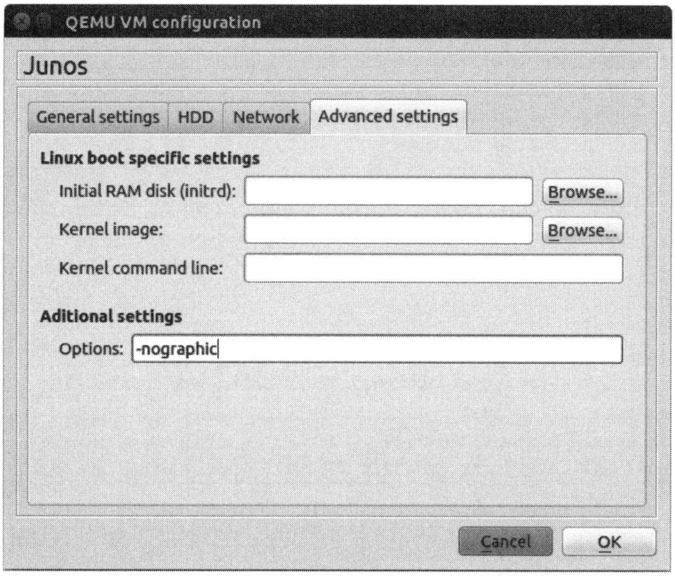

Figure 6-18: QEMU advanced options

The -nographic option prevents the QEMU GUI interface from displaying when you start your QEMU virtual machine. Although the GUI can be useful in troubleshooting a virtual machine, it's more often a nuisance and should be disabled. This option can be used with any QEMU virtual machine, not only Juniper. When you're done, click **OK** to close the window and then click **Apply** and **OK** to save all your changes.

Testing a Juniper Router

Before creating projects that include Juniper routers, it's a good idea to test connectivity between a Cisco router and a Juniper router. If you're unable to successfully ping between the devices, there might be a problem with your installation, and it's better to find out early before you spend hours designing a project that doesn't work.

Drag a Cisco router node and a Juniper router node to your workspace from the Devices toolbar, and create a link from the Cisco router to interface e0 of the Juniper router, as shown in Figure 6-19.

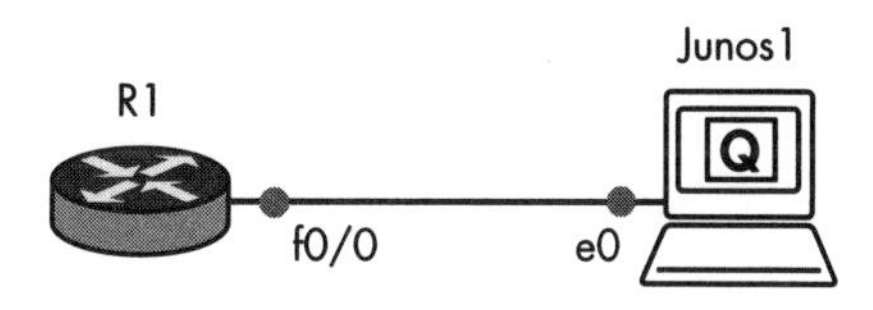

Figure 6-19: Connecting a Cisco router to a Juniper router

Start the routers and open a console to the Cisco router. Assign an IP address to the interface that's connected to your Juniper router (f0/0, in this example).

```
R1> enable
R1# configure-terminal
R1(config)# interface f0/0
R1(config-if)# ip address 10.10.10.1 255.255.255.0
R1(config-if)# no shutdown
```

Now open a console to your Juniper router, log on, and configure an IP address using the same subnet as your Cisco router.

```
Login: root
root@% cli
root> edit
❶ root# set system root-authentication plain-text password
New password: olive1
Retype new password: olive1
root# set interfaces em0 unit 0 family inet address 10.10.10.2/24
root# commit
commit complete
```

For security, Junos OS requires that you assign a root password ❶ before you can commit any other configuration changes to the router, so do that now. I set the password to *olive1*, but you can enter any password you want.

NOTE *In this example, you can see that Juniper syntax is entirely different from Cisco syntax. If Juniper syntax is new to you, visit the Juniper website* (http://www.juniper.net/) *for detailed information about configuring Juniper routers.*

After configuring both devices, ping your Cisco router to test connectivity.

```
root# exit
root> ping 10.10.10.1
```

If the ping test fails, there could be a problem with your IP addresses or QEMU installation. If you compiled QEMU from source code, verify that you installed a version known to work with Juniper Olive. If necessary, compile and reinstall QEMU again. If the problem persists, try installing or compiling another version of QEMU.

You can also create an Olive using VirtualBox. The procedure is basically the same as QEMU, but you'll use the VirtualBox GUI tools instead of the command line. When you create your VirtualBox virtual machine, set Type to BSD and set Version to FreeBSD (32-bit).

Running Juniper vSRX Firefly

In addition to Junos OS, you can run a virtual version of Juniper's SRX Firewall, called *vSRX Firefly*. If you register with Juniper, you can download an evaluation of Firefly from the website for free (*http://www.juniper.net/*). You'll want to download the Firefly VMware Appliance - FOR EVALUATION!

package. As you can see from the name, it's designed to run on VMware, but you can tweak it to run on VirtualBox or QEMU. I'm covering VirtualBox here, so make sure the VirtualBox program is installed on your system before you begin.

After you've downloaded the Firefly software, notice that it's an Open Virtual Appliance (OVA) file, named something like *junos-vsrx-ver.x-domestic .ova*. An OVA file is a special package file that can be unarchived using the `tar` command. To extract the contents from the file on Linux or OS X, use the following command:

```
$ tar xvf junos-vsrx-ver.x-domestic.ova
```

NOTE *If you're running Windows, you can use the 7-zip application* (http://www.7-zip .org/) *to extract the files.*

After all the files have been extracted, you need to convert the VMware virtual machine disk file (the file with extension *.vmdk*) to a virtual disk image (VDI) file that can be used by VirtualBox. To convert the file, use the `vboxmanage` utility that comes with VirtualBox.

```
$ vboxmanage clonehd -format VDI junos-vsrx-ver.x-domestic-disk1.vmdk
junos-vsrx-ver.x-domestic-disk1.vdi
```

After converting the disk image, you can delete all the Firefly files except the new VDI image file (*junos-vsrx-ver.x-domestic-disk1.vdi* in this example). This is the hard disk image file that you will import into VirtualBox.

Creating a Firefly Virtual Machine with VirtualBox

You need to create a new virtual machine in VirtualBox and import the Firefly hard disk image file. Launch VirtualBox and click **New** to open the Create Virtual Machine dialog, shown in Figure 6-20.

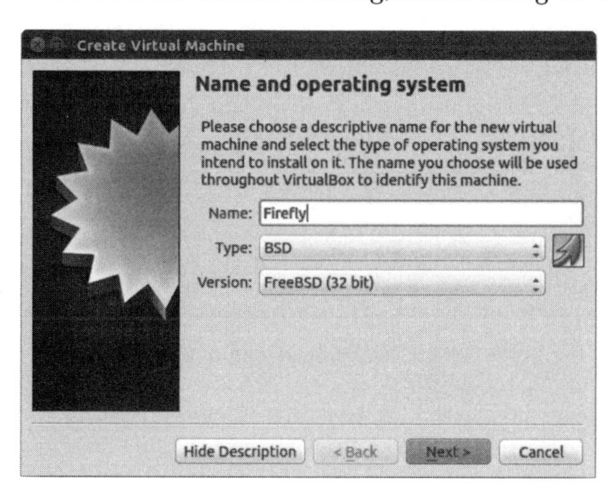

Figure 6-20: Create Virtual Machine dialog

Give the virtual machine a name (*Firefly* in this example), set Type to **BSD**, and set Version to **FreeBSD (32-bit)**. When you're done, click **Next** to assign the memory size, as shown in Figure 6-21.

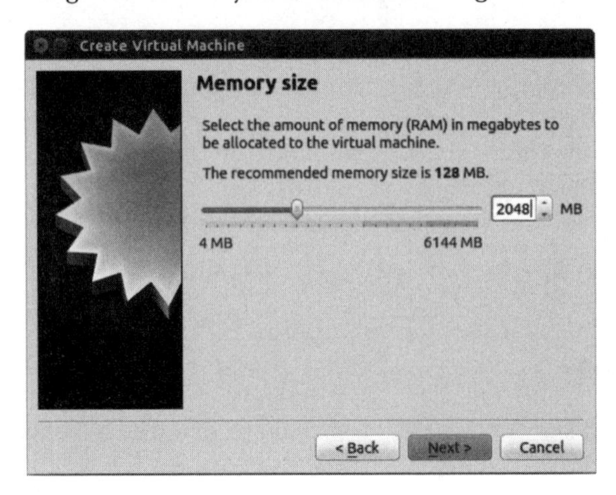

Figure 6-21: Adjust the memory size.

Follow the instructions from Juniper to set the proper memory size. In this example, I've chosen 2048 MB, because that's what Juniper recommends for my version of Firefly. When you're done, click **Next**, and check **Use an existing virtual hard drive file**, as shown in Figure 6-22.

Use the browse icon to locate and choose the VDI image file you created previously. When you're finished, click the **Create** button to create the virtual machine.

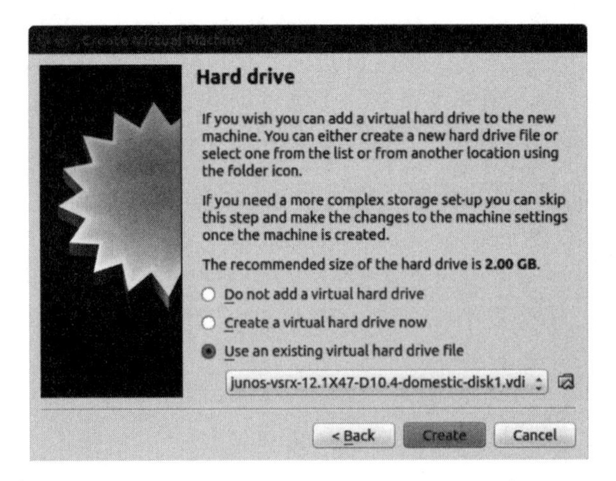

Figure 6-22: Choose the Junos vSRX Firefly VDI hard disk image file.

Giving Your Virtual Machine More Processors

After creating the virtual machine, you have to increase the number of processors to two because vSRX Firefly needs two processors to run properly. If your virtual machine is configured with only one processor, Firefly will boot and run, but you will not be able to see or configure any Ethernet interfaces.

Select your virtual machine name in VirtualBox, go to **Settings ▸ System**, and click the **Processor** tab, shown in Figure 6-23.

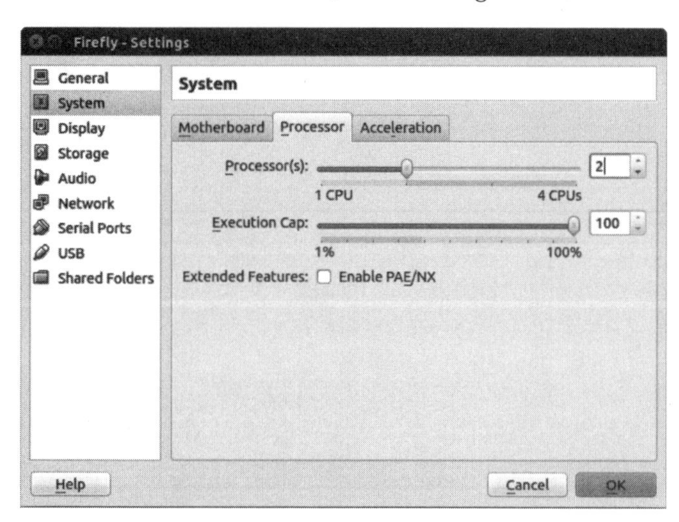

Figure 6-23: The Processor tab under System

Use the slider tool to select two processors, and click **OK**. After you've configured your Firefly virtual machine, right-click your virtual machine in VirtualBox and select **Clone** to create a copy of it to work with in GNS3. The original virtual machine will remain unused, and you'll always have a clean, unconfigured master of your virtual machine.

Once you're done creating the Firefly virtual machine, you'll need to add it to GNS3 before you can use it in your projects.

Adding vSRX Firefly to GNS3

Launch GNS3 and select **Edit ▸ Preferences** on Windows and Linux or **GNS3 ▸ Preferences** on OS X. Double-click **VirtualBox** in the pane on the left, and select **VirtualBox VMs** to open the VirtualBox VMs preferences window, shown in Figure 6-24.

To add your Firefly VirtualBox virtual machine to GNS3, click **New** to start the New Virtual VM wizard. Select your Firefly virtual machine from the drop-down menu and click **Finish**. Next, click **Edit**.

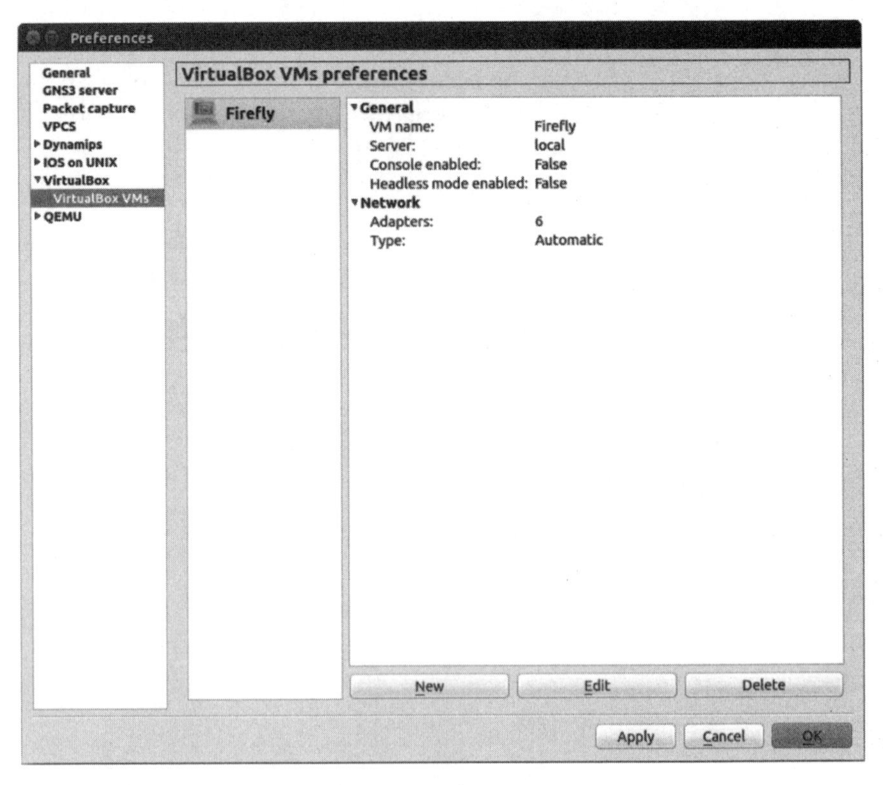

Figure 6-24: VirtualBox VMs preferences window

On the General settings tab, place a check next to **Enable remote console** and **Start VM in headless mode**. This will allow you to use the console to log on to Firefly. Finally, click the **Network** tab, change the number of interfaces to 6, and set the network type to **Paravirtualized Network (virtio net)**. You're now ready to create a project using Firefly.

Creating a Project with a Zone-Based Firewall

In this section, you'll create a simple project using vSRX Firefly as a network firewall. Firefly is similar in functionality to Cisco's ASA firewall, but it's different to configure. I won't go into a lot of detail, but this project should get you started. If you want to learn more about Juniper SRX, you can find plenty of detailed documents at Juniper's website (*https://www.juniper.net/*).

Let's start by creating the GNS3 project shown in Figure 6-25. Drag a Firefly device from the End Devices toolbar to your workspace. Next, drag two Cisco routers to your workspace and link the devices together. Link R1's interface f0/0 to interface e1 of vSRX Firefly. Link R2's interface f0/0 to interface e0 of vSRX Firefly.

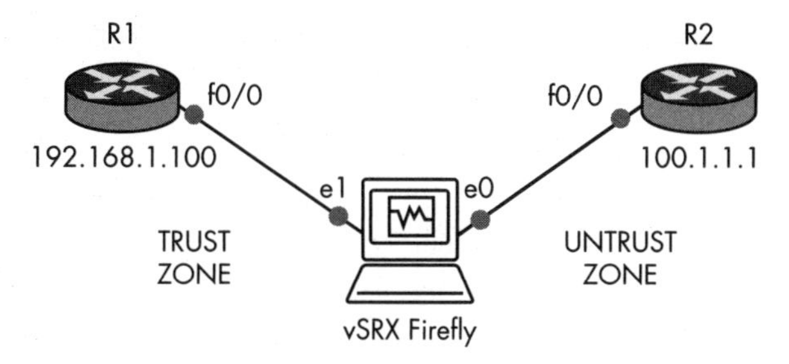

Figure 6-25: vSRX Firefly project

Router R1 will be configured to use a Firefly trust zone. R1 represents a trusted host on your LAN. Router R2 will be configured to use a Firefly untrust zone. The untrust zone represents an untrusted network, like the Internet. You'll configure Firefly so that your trusted host (R1) can ping your untrusted host (R2) through the vSRX Firefly firewall using NAT.

Begin by configuring router R1 with an IP address and default gateway.

```
R1(config)# interface f0/0
R1(config-if)# ip address 192.168.1.100 255.255.255.0
R1(config-if)# no shutdown
R1(config-if)# ip route 0.0.0.0  0.0.0.0 192.168.1.1
```

Next, configure an IP address on the untrusted router R2. No gateway configuration is necessary here.

```
R2(config)# interface f0/0
R2(config-if)# ip address 100.1.1.1 255.255.255.0
R2(config-if)# no shutdown
```

With the router IP addresses configured, you can turn your attention to Firefly. Log on using the root account to configure the vSRX Firefly firewall. Because this is a new installation, you should not be asked for a password. After logging on, enter the following commands to create your firewall; you'll start by creating a password and configuring the network settings:

```
  root@%cli
  root>edit
❶ root#set system root-authentication plain-text-password
  New password:firefly1
  Retype new password:firefly1
❷ root#set interface ge-0/0/0.0 family inet address 100.1.1.2/24
❸ root#set interface ge-0/0/1.0 family inet address 192.168.1.1/24
❹ root#set routing-options static route 0.0.0.0/0 next-hop 100.1.1.1
```

Like a Juniper router, you cannot save any configuration changes on an SRX device until you've assigned a password to the root account, so start by going to edit mode and creating a root password ❶. I've entered *firefly1*, but you can choose any password you'd like.

Next, at ❷, you set the IP address on the WAN interface (ge-0/0/0.0), and at ❸, you set the LAN interface (ge-0/0/1.0). Finally, at ❹, set the default gateway address using the untrusted router's IP address (100.1.1.1).

Complete the configuration by defining your security zones and security trust policies.

```
❶ root#set security zones security-zone trust interfaces ge-0/0/1.0
❷ root#set security nat source rule-set interface-nat from zone trust
❸ root#set security nat source rule-set interface-nat to zone untrust
❹ root#set security nat source rule-set interface-nat rule rule1 match
  source-address 0.0.0.0/0 destination-address 0.0.0.0/0
❺ root#set security nat source rule-set interface-nat rule rule1 then source-nat
  interface
❻ root#set security policies from-zone trust to-zone untrust policy permit-all
  match source-address any destination-address any application any
❼ root#set security policies from-zone trust to-zone untrust policy permit-all
  then permit
❽ root#commit
```

Assign your LAN interface to the trust zone ❶. Set the interface-nat source zone to trust ❷ and the interface-nat destination zone to `untrust` ❸, and create a rule that matches any source and destination IP addresses (0.0.0.0/0) ❹. In a production environment, you would tighten this up a bit, but for your practice GNS3 lab, it's fine. Now configure NAT overloading on the WAN interface ❺.

NOTE *vSRX Firefly's* `interface-nat` *command is used to achieve the equivalent of Cisco NAT/PAT overloading.*

To finish the configuration, define the type of traffic that's allowed to go between the zones ❻. In this case, you're allowing all protocols and applications from the trust zone to the `untrust` zone. Finally, create the security policy ❼ and commit your changes ❽, and you're done!

Verify your configuration by entering the `show security nat source summary` command.

```
root>show security nat source summary
Total port number usage for port translation pool: 0
Maximum port number for port translation pool: 33554432
Total pools: 0

Total rules: 1
Rule name      Rule set        From       To          Action
rule1❶         interface-nat❷  trust❸     untrust❹    interface❺
```

This information indicates that `rule1` ❶ allows packets via NAT ❷ from the `trust` zone ❸ to the `untrust` zone ❹, and IP data sourced from the `trust` zone will be overloaded onto the untrusted interface ❺. By default, that's interface ge-0/0/0.0 (your WAN interface). If your summary matches the one in this book after entering the command, then you're ready to test the connection. If your output looks different, then you've probably mistyped something, so you need to go back and check all your configuration settings.

Log on to router R1 and enter the `ping` command to test connectivity with router R2.

```
R1#ping 100.1.1.1

Type escape sequence to abort.
Sending 5, 100-byte ICMP Echos to 100.1.1.1, timeout is 2 seconds:
!!!!!
Success rate is 100 percent (5/5), round-trip min/avg/max = 4/10/24 ms
```

If your ping is successful, as indicated by `!!!!!`, then you've done everything correctly. If it failed, then you may need to go back and check your configuration settings. You should also make sure your Cisco routers have the correct IP addresses and subnet masks and that the Ethernet interfaces are not shut down.

Final Thoughts

In this chapter, you learned about Juniper and Juniper Olive, and I showed you how to create a Juniper Olive using QEMU and VirtualBox. I also introduced you to vSRX Firefly, and I provided some insight about how to configure a basic zone-based firewall using an SRX device.

In most cases, Juniper runs a little slower using QEMU than using VirtualBox. However, QEMU allows you to add an unlimited number of Juniper routers to your projects without cloning, and GNS3 will store your Juniper configurations with your projects. As a rule, VirtualBox loads and runs devices faster than QEMU, but your configurations are saved with each virtual machine instance in VirtualBox, not in GNS3. Because of this, you have to create a unique virtual machine instance of your devices using the VirtualBox clone feature. The cloned devices are then used in your GNS3 projects.

Juniper is less popular than Cisco in the corporate world, but it's a big player in larger environments, like campus sites and the ISP routing and switching market. If you take your networking career into one of those realms, Juniper certification could set you apart from other applicants, and GNS3 is a great way to learn Juniper routers and SRX devices! You should start with JNCIA certification, which is the entry-level Juniper certification (Juniper's equivalent to Cisco CCNA), and it's a prerequisite for more advanced certifications. Juniper's training website (*http://www.juniper.net/us/en/training/*) provides all the information you need to get started.

7

DEVICE NODES, LIVE SWITCHES, AND THE INTERNET

In this chapter, I'll demonstrate how GNS3 device nodes are used with Cisco IOS routers. GNS3 provides a Hub node and various Switch nodes, including an Ethernet switch, EtherSwitch router, ATM switch, and Frame Relay switch. In addition, we'll take a look at how to create your own Frame Relay switch using a Cisco IOS router.

We'll also explore a very powerful feature known as a *Cloud node*. A Cloud node is used to expand your networks beyond the GNS3 program. With Cloud nodes, you'll soon be able to connect your GNS3 projects to live Cisco switches and access the Internet using GNS3 routers.

Built-in Device Nodes

Built-in device nodes *simulate* the features of a specific device type (like a switch). They're easy to configure and can be useful if you need to save time and PC resources or if you just want to get something done without knowing all the details of the underlying technology.

If you create a topology that uses VLANs, you can drag a GNS3 Ethernet switch node to your workspace and use a simple menu to quickly create VLANs or VLAN trunks. Of course, if you're studying for a Cisco exam that involves switching, you need to know how to configure actual Cisco IOS switches.

Node Configurator

By now, you already know that the Node configurator can be used to configure the features of a single device node, but it can also be used to modify multiple devices at the same time. As your projects grow and you use more devices, this feature can save you a lot of time.

To open multiple devices at the same time, use your mouse to select those devices in your workspace, and then right-click any device and choose **Configure**. The selected devices display in the Node configurator, as shown in Figure 7-1.

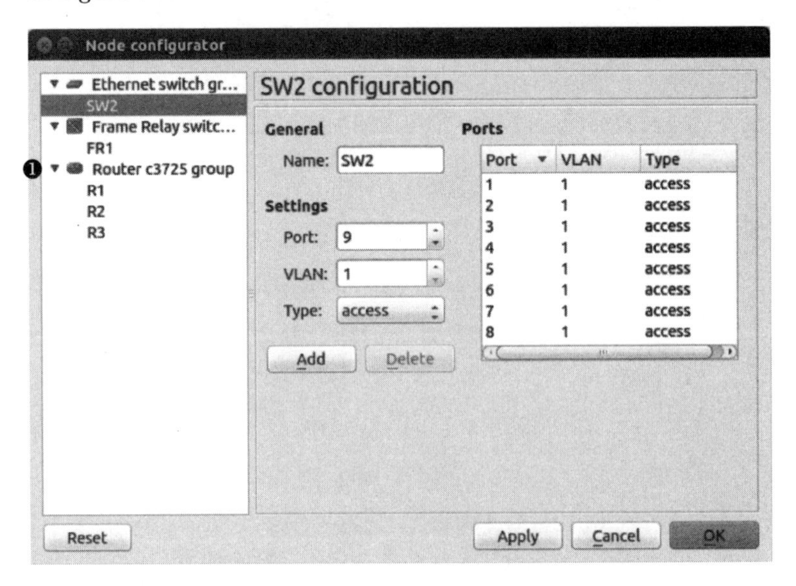

Figure 7-1: Modifying multiple devices using the Node configurator

To configure a single device, select that device from the column on the left. Configure each device and click **Apply**. When you're finished configuring all the devices, click **OK** to complete the process.

To modify multiple devices, use the SHIFT key to select several at once from the column on the left and then configure them in the same manner as you would a single device. Let's say you have ten 7200 series routers and you want to add the same network module to slot 0 on all 10 routers. Use the SHIFT key to select all the routers, add the module to slot 0, and then click **Apply** and **OK** to make the change to all 10 devices.

You can also select an entire group of routers by clicking their group name. In the previous figure, you could configure R1, R2, and R3 at the same time by selecting the group name *Router c3725 group* ❶.

Ethernet Hub

GNS3 provides an Ethernet hub (see Figure 7-2) as a tool that networking instructors can use to teach students about the perils of Ethernet loops, excessive broadcasts, and multiport repeating.

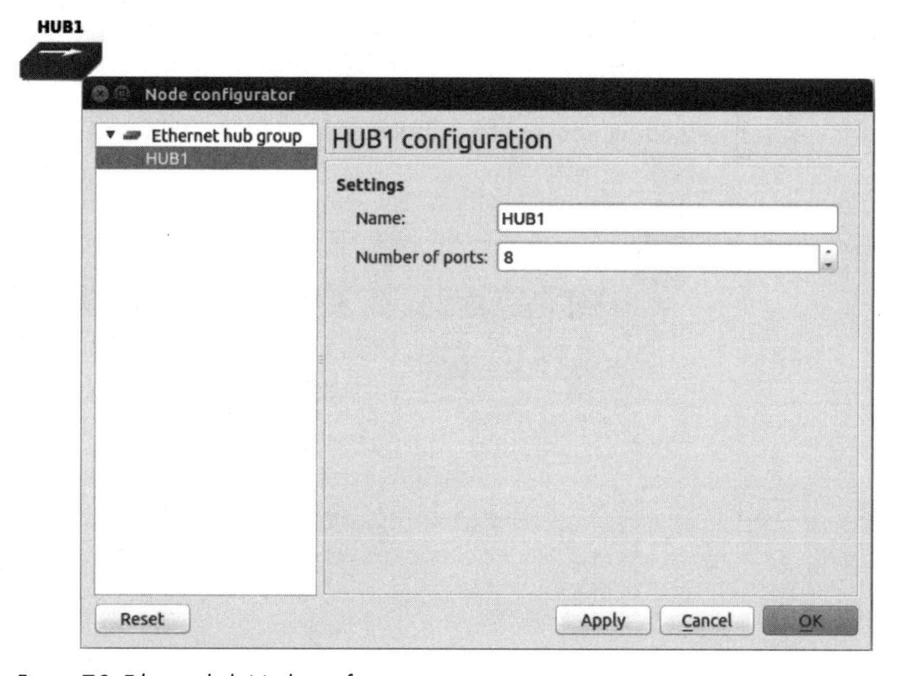

Figure 7-2: Ethernet hub Node configurator

As a general rule, you should stick with GNS3 switches and avoid including hubs in your projects. But if you do need to use an Ethernet hub, you can change the number of available Ethernet ports by pulling up the Node configurator and selecting your hub from the list on the left. The default value is eight ports, so if you want a different amount, enter that number in the Settings field on the right.

EtherSwitch Router

GNS3 provides two types of Dynamips switches, the Ethernet switch node and the EtherSwitch router. I discussed the Ethernet switch node in Chapter 4, so I'll only cover the EtherSwitch router here.

An *EtherSwitch router* is not a simulated device like an Ethernet hub or Ethernet switch node. Instead, it's a Dynamips router running Cisco IOS that's been configured with a 16-port switch module (NM-16ESW). This is the same switch module that can be installed on an actual Cisco router, and it has the same features and limitations (see Appendix C for details). Although the switch module has limited functionality, it's perfectly suited for CCNA and many CCNP studies. For more advanced switching features, you need to integrate real switches into your GNS3 projects or use Cisco IOU switches.

NOTE *The EtherSwitch router requires that you configure a c3745 router with an IOS.*

To add additional switch ports to your EtherSwitch router, right-click the switch icon and select **Configure**, as shown in Figure 7-3.

The EtherSwitch router allows you to add additional switch modules. Adding another NM-16ESW module in slot 2 increases the number of switch ports to 32.

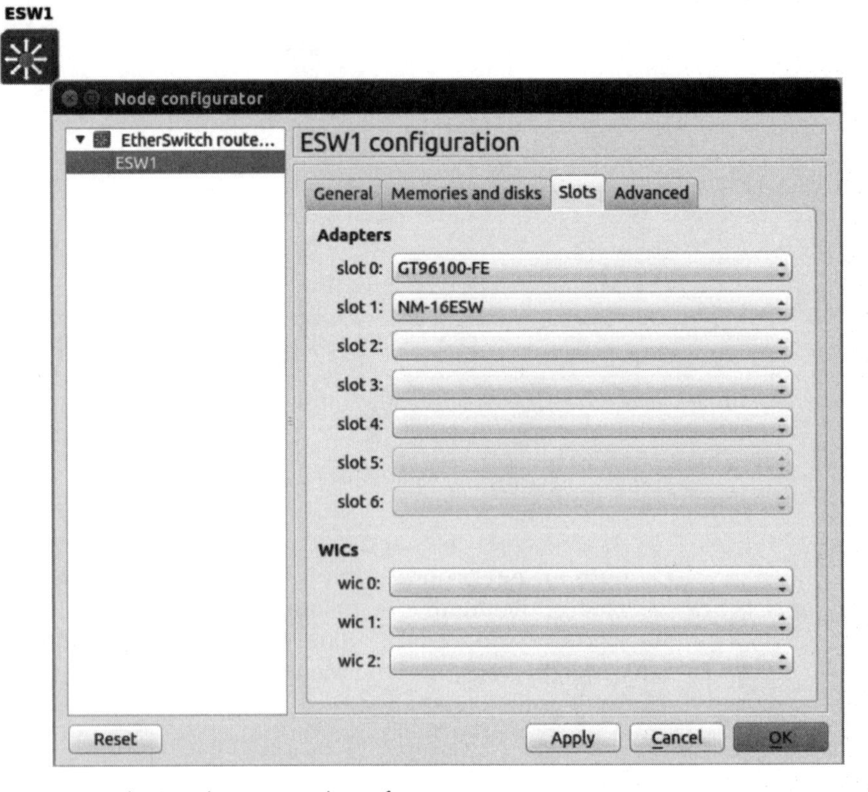

Figure 7-3: EtherSwitch router Node configurator

Frame Relay Switch

GNS3 provides a simple *Frame Relay switch node*, capable of emulating the basics of a generic Frame Relay switch. The nice thing about the GNS3 Frame Relay switch node is that it requires very little configuration. The downside is that it can sometimes be unstable.

WARNING *The GNS3 Frame Relay switch node only supports the ANSI LMI type, and* Cisco *is the default LMI type on Cisco IOS. You must use the command* `frame-relay lmi-type ansi` *on your router interfaces. Otherwise your frame cloud will not work. You can verify your LMI type using the* `show frame-relay lmi` *command (after configuring Frame Relay encapsulation).*

In Frame Relay, *data link connection identifiers (DLCIs)* are used to assign frames to a *permanent virtual circuit (PVC)* using serial port connections. To configure DLCI to serial port mappings, right-click the Frame Relay switch icon and open the Node configurator. Use the Source and Destination fields to create a mapping and click **Add**. When you're finished, click **Apply** and **OK** to complete the configuration.

The example configuration in Figure 7-4 will be used later to create a simple Frame Relay network. In the Mapping panel on the right, notice that FR1 is configured using two serial ports. Each serial port is used to link the Frame Relay switch to a router in your GNS3 project.

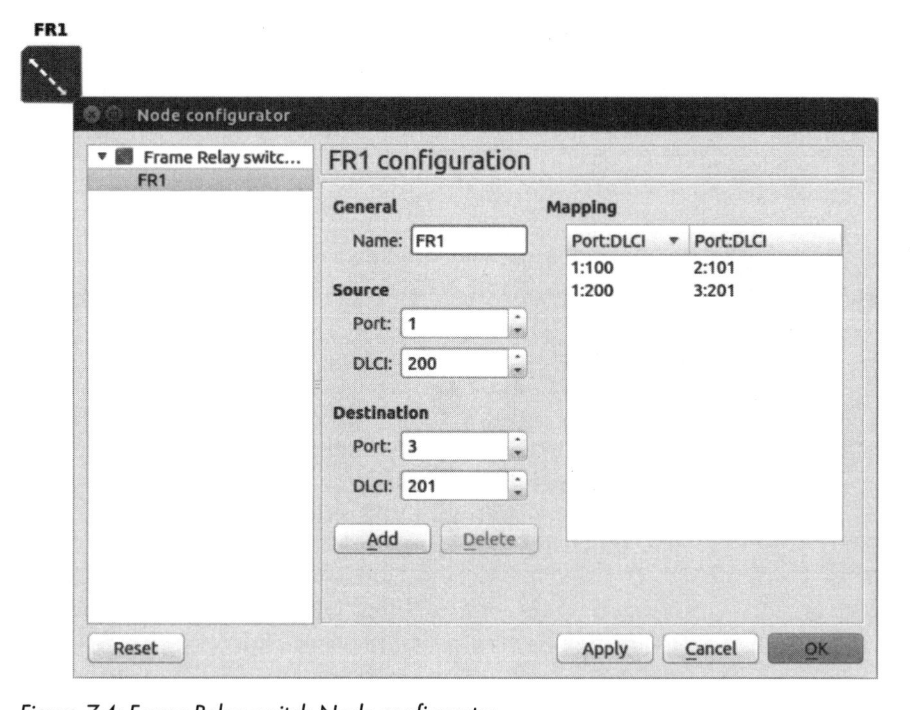

Figure 7-4: Frame Relay switch Node configurator

Port 1 has been assigned two DLCI numbers (100 and 200). Each DLCI on port 1 is mapped to a DLCI number on another serial port, and each mapping forms a Frame Relay PVC. Mapping is read from left to right, so in the first row, port 1 DLCI 100 is mapped to port 2 DLCI 101, and in the second row, port 1 DLCI 200 is mapped to port 3 DLCI 201. We'll use these mappings to configure a simple Frame Relay network.

Simple Frame Relay Hub and Spoke Configuration

There are several ways to configure a Frame Relay network, and understanding DLCI to serial port mapping is critical for understanding and configuring any of them. To better understand the mapping relationship, let's configure a simple network using the previously discussed DLCI to serial port mappings. I won't go into a lot of theory, but I'll explain enough to get you started.

We'll create our sample network using the topology in Figure 7-5. The network is divided into two subnets, 10.10.10.0 and 10.10.10.32, using the subnet mask 255.255.255.224.

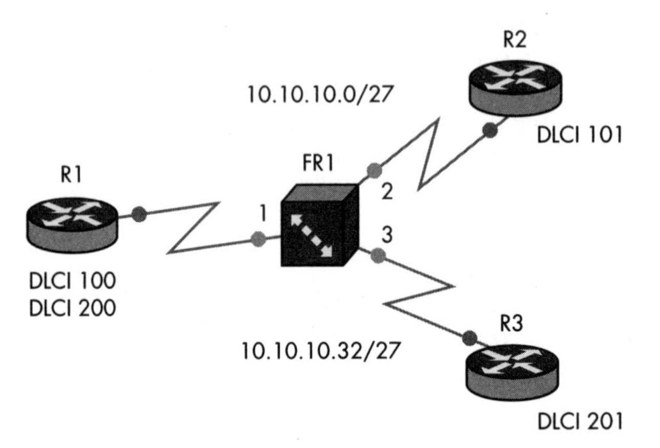

Figure 7-5: Sample hub and spoke Frame Relay network

This simple network is an example of a Frame Relay hub and spoke topology and should give you a good idea of how DLCI mappings work in a Frame Relay network. Router R2 will be on the 10.10.10.0 subnet, and router R3 will be on the 10.10.10.32 subnet. Router R1 is the hub in our hub and spoke topology. It will be connected to both subnets and will forward packets between them through the Frame Relay switch. This configuration will allow router R2 to ping router R3 and vice versa.

To create the project, add a Frame Relay switch node to your workspace and set it up the way we did in Figure 7-4. Add three routers and configure each of them with a serial interface card such as a WIC or NM-4T. Link the routers to the FR1 switch as shown. Be sure R1 is connected to Port 1 on FR1, R2 is connected to Port 2, and R3 is connected to Port 3. After linking the devices and configuring the Port:DLCI mapping on the FR1 switch, configure the hub router R1, as shown in the following code.

```
  R1(config)# interface Serial0/0
❶ R1(config-if)# encapsulation frame-relay
❷ R1(config-if)# frame-relay lmi-type ansi
❸ R1(config-if)# clock rate 64000
  R1(config-if)# no shutdown
  R1(config-if)# no ip address
```

On the serial interface, enable Frame Relay encapsulation ❶, and set the LMI type to ANSI ❷. Although not required for GNS3, I've also set the clock rate ❸ because, depending on your IOS, the command may be required on an actual Frame Relay switch.

Next, configure point-to-point interfaces and DLCIs.

```
❶ R1(config-if)# interface Serial0/0.100 point-to-point
❷ R1(config-subif)# frame-relay interface-dlci 100
❸ R1(config-subif)# ip address 10.10.10.1 255.255.255.224
❹ R1(config-subif)# interface Serial0/0.200 point-to-point
❺ R1(config-subif)# frame-relay interface-dlci 200
❻ R1(config-subif)# ip address 10.10.10.33 255.255.255.224
```

Configure a point-to-point subinterface ❶ on serial interface `Serial0/0.100` using DLCI 100 ❷ and assign the interface an IP address from the first subnet ❸ (10.10.10.0/27).

Complete the configuration by adding a second point-to-point subinterface ❹ in the same manner, but use DLCI 200 ❺, and assign the interface an IP addresses from the second subnet ❻ (10.10.10.32/27). In this example, I'll use the first valid address from the subnet, which is 10.10.10.33.

NOTE *It's considered a Cisco best practice to use the DLCI number for your subinterface number.* `Serial0/0.100` *is an example of a subinterface for DLCI 100.*

The following listing contains all of the commands you need to configure router R2.

```
  R2(config)# interface Serial0/0
❶ R2(config-if)# encapsulation frame-relay
❷ R2(config-if)# frame-relay lmi-type ansi
❸ R2(config-if)# clock rate 64000
  R2(config-if)# no shutdown
  R2(config-if)# no ip address
❹ R2(config-if)# interface Serial0/0.101 point-to-point
❺ R2(config-subif)# frame-relay interface-dlci 101
❻ R2(config-fr-dlci)# ip address 10.10.10.2 255.255.255.224
  R2(config-subif)# exit
❼ R2(config)# ip route 0.0.0.0 0.0.0.0 10.10.10.1
```

To configure R2, go under the serial interface and enable Frame Relay encapsulation ❶, then set the LMI type to ANSI ❷, set the clock rate ❸, and bring up the interface. Configure a point-to-point subinterface ❹ using

DLCI 101 ❺ and assign the subinterface an IP address from the first subnet ❻ (10.10.10.0 /27 in this example). Lastly, set the router's default gateway using the IP address configured under interface DLCI 100 of router R1 ❼ (IP address 10.10.10.1). Because R1 is the hub of our Frame Relay hub and spoke topology, it's used as the default gateway for our two subnets so that data can be routed between routers R2 and R3.

Finally, add a configuration to router R3 to complete the project.

```
  R3(config)# interface Serial0/0
  R3(config-if)# encapsulation frame-relay
  R3(config-if)# frame-relay lmi-type ansi
  R3(config-if)# clock rate 64000
  R3(config-if)# no shutdown
  R3(config-if)# no ip address
  R3(config-if)# interface Serial0/0.201 point-to-point
❶ R3(config-subif)# frame-relay interface-dlci 201
❷ R3(config-fr-dlci)# ip address 10.10.10.34 255.255.255.224
  R3(config-subif)# exit
❸ R3(config)# ip route 0.0.0.0 0.0.0.0 10.10.10.33
```

Router R3 is configured in nearly the same way as R2, but it uses DLCI 201 ❶ and an IP address ❷ from the second subnet. Also, you need to set the default gateway using the IP address configured under interface DLCI 200 of router R1 ❸ (IP address 10.10.10.33).

That's it! All three routers should now be able to ping each other. In a nutshell, each router encapsulates data frames and identifies them with a Frame Relay DLCI number as they leave their serial interfaces. When the Frame Relay switch receives data from a router, the data frames are forwarded to other routers through the switch based on the DLCI to serial port mapping. Because R1 is configured as a Frame Relay hub and knows about both subnets, it can forward data between the two subnets using the two PVCs. In this example, one PVC is made up of DLCI 100 mapped to DLCI 101, and the other is made up of DLCI 200 mapped to DLCI 201.

To verify that your Frame Relay circuit is active, enter the command `show frame-relay pvc` on each of your routers.

```
R1# show frame-relay pvc

PVC Statistics for interface Serial0/0 (Frame Relay DTE)

              Active     Inactive      Deleted       Static
  Local       ❶2            0             0             0
  Switched      0            0             0             0
  Unused        0            0             0             0
```

If you've set everything up correctly, your PVCs should be displayed under `Active` ❶.

Creating a Frame Relay Switch Using IOS

As handy as the Frame Relay switch node is, sometimes you might need to create your own Frame Relay switch using an IOS router. Maybe you want to use a different LMI type (like Cisco or q933a), or perhaps your studies require knowing the details of an actual Cisco Frame Relay switch. In any case, an IOS switch is fairly easy to set up.

The following listing creates an IOS Frame Relay switch using DLCI mappings identical to the GNS3 Frame Relay switch node you configured earlier. It may look intimidating at first glance, but it's not; you just need to understand how Frame Relay `connect` commands are used to configure the DLCI to serial port mappings.

```
❶ FRSW(config)# frame-relay switching
  FRSW(config)# interface Serial0/0
  FRSW(config-if)# description Serial connection to Router R1 (Hub)
  FRSW(config-if)# no shutdown
  FRSW(config-if)# no ip address
❷ FRSW(config-if)# encapsulation frame-relay
❸ FRSW(config-if)# clock rate 64000
❹ FRSW(config-if)# frame-relay lmi-type ansi
❺ FRSW(config-if)# frame-relay intf-type dce
  FRSW(config-if)# interface Serial0/1
  FRSW(config-if)# description Serial connection to Router R2 (Spoke)
  FRSW(config-if)# no shutdown
  FRSW(config-if)# no ip address
  FRSW(config-if)# encapsulation frame-relay
  FRSW(config-if)# clock rate 64000
  FRSW(config-if)# frame-relay lmi-type ansi
  FRSW(config-if)# frame-relay intf-type dce
  FRSW(config-if)# interface Serial0/2
  FRSW(config-if)# description Serial connection to Router R3 (Spoke)
  FRSW(config-if)# no shutdown
  FRSW(config-if)# no ip address
  FRSW(config-if)# encapsulation frame-relay
  FRSW(config-if)# clock rate 64000
  FRSW(config-if)# frame-relay lmi-type ansi
  FRSW(config-if)# frame-relay intf-type dce
  FRSW(config-if)# exit
❻ FRSW(config)# connect PVC1 Serial0/0 100 Serial0/1 101
❼ FRSW(config)# connect PVC2 Serial0/0 200 Serial0/2 201
```

When configuring a Frame Relay switch, you must first enable Frame Relay switching with the `frame-relay switching` command ❶. You'll also configure Frame Relay encapsulation on each serial interface with the `encapsulation frame-relay` command ❷. Then, use the `clock rate` command ❸ to set up clocking, choose an LMI type with `frame-relay lmi-type` ❹, and set the interface type to DCE using the `frame-relay intf-type dce` command ❺. After bringing up the interfaces, you're ready to define your PVCs.

NOTE *On some IOS versions, the* `clock rate` *command may need to be entered as* `clockrate`.

DLCI to port mapping is configured using `connect` *`connection-name interface dlci interface dlci`* commands. The last two commands in this configuration define a connection mapping between two Frame Relay PVCs. The command `connect PVC1 Serial0/0 100 Serial0/1 101` ❻ defines a PVC between routers R1 and R2 and is used for creating our first subnet. The source interface is Serial0/0 and the source DCLI is 100. The PVC is completed using interface Serial0/1, and DLCI 101 configured on router R2.

The command `connect PVC2 Serial0/0 200 Serial0/2 201` ❼ uses the same syntax to create a second PVC between routers R1 and R3 (used for the second subnet).

That's all there is to creating your own Frame Relay switch. When configuring a Frame Relay switch with Cisco IOS, the LMI type can be set to `cisco`, `ansi`, or `q933a`, but you must be consistent on all routers participating in the Frame Relay network.

ATM Switch

GNS3 provides an easy way to configure an *Asynchronous Transfer Mode (ATM)* switch. ATM is similar to Frame Relay in that it's a layer 2 protocol that maps physical ports to logical circuits.

To configure a VPI/VCI to port mapping, right-click the ATM switch icon and select **Configure**, as shown in Figure 7-6. Here, I've configured a simple virtual circuit using two ports on the ATM1 switch node.

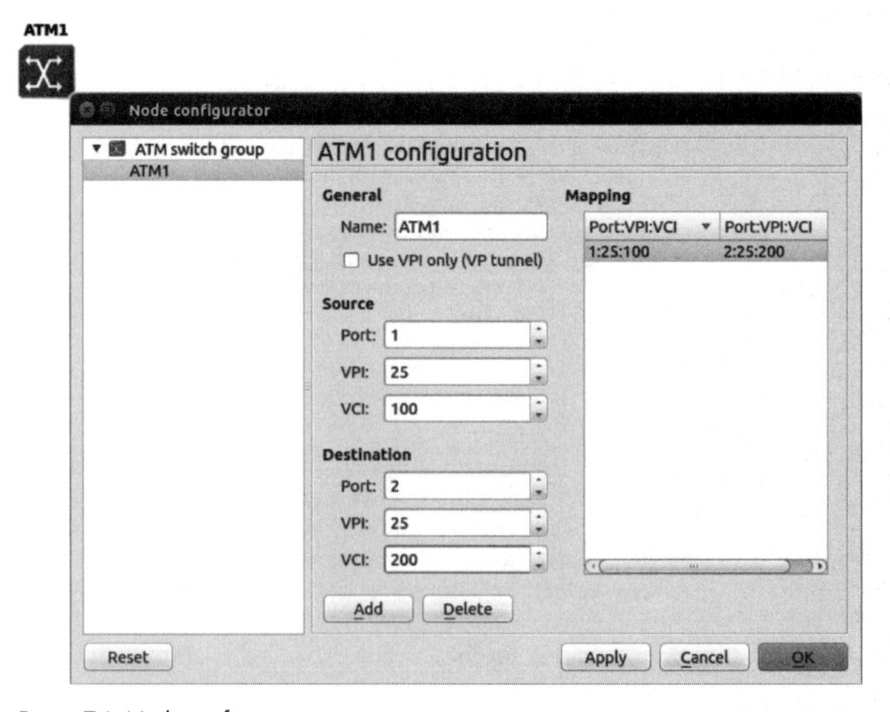

Figure 7-6: Node configurator

Use the Source and Destination fields to create your port mapping, and then click **Add**. When you're finished with all the port mapping, click **Apply** and **OK** to complete the configuration.

Now let's run through a quick example of creating a simple point-to-point WAN connection using an ATM switch. Start by creating the topology shown in Figure 7-7.

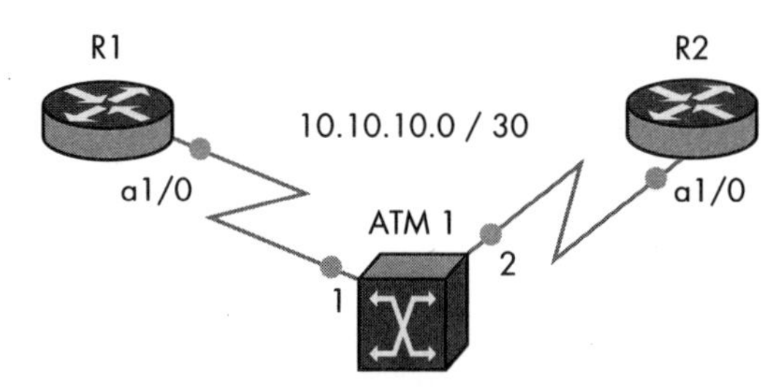

Figure 7-7: Sample ATM network

Add an ATM switch to your workspace and configure it using the information from Figure 7-6. Next, add two routers and create a link between each router and the switch. You need to use *7200 series routers* that are each configured with an *ATM port adapter* (PA-A1) in slot 1. Create a link from *a1/0* on each router to the ATM switch, as shown in Figure 7-7, and then enter the following commands to configure ATM on router R1.

```
R1(config)# interface ATM1/0
R1(config)# no shutdown
R1(config)# interface ATM1/0.100 point-to-point
R1(config-subif)# ip address 10.10.10.1 255.255.255.252
R1(config-subif)# pvc 25/100
R1(config-if-atm-vc)# protocol ip 10.10.10.2 broadcast
R1(config-if-atm-vc)# encapsulation aal5snap
```

Next, apply a similar configuration to router R2.

```
R2(config)# interface ATM1/0
R2(config)# no shutdown
R2(config)# interface ATM1/0.200 point-to-point
R2(config-subif)# ip address 10.10.10.2 255.255.255.252
R2(config-subif)# pvc 25/200
R2(config-if-atm-vc)# protocol ip 10.10.10.1 broadcast
R2(config-if-atm-vc)# encapsulation aal5snap
```

To verify that your ATM circuit is up, enter the `show atm pvc` command.

```
R1# show atm pvc
```

If the PVC status displays `UP`, then the two routers should now be able to ping each other.

Cloud Nodes

The Cloud node is a highly configurable device node that doesn't simulate a particular piece of hardware. Instead, it provides a wide range of *Network Input/Output (NIO)* connection options that allow GNS3 virtual devices to communicate with other programs or real hardware, like your PC's Ethernet adapter.

You connect to a Cloud node by creating a standard link from a GNS3 device (like a router) to the Cloud. Once this is done, any data leaving a virtual interface passes through the Cloud node's NIO connection to a destination outside GNS3, like a physical Ethernet adapter. Keep in mind that throughput limitations presented in GNS3 also apply to the virtual interface connected to the Cloud mode, meaning those limitations will affect your overall performance.

To configure an NIO connection (shown in Figure 7-8), right-click the Cloud icon and select **Configure**.

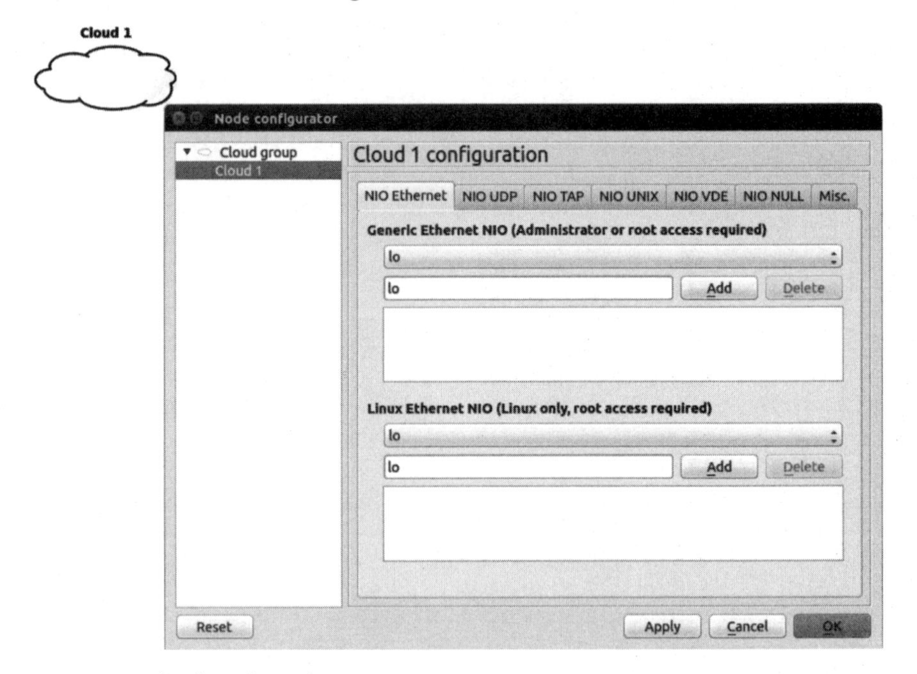

Figure 7-8: Cloud Node configurator

The Node configurator provides six connection options:

NIO Ethernet Creates a connection to one or more physical or logical interfaces in your PC. The NIO Ethernet configuration lets you set up both a generic NIO and a Linux-only NIO.

NIO UDP Creates a UDP socket in order to form a link between GNS3 and other programs.

NIO TAP Creates a connection to a virtual TAP interface. TAP interfaces are often bridged to physical interfaces in your PC.

NIO UNIX Creates a UNIX Socket connection between GNS3 and some other application.

NIO VDE Creates a link between GNS3 and a Virtual Distributed Ethernet device.

NIO NULL Creates a link between GNS3 and a NULL device to form a dummy link.

Misc. Allows you to rename a Cloud node.

To configure a connection, select the NIO connection type, choose the options you want, and select **Add**. You can configure more than one connection per Cloud node, allowing you to link multiple GNS3 devices, just as you can use multiple interfaces on a GNS3 switch or router.

On Linux systems, you may want to use a generic NIO connection, which may work more reliably than a Linux-specific NIO. One reason is that the Linux-specific NIO may strip incoming VLAN tags. If you're having difficulty with a connection on Linux, try both to see which works better.

Connecting GNS3 Devices to Physical Hardware

The ability to connect projects to physical hardware is what transforms GNS3 from a diamond in the rough to the Great Star of Africa. Using the Cloud node, you can establish trunk links with live Cisco switches and even access the Internet from your GNS3 devices. This gives GNS3 nearly limitless networking possibilities. Connecting GNS3 to real devices is easier on some systems than others, but it should work on all major operating systems.

Dynamips Permissions

Before connecting GNS3 devices to a physical Ethernet adapter, you may need to make a few changes on your PC. If your Cloud node is configured using NIO Ethernet on a Windows system, you should run GNS3 using administrator privileges by right-clicking the GNS3 icon and selecting **Run as Administrator**. To make this option permanent, right-click the GNS3 icon and choose **Properties**. Select the Compatibility tab and place a check next to **Run this program as an administrator**.

On Unix-based systems, you need to elevate the permissions of Dynamips before using NIO Ethernet or NIO TAP connections. If you skip this step, you'll have to run GNS3 using the root account. Otherwise, NIO connections will fail and GNS3 will display an error message in the GNS3 Console window.

To set the correct Dynamips permissions on OS X, use the following commands:

```
$ sudo chown root /Applications/GNS3.app/Contents/Resources/dynamips*
$ sudo chmod 4755 /Applications/GNS3.app/Contents/Resources/dynamips*
```

Setting permissions on most Linux distributions works the same way; just replace the file path with the correct location for your `dynamips` file, as shown in the following code. If you're running a Debian-based Linux system like Ubuntu, use the `setcap` command instead because it's more secure.

```
$ sudo apt-get install libcap2
$ sudo setcap cap_net_raw,cap_net_admin+eip /usr/local/bin/dynamips*
```

After changing the Dynamips permissions, you can run GNS3 as a regular user, but Dynamips will be treated as though it's being run by the root account.

Preparing Your PC for a Bridge

Some operating systems don't allow GNS3 to communicate directly with your PC's Ethernet hardware, and Wi-Fi adapters usually don't work, either. Before using GNS3 with an Ethernet adapter on those systems, you might need to install additional software to make it work.

A common solution is to install a virtual interface driver and use a bridge to associate it with your PC's physical Ethernet adapter. GNS3 then passes network data to the virtual interface, which hands it off to the physical Ethernet interface via the bridge. On Unix-based systems, virtual interfaces are often provided using TUN/TAP drivers. On Windows, you'll use a loopback adapter that's bridged to your physical Ethernet adapter.

Even if your PC's Ethernet hardware works directly with GNS3, the following methods are recommended and predictable ways to connect GNS3 to the outside world.

Using a Loopback Adapter on Windows

In Windows, a *loopback adapter driver* provides a virtual network interface that can be bridged to a physical Ethernet adapter in your PC. To add a loopback adapter to Windows, go to **Control Panel ▸ Device Manager**. Right-click your computer name from the list, and select **Add legacy hardware**. Click **Next**, select **Install the hardware that I manually select from a list (Advanced)**, and click **Next** again. Choose **Network Adapters** from the list and click **Next**. From the Add Hardware wizard, shown in Figure 7-9, select **Microsoft** under Manufacturer, and then scroll down and select the Network Adapter named **Microsoft Loopback Adapter**. Click **Next** and **Finish** to complete the installation. You must reboot Windows after installing the Microsoft Loopback Adapter.

The Microsoft loopback adapter can also be installed by running the `loopback-manager.cmd` command from your GNS3 installation directory.

To create a bridge between the loopback adapter and Ethernet adapter, go to **Control Panel ▸ Network and Sharing Center** and choose **Change Adapter Settings**. Select the two adapters and right-click to bring up the menu shown in Figure 7-10. Select **Bridge connections** to create the bridge interface between the two adapters. When you're finished, restart Windows to allow the changes to take effect.

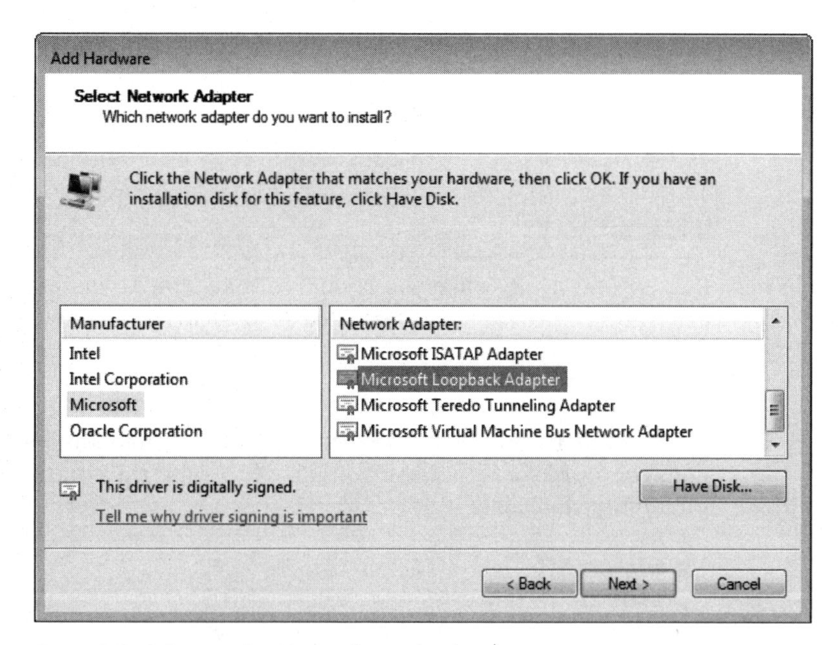

Figure 7-9: Selecting the Microsoft Loopback Adapter

Figure 7-10: Creating a bridge using a Microsoft Loopback Adapter and an Ethernet adapter

To allow GNS3 to use your physical Ethernet adapter on a Windows system, you'll need to configure a Cloud node with the loopback adapter (see "Connecting GNS3 Devices to Physical Hardware" on page 105). It's a good idea to rename your loopback adapter, so it can be clearly identified within GNS3. In this example, I recommend changing *Local Area Connection 2* to *Loopback.*

TUN/TAP Drivers on OS X

If you're using OS X, you need to install a virtual interface driver before GNS3 can access a physical Ethernet Interface. To install TUN/TAP drivers on OS X, download the driver software for your version of OS X from SourceForge (*http://tuntaposx.sourceforge.net/*), run the installer, and follow the instructions.

The drivers should be installed under */Library/Extensions* and should load automatically when you restart your system. To manually load the driver, change to the */Library/Extensions* directory and enter the following:

```
$ sudo kextload tap.kext
```

Before launching GNS3, enter the following command to set permissions on your TAP interfaces. You'll have to enter the command each time you reboot your Mac.

```
$ sudo chown $(id -un):$(id -gn) /dev/tap*
```

To activate a TAP interface and bridge it to a physical Ethernet port in your PC, you must enter the following commands *after* you add a Cloud and attach a router to the nio_tap interface, configured using */dev/tap0*. If you enter the commands beforehand, they will fail and your bridge won't work. You will have to enter these commands every time you load a project that includes a cloud node.

```
$ sudo ifconfig bridge0 create
$ sudo ifconfig bridge0 addm en0
$ sudo ifconfig bridge0 addm tap0 up
```

After entering the commands from a terminal, OS X should bridge the tap0 interface to the physical Ethernet interface in your Mac, which is en0 in this example. You should use the `ifconfig` command to verify the name of your Mac's Ethernet interface and then replace en0 with that name.

NOTE *If you change the maximum transmission unit (MTU) size of an interface, you may see the error "ifconfig: BRDGADD tap0: Invalid argument" when you go to create the bridge. In this case, you need to make sure that the MTU size of your physical interface matches the MTU size of the TAP interface.*

I recommend adding an annotation to your project that includes these commands as a reminder to create the bridge when you open a project. Then, after opening the project you can copy the annotation and paste it into a terminal window to save time. Don't forget to enter those commands *every time you open a project* that bridges Ethernet to a TAP interface, or it won't work.

TUN/TAP Drivers on Ubuntu Linux

On Linux, you should be able to connect a Cloud node directly to your Ethernet interface using the NIO Ethernet tab under the Cloud configurator, but if you find that you need TUN/TAP drivers for Ubuntu, update your package manager and enter the following command to install the package.

```
$ sudo apt-get install uml-utilities
```

If you're running some other version of Linux, you may have to install a different package, but this package should work on most Debian-based distributions.

Connecting to Live Switches

GNS3 is great software, but it has some limitations. For example, the NM-16ESW switch module doesn't include all the advanced features of an actual layer 2 or layer 3 switch. If you want to work with advanced switching, you have to use additional software like Cisco IOU or use physical Cisco switches. If you're creating CCNA labs, then one live Cisco switch might be enough, but if you're creating CCNP or CCIE labs, you'll probably use multiple live switches. Often the goal is to have a GNS3 router connected to each external switch. This is tricky because most PCs have only one Ethernet adapter. Fortunately, GNS3 and IOS have this sorted out. Your options are to trunk VLANs to the switch over a single Ethernet adapter in your PC or to install multiple Ethernet adapters in your PC.

In this section, I'll cover two ways to connect GNS3 devices to live Cisco switches.

Standard 802.1Q Trunk This method uses a standard 802.1Q trunk to allow GNS3 devices to communicate with a live Cisco switch via your PC's Ethernet adapter.

Breakout Switch This method uses a specially configured Ethernet switch called a breakout switch to allow GNS3 devices to connect to multiple live switches using only a single Ethernet adapter in your PC. To create a breakout switch, you must have a second physical Ethernet switch on hand to use as the breakout switch.

The option you choose depends on how many switches you own, your PC's operating system, and what Ethernet adapters are already installed in your PC. Let's start by looking at how an 802.1Q trunk works to reach a Cisco switch.

Configuring a Standard 802.1Q Trunk

In my opinion, an 802.1Q trunk is the best way to attach live switches to your GNS3 projects. The advantages of a standard 802.1Q trunk are that it is easy to set up and works the same as connecting a switch to a physical network. The disadvantage is that your PC operating system or your PC's

Ethernet drivers might not support it. Often they strip the 802.1Q tags from packets coming from the switch into your PC. Without the proper tags, GNS3 has no way of knowing which VLANs your packets belong to and in turn doesn't know where to forward the packets, which breaks your network.

If you poke around the Internet, you'll find all sorts of creative solutions that people have come up with to circumvent this problem, but they are generally platform-specific and vary from machine to machine.

NOTE *One way to prevent tag stripping on OS X and Linux is to use a USB Ethernet adapter that supports 802.1Q tagging and jumbo frames. One such adapter that works well is the StartTech USB31000SW adapter, but any adapter that uses the ASIX AX88772A chipset should work.*

In this example, you'll place either an EtherSwitch router or Ethernet switch node in your workspace and configure it with the 802.1Q trunking protocol. Next, you'll add a Cloud node to your workspace and configure it using an NIO interface, and link it to the GNS3 switch. The Cloud node can either be directly connected, or bridged, to your PC's Ethernet adapter (depending on your OS). You'll then plug an Ethernet cable from your PC's Ethernet adapter into a port on the live Cisco switch. The switch port you choose also needs to be configured with 802.1Q trunking. After both the GNS3 switch and physical switch have been configured, you should be able to route GNS3-generated VLAN packets through the trunk to the live switch.

In this section, we'll create a simple project that connects our GNS3 network to a live c3550 switch using two VLANs (10 and 20). Begin by creating the topology shown in Figure 7-11. When configuring the Cloud node, choose your PC's Ethernet adapter name, found under the NIO Ethernet tab.

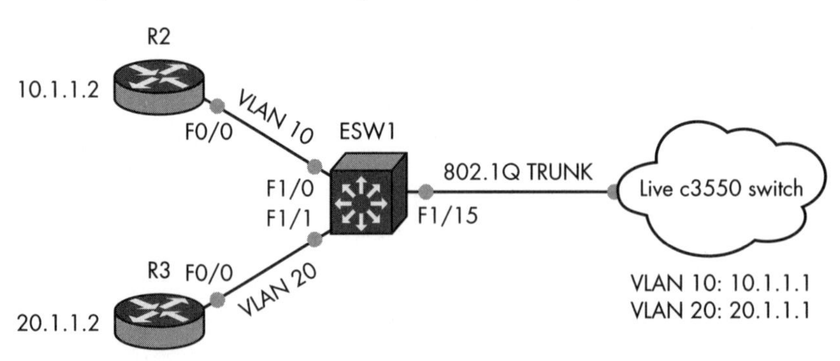

Figure 7-11: Sample topology using a standard dot1q trunk to live switch

To configure VLANs and an 802.1Q trunk using the *EtherSwitch router*, open a console on ESW1 and enter the following commands:

```
  ESW1# vlan database
❶ ESW1(vlan)# vlan 10
❷ ESW1(vlan)# vlan 20
```

```
  ESW1(vlan)# apply
  ESW1(vlan)# exit
  ESW1# configure terminal
  ESW1(config)# int f1/15
❸ ESW1(config-if)# switchport mode trunk
❹ ESW1(config-if)# switchport trunk encapsulation dot1q
  ESW1(config-if)# int f1/0
  ESW1(config-if)# switchport mode access
❺ ESW1(config-if)# switchport access vlan 10
  ESW1(config-if)# int f1/1
  ESW1(config-if)# switchport mode access
❻ ESW1(config-if)# switchport access vlan 20
```

The previous commands create VLAN 10 ❶ and 20 ❷ on the switch, configure a trunk port ❸ using the dot1q protocol ❹, and assign access ports to VLAN 10 ❺ (for router R2) and VLAN 20 ❻ (for router R3).

If instead you choose to use an Ethernet switch node, configure one port as an 802.1Q trunk and the others as VLAN access ports, as shown in Figure 7-12.

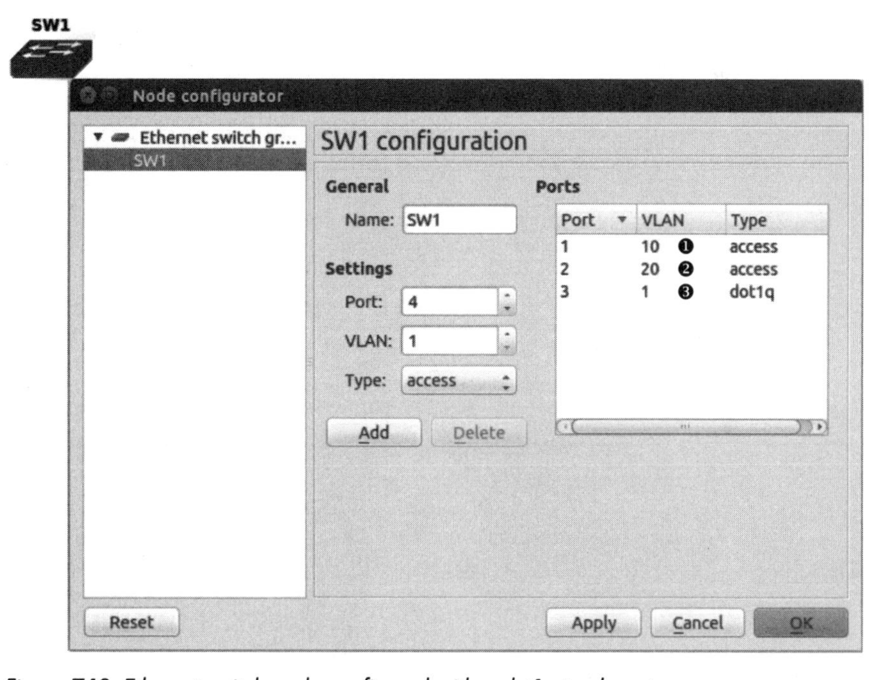

Figure 7-12: Ethernet switch node configured with a dot1q trunk port

Ports 1 and 2 are configured as access ports using VLAN 10 ❶ and 20 ❷, and port 3 is the dot1q trunk port ❸ that's connected to the Cloud node.

Next, log on to your live Cisco switch and create the same VLANs. Then, configure the 802.1Q trunk port and cable it to your PC's Ethernet adapter. The following listing is an example of how to configure a c3550 switch, using commands you've seen throughout the chapter.

```
c3550# configure-terminal
c3550(config)# ip routing
c3550(config)# interface vlan 10
c3550(config-vlan)# ip address 10.1.1.1
c3550(config-vlan)# interface vlan 20
c3550(config-vlan)# ip address 20.1.1.1
c3550(config-vlan)# exit
c3550(config)# Interface f0/1
c3550(config-if)# switchport trunk encapsulation dot1q
c3550(config-if)# switch port mode trunk
c3550(config-if)# switchport trunk allowed vlan all
c3550(config-if)# speed 100
c3550(config-if)# duplex full
```

To complete the project, configure routers R2 and R3. Log on to router R2 and configure an IP address and default gateway for VLAN 10.

```
R2(config)# interface f0/0
R2(config-if)# description Using VLAN 10
R2(config-if)# ip address 10.1.1.2 255.255.255.0
R2(config-if)# no shutdown
R2(config-if)# exit
R2(config)# ip route 0.0.0.0 0.0.0.0 10.1.1.1
```

Now, log on to router R3 and configure an IP address and default gateway for VLAN 20.

```
R3(config)# interface f0/0
R3(config-if)# description Using VLAN 20
R3(config-if)# ip address 20.1.1.2 255.255.255.0
R3(config-if)# no shutdown
R3(config-if)# exit
R3(config)# ip route 0.0.0.0 0.0.0.0 20.1.1.1
```

Test VLAN routing through the switch by entering a `ping` command from one VLAN to another.

```
R3# ping 10.1.1.2
!!!!!
```

When you're finished with the project, you can further verify the configuration using tools like CDP or Wireshark.

Creating the Elusive Breakout Switch

A *breakout switch* is another way to connect real switches to GNS3 projects, and it's common to set one up using Ubuntu Linux. Although a breakout switch does work on other systems, it's easiest to set up on Linux. As mentioned earlier, other operating systems like Windows and OS X might remove VLAN information from the packets. For this reason, it's best to install Ubuntu on real hardware if you plan to create a breakout switch.

If you use a virtual machine, your underlying host OS may strip the VLAN tags, and the breakout switch won't work. You can sometimes get around this by using a USB Ethernet adapter, like the StartTech USB31000SW mentioned in "Configuring a Standard 802.1Q Trunk" on page 109.

This switching method requires a minimum of two real Cisco switches; one is the breakout switch, and the other is one or more live Cisco switches that are used in your GNS3 project. The breakout switch is used to fool the live Cisco switches into thinking that each of your GNS3 routers is *directly connected* to a live switch with an Ethernet cable. In reality, only one Ethernet adapter is used in your PC to connect all your GNS3 routers to the live switches, and that adapter is connected to the breakout switch. The breakout switch is then configured to *break out all the VLANs* into individual interfaces that you plug into other live Cisco switches using Ethernet cables (one per VLAN). I call these *breakout cables*. Figure 7-13 shows the physical layout of your PC and switches.

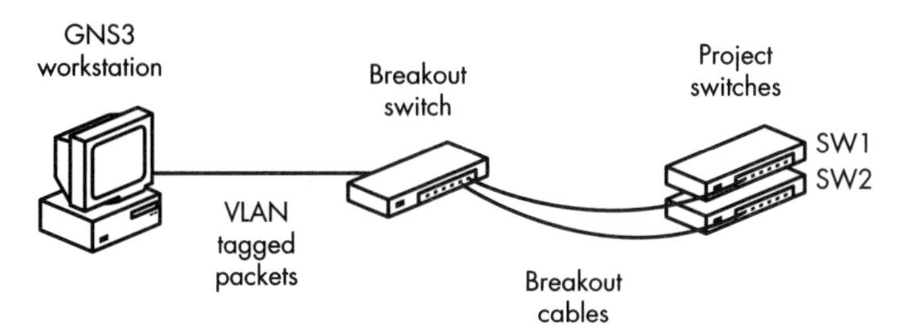

Figure 7-13: Physical layout using a breakout switch and live Cisco switches

Here's the flyby view of how it works. Breakout VLANs are configured on your Linux Ethernet adapter using the `vlan` package, and an 802.1Q trunk is configured on the breakout switch. In GNS3, you'll add one or more Cloud nodes that are configured with the Linux breakout VLANs using NIO Ethernet interfaces. In your GNS3 project, a router is connected to each of the Cloud node's VLAN interfaces (one router per interface). Packets leaving the routers go into the Cloud node, where Linux tags them with a VLAN ID and passes them to the breakout switch using your PC's Ethernet adapter. The breakout switch receives the packets on a standard 802.1Q trunk port. From there, the breakout switch uses the VLAN IDs to identify and transparently pass the packets to one (or more) live Cisco switches. What makes this so ingenious is that each GNS3 router has a separate Ethernet cable that is connected to a port on the live Cisco switch, even though your PC has only a single Ethernet adapter.

Breakout switches are fairly straightforward to set up on Linux. Start by updating your package manager and installing VLAN support on your Ubuntu system.

```
$ sudo apt-get install vlan
```

Now, enable the `8021q` Linux module using the `modprobe` command.

```
$ sudo modprobe 8021q
```

Next, increase the MTU frame size on the Ethernet interface, and create your breakout VLANs using the vconfig command. Be sure to substitute *eth0* with the name of your interface.

```
❶ $ sudo ifconfig eth0 mtu 1546
❷ $ sudo vconfig add eth0 10
❸ $ sudo vconfig add eth0 20
```

NOTE *Your Ethernet adapter must support frame sizes above the standard maximum of 1500 bytes.*

The increased frame size ❶ makes room for the additional VLAN tags. Create one breakout VLAN for each router in your project. In the previous listing, I created two breakout VLANs (10 ❷ and 20 ❸) on my Linux PC's *eth0* interface.

NOTE *Don't confuse breakout VLANs with VLANs you create in your GNS3 projects. It's important to understand that breakout VLANs should be used only by Linux and the breakout switch—they are not to be used in your GNS3 project or live Cisco switches.*

Start configuring the breakout switch by increasing the system-wide MTU size. After the command is entered, you must reload the switch for the change to take effect.

```
Breakout(config)# system mtu 1546
```

After the switch reboots, log on and configure an 802.1Q trunk link as follows:

```
  Breakout# configure terminal
  Breakout(config)# interface FastEthernet 0/1
❶ Breakout(config-if)# switchport trunk encapsulation dot1q
❷ Breakout(config-if)# switchport mode trunk
❸ Breakout(config-if)# switchport trunk allowed vlan all
```

The interface you configure as the trunk is then connected to your PC's physical Ethernet adapter using an Ethernet cable. As shown here, dot1q encapsulation ❶ is configured on the trunk port ❷, and all VLANs ❸ are allowed through the trunk.

Next, go under each interface that you plan to connect to a live switch, and configure a breakout VLAN and a dot1q tunnel for each VLAN, as shown in the following listing:

```
Breakout(config)# vlan 10
Breakout(config-vlan)# vlan 20
Breakout(config-vlan)# exit
```

```
Breakout(config)# interface FastEthernet 0/2
Breakout(config-if)# description GNS3 R1 Physical Uplink to Live Switch SW1
❶ Breakout(config-if)# switchport access vlan 10
❷ Breakout(config-if)# switchport mode dot1q-tunnel
❸ Breakout(config-if)# l2protocol-tunnel cdp
Breakout(config-if)# interface FastEthernet 0/3
Breakout(config-if)# description GNS3 R2 Physical Uplink to Live Switch SW2
❹ Breakout(config-if)# switchport access vlan 20
Breakout(config-if)# switchport mode dot1q-tunnel
Breakout(config-if)# l2protocol-tunnel cdp
```

Here, our breakout switch's FastEthernet 0/2 interface is configured for VLAN 10 ❶, dot1q tunneling ❷, and Cisco discovery protocol tunneling ❸. FastEthernet 0/3 is configured the same way, but for VLAN 20 ❹. These are the interfaces used to connect GNS3 routers to your live Cisco switches.

We already know that Cisco Discovery Protocol (CDP) is used to share and gather information with directly connected Cisco equipment, often called *neighbors*. However, our live Cisco switch is not directly connected to GNS3; instead, it's connected to the breakout switch. In this instance, the only way to use CDP is by tunneling the protocol through the breakout switch to a live Cisco switch with the `l2protocol-tunnel cdp` command. (You can also tunnel STP and VTP.) This is where things get tricky because CDP tunneling does not work on all switches. If you need to use CDP, be sure to choose a breakout switch that fully supports CDP tunneling. Table 7-1 lists a few common Cisco switches and their CDP tunneling capabilities.

Table 7-1: Common Cisco Switches and Their CDP Tunneling Compatibility

Switch	CDP tunneling compatibility
Cisco 2950	CDP will not work in either direction. Layer 2 tunneling is not supported on this switch.
Cisco 3550	CDP works only in one direction. Neighbors cannot be seen on the switches regardless of the IOS version.
Cisco 3560	CDP works only in one direction. Neighbors cannot be seen on the switches regardless of the IOS version.
Cisco 3750	Bidirectional CDP and fully functional (layer 2 and layer 3) using IP Services image. IP Base image does not support tunneling.
Cisco 4948	Bidirectional CDP and fully functional (layer 2 and layer 3) using a minimum IP Services image.

The Cisco 3750 switch works well, both as a breakout switch and for tunneling CDP, but it's not the cheapest switch available. If you don't have the cash to spring for this model, you can choose a cheaper model that should work as a breakout switch, but you won't have complete transparency in your GNS3 project.

Before continuing, be sure that Fa0/1 on the breakout switch is connected to your PC's Ethernet port, and that Fa0/2 and Fa0/3 are connected to Ethernet ports on your live project switches. After checking those connections, start GNS3 and configure a Cloud node using the Linux VLANs you created previously, as shown in Figure 7-14.

Figure 7-14: Configuring a Cloud node using Linux VLANs

NOTE *Even though you're using Linux, it's important to use the Generic Ethernet NIO and not the Linux Ethernet NIO. Otherwise, VLAN tagging may not work.*

When you're finished adding breakout VLANs to the Cloud node, add a couple of routers to your workspace and create a link from each router to a breakout VLAN on the Cloud node. In Figure 7-15, router R1 (F0/0) is linked to VLAN 10 in the Cloud using *nio_gen_eth:eth0.10*, and R2 (F0/0) is linked to VLAN 20 using *nio_gen_eth:eth0.20.*

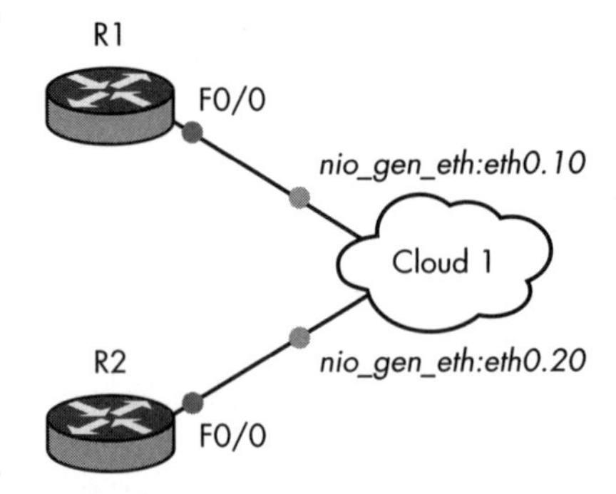

Figure 7-15: Virtual routers connected to Linux VLANs using a Cloud node

Because the breakout switch is only used to split VLANs into multiple physical ports, it requires no further configuration. In this example, router R1 is now linked to any live switch plugged into breakout switchport f0/2, and R2 should be linked to any live switch plugged into port f0/3.

NOTE *If you create large projects using many VLANs, you may want to assign only one Linux VLAN interface per Cloud node to help clarify the layout in your workspace.*

Your GNS3 routers should now be able to communicate with one or more real Cisco switches.

Optional Breakout Switch Configuration

If you're running Windows or OS X, you may be able to use a GNS3 Switch node to link your project to a breakout switch, as shown in Figure 7-16. In this setup, the breakout switch is configured in the same way as previously, but you'll need to make some tweaks to your PC. The Ethernet switch node connects to a Cloud node using an NIO interface configured with a loopback adapter on Windows or a TAP interface on OS X. The virtual adapter is bridged to your PC's physical Ethernet adapter. This allows Cloud 1 to connect to the breakout switch using your PC's Ethernet adapter.

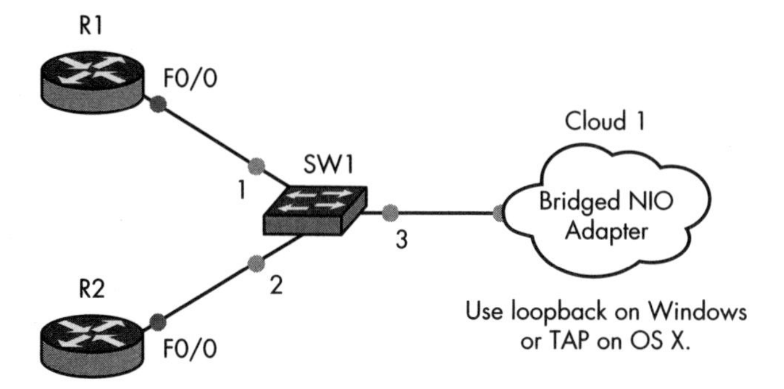

Figure 7-16: Breakout switch configuration using an Ethernet switch node

For the breakout switch to work, you should increase the MTU size on your PC's physical Ethernet adapter, but not all adapters support this feature.

If you're a OS X user, the MTU size must be increased on both your physical adapter and virtual adapter. To increase the MTU size from the command line, use the following example:

```
$ sudo ifconfig en0 mtu 1546
$ sudo ifconfig tap0 mtu 1546
```

NOTE *On OS X, configure the virtual and physical adapter using the same MTU size, or the bridge creation will fail.*

You may have to check your Ethernet adapter documentation to configure your adapter on Windows. On many adapters, however, the MTU setting can be found under the Advanced properties of the adapter, as shown in Figure 7-17. In this example the `Jumbo Packet` value is set to 9014 bytes on an Intel PRO/1000 MT card.

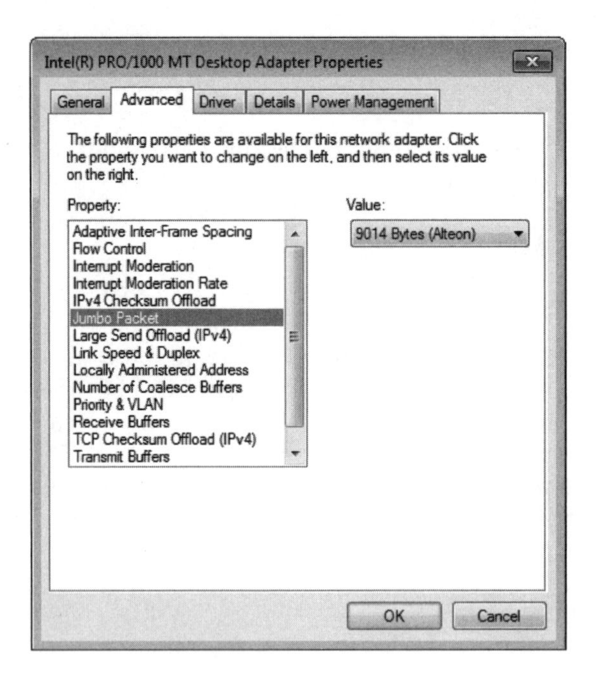

Figure 7-17: Setting the Jumbo Packet size on Windows

Next, bring up the Node configurator for the Ethernet switch node to define VLANs and the dot1q trunk port, as shown in Figure 7-18.

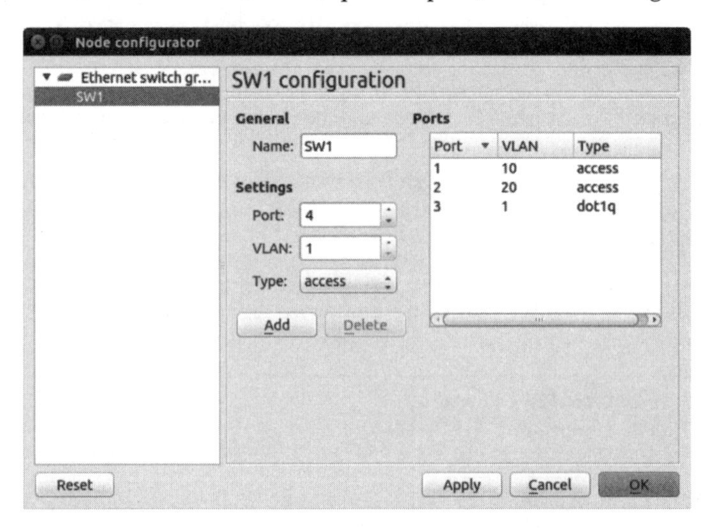

Figure 7-18: Ethernet switch node configured for breakout switch

In this example, R1 is connected to access Port 1 (VLAN 10), R2 is connected to access Port 2 (VLAN 20), and Port 3 is the dot1q trunk to the breakout switch. After everything is configured in GNS3, you can log on and configure the breakout switch with VLANs and dot1q tunneling as previously described.

Using Multiple Adapters in Your PC

Instead of using an 802.1Q trunk or a breakout switch, you could use one physical Ethernet interface for each router in GNS3. If you have a laptop, you could use a USB hub and connect multiple USB Ethernet adapters to your PC; with a desktop, you could use the USB hub method or purchase a multiport Ethernet card. Figure 7-19 shows the physical layout of the design.

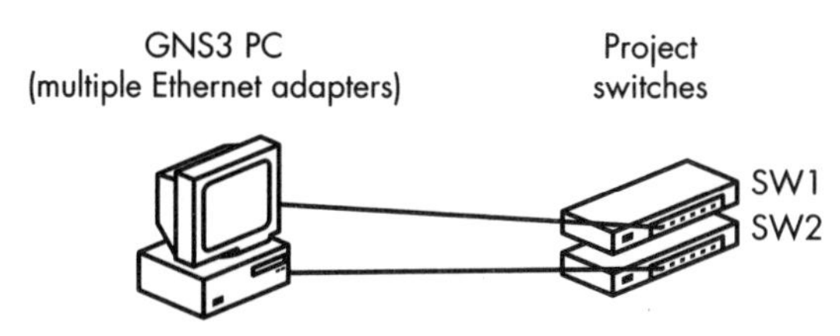

Figure 7-19: Physical layout using multiple adapters in a PC

Connect each Ethernet adapter in your PC to a physical port on a live Cisco switch. Log on to each switch and configure an access port using the `switchport mode access` command. Then, assign a unique VLAN number to the port by entering `switchport access vlan {vlan number}`, as in the following listings.

Start with the first switch (c3550_swl):

```
c3550_sw1(config)# interface f0/1
c3550_sw1(config-if)# description VLAN used for PC Ethernet Adapter 1
c3550_sw1(config-if)# switchport mode access
c3550_sw1(config-if)# switchport access vlan 10
```

Next, configure switch two (c3550_sw2):

```
c3550_sw2(config)# interface f0/1
c3550_sw2(config-if)# description VLAN used for PC Ethernet Adapter 2
c3550_sw2(config-if)# switchport mode access
c3550_sw2(config-if)# switchport access vlan 20
```

To connect GNS3 devices to the switches, add a Cloud node to your workspace and assign one NIO Ethernet interface for each Ethernet adapter in your PC. Connect your GNS3 routers to each NIO interface using one router per interface.

NOTE *OS X users will have to create a unique bridge interface for each adapter and bridge each Ethernet interface to a unique TAP interface. OS X supports up to 16 TAP devices (tap0 through tap15).*

After all the devices in your project have been configured, your GNS3 devices should be able to communicate with the live Cisco switches. Further configuration is required on the switches to enable routing between GNS3 routers and is determined by the switch block design you create.

Now let's take a look at connecting GNS3 to the Internet.

Connecting GNS3 Devices to the Internet

To connect GNS3 devices to the Internet, you need to use an Ethernet adapter in your PC. Wireless network adapters are not supported if you use them directly, though one may work if bridged to a loopback adapter or TAP interface (but don't count on it). Make the GNS3 to Ethernet connection the same way that you connect to a physical switch: add a Cloud node to your project and configure it with either an NIO TAP or NIO Ethernet interface.

Configuring Windows

On Windows systems, create a bridge using a loopback adapter and your PC's physical Ethernet adapter. Then, in GNS3, use a Cloud node configured using NIO Ethernet and select the loopback adapter. Because the loopback adapter is bridged to the physical Ethernet adapter, you can use the Cloud to connect to networks outside GNS3—including the Internet.

On Windows 8.*x*, install a loopback adapter, but do not add it to a bridge. Instead, configure Internet Connection Sharing (ICS) on your physical interface (Ethernet or Wi-Fi). To do so, right-click the **Start** button and select **Network Connections**. Next, right-click your physical Interface and select **Properties**. Select the **Sharing** tab, and check the **Allow other network users to connect through this computer's Internet connection** option. Lastly, select your loopback adapter from the Home Networking Connection drop-down menu, and click **OK**.

Configuring Unix-Based Systems

On Ubuntu Linux, create an NIO Ethernet connection using your PC's Ethernet interface. On OS X and some Linux systems, use an NIO TAP connection configured with */dev/tap0* and bridge the TAP interface to your PC's Ethernet interface.

Creating a Simple Network

Create a project by adding a router and a Cloud node to your workspace and adding a link from the router to the Cloud. In Figure 7-20, the Cloud is configured using the Windows loopback adapter, named `Local Area Connection 2`.

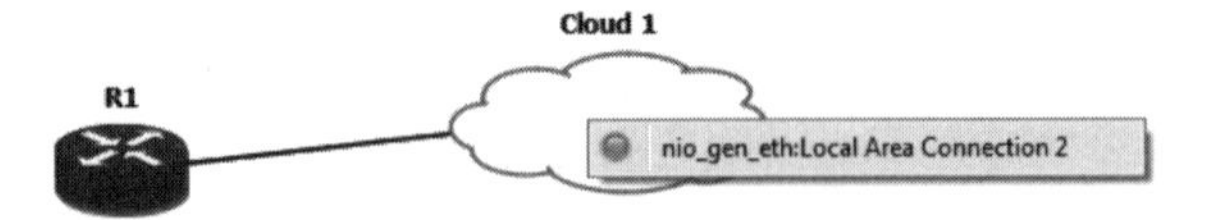

Figure 7-20: Connecting to a Cloud using a Windows loopback adapter

To test Internet connectivity, attach an Ethernet cable from your PC to an Internet device, like a cable modem, and configure an IP address on your GNS3 router. If you use DHCP to assign an IP address as I did here, you may have to wait a moment for the router to receive an IP address before you can test connectivity.

```
R1(config)# ip domain-lookup
R1(config)# ip name-server 8.8.8.8
R1(config)# interface f0/0
R1(config)# no shutdown
R1(config-if)# ip address dhcp

*Mar  1 00:01:08.875: %DHCP-6-ADDRESS_ASSIGN: Interface FastEthernet0/0 assigned
DHCP address 192.168.1.101, mask 255.255.255.0, hostname R1
```

After your router has obtained an IP address, you should be able to ping a host on the Internet. Try to ping *www.gns3.net*! You're not limited to using a router to connect to the Internet; you can also use an ASA device, Juniper router, or any other device that supports TCP/IP.

NOTE *If you have other devices behind router R1, you need to configure NAT on R1 before they can route to the Internet. For more information, visit Cisco's website* (http://www.cisco.com/en/US/tech/tk648/tk361/technologies_tech_note09186a0080094e77.shtml#topic6).

Final Thoughts

In this chapter, we looked at configuring GNS3 device nodes and integrating them into your projects using Cisco IOS. They're simple to set up and well suited for large projects because they greatly reduce the load on your PC. Compared to Dynamips devices, GNS3 device nodes use almost no PC resources.

Connecting a GNS3 device to a live Cisco switch is tricky. If you choose to create a standard 802.1Q trunk to connect with a live switch, you can use either an EtherSwitch router or an Ethernet switch node, but your PC operating system and Ethernet adapter drivers must both support 802.1Q tagging. Without the proper VLAN tags, trunking won't work.

If you have an extra IOS switch, you can create a breakout switch, which is a very reliable way to integrate multiple real Cisco switches into your GNS3 projects. A breakout switch works most reliably on Linux systems but can also be configured using Windows and OS X.

In the next chapter, we'll look at some more advanced features including Cisco, ASA, and IDS/IPS.

8

CISCO ASA, IDS/IPS, AND IOS-XRV

You've already seen some of the ways GNS3 can interact with other software and operating systems. In this chapter, you'll delve deeper into the advanced features of GNS3 and explore how you can expand your projects by interacting with additional Quick Emulator (QEMU) virtual devices and software.

Knowing about technologies such as Cisco's ASAs, Intrusion Detection Systems/Intrusion Prevention Systems (IDSs/IPSs), and IOS-XR broadens your view of Cisco and GNS3 and can be useful when choosing a network certification path. Plus, it's a lot of fun to play with virtualized Cisco products that are otherwise inaccessible to most people. It's also important to learn how to use some of Cisco's GUI-based tools.

I'll begin by showing you how to install Cisco Configuration Professional (CCP) software, a web-based alternative to configuring routers via the Cisco command line interface. Next, you'll learn how to configure and run an ASA. I'll discuss using Cisco's Adaptive Security Device Manager (ASDM) software, which is similar to the CCP software mentioned earlier but used to configure ASAs. By the end of the chapter, you'll learn that patience is not only a virtue but a prerequisite when you set up a Cisco IDS/IPS. Finally, I'll show you how to configure and use Cisco IOS-XRv devices in GNS3.

Cisco Configuration Professional

Most engineers use IOS commands to configure routers and switches, but there are other ways. CCP is a web-based alternative that uses "smart wizards" to simplify router configuration, and it provides tools to help you monitor and troubleshoot networks and VPNs. In a nutshell, CCP allows less experienced users to get their equipment up and running.

Project Configuration

To use CCP with GNS3, you'll create a simple project using one router and a VirtualBox virtual machine running Microsoft Windows, as in Figure 8-1. Although there are other methods to do this, I've chosen to demonstrate this method because it should work on any PC that's running GNS3 (Windows, Linux, and OS X).

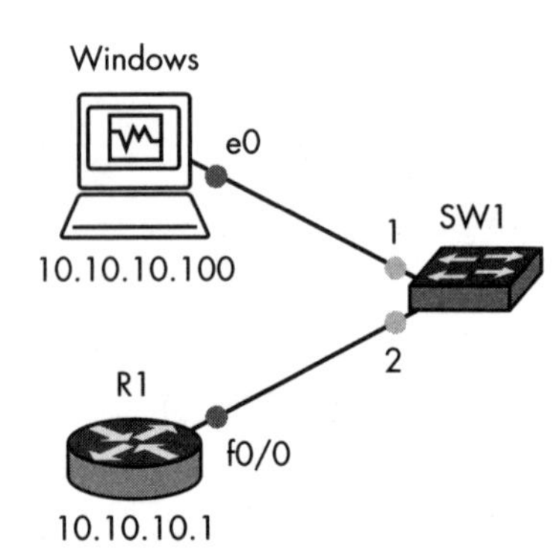

Figure 8-1: CCP topology with a router and Windows host

Log on to the Windows computer and disable the firewall to ensure that CCP has unrestricted communication with your router. (This isn't mandatory, but it may prevent headaches later.) Assign the Windows guest an IP address on the same subnet as your router (in this example, 10.10.10.100).

Next, create a basic configuration on your router.

```
❶ R1(config)# ip http server
  R1(config)# ip http secure-server
  R1(config)# ip http authentication local
❷ R1(config)# username admin privilege 15 secret cisco
  R1(config)# interface f0/0
❸ R1(config-if)# ip address 10.10.10.1 255.255.255.0
  R1(config-if)# no shutdown
```

You need to enable the router's web server ❶, create a user with full EXEC mode privileges ❷, and assign an IP address to the interface ❸. In this example, the router is assigned IP address 10.10.10.1.

NOTE *You have to create a Cisco admin account with full EXEC mode privileges (privilege 15) so that later you'll have sufficient rights to configure the router using CCP.*

After configuring the router, test connectivity between the Windows guest and the router using a `ping` command.

```
C:> ping 10.10.10.1
```

If you can successfully ping the router, then it's safe to proceed. If you cannot ping the router, check your IP addresses and interfaces.

CCP Installation

CCP is a Java-based application that interacts with a web browser, so before you begin, download and install Java if you don't have it already (*http://www.java.com/*). Make sure you also have the latest version of Adobe Flash Player (*http://www.adobe.com/*). You can download Cisco Configuration Professional from the Cisco website (*http://www.cisco.com/*).

To install CCP, log on to your Windows virtual machine and launch the setup program; you should see the CCP installation wizard. Click **Next** and follow the instructions to complete the setup.

Running CCP

Launch Cisco Configuration Professional by right-clicking the program icon and choosing **Run as Administrator**. When the program opens, you'll be asked for the IP address of a router you want to manage. You should see the CCP Device Manager, shown in Figure 8-2.

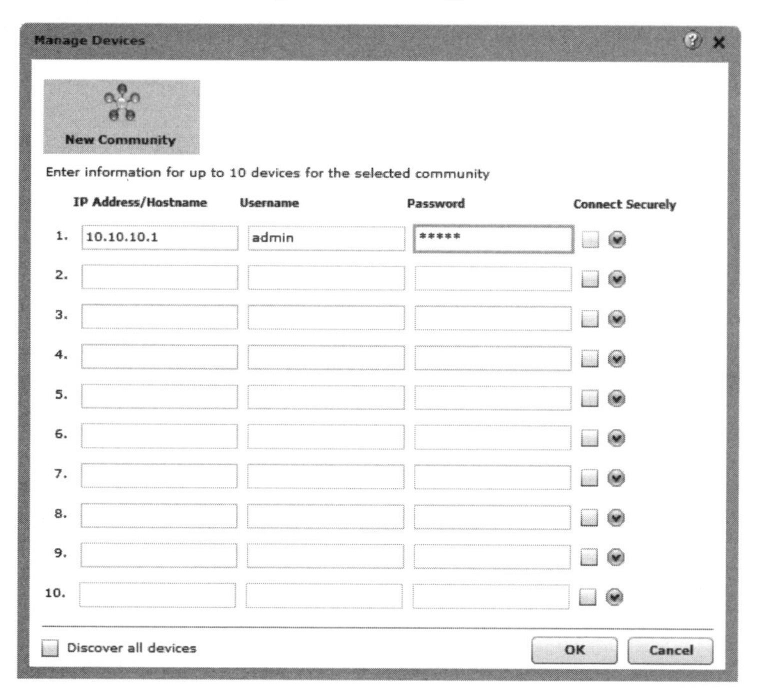

Figure 8-2: CCP Device Manager

Enter the IP address you assigned to the router (**10.10.10.1**), enter the administrator username and password you assigned earlier (**admin** and **cisco**), and then click **OK**. After logging on, you should see the CCP management screen, shown in Figure 8-3.

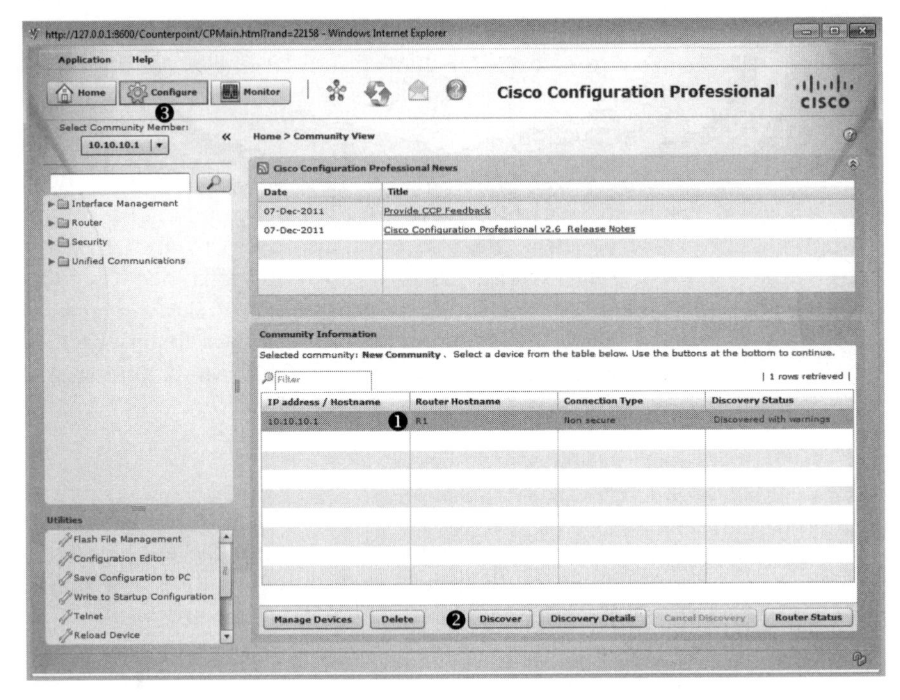

Figure 8-3: Cisco CCP management screen

Before you can manage your router, you have to select it by first clicking the router hostname R1 ❶ and then clicking **Discover** ❷ so CCP can discover its features and capabilities. After it's been discovered, you can set up your router by clicking **Configure** ❸ in the toolbar. The advantage of using CCP is that it guides you through the process of assigning IP addresses, NAT, VPNs, and other Cisco features without you having to know any IOS commands. Be aware that Cisco certification exams primarily focus on IOS commands, and not CCP, to configure devices.

Cisco ASA Firewall

Cisco's ASA is an improved version of the old PIX firewall. GNS3 emulates a Cisco ASA model 5520. Although it's not a router, you may be surprised to learn that the ASA supports several routing protocols, including RIP, EIGRP, and OSPF, allowing you to easily network them with other GNS3 routed devices.

Acquiring an Image

Before you can use an ASA virtual machine with GNS3, you need an image file of the ASA operating system. The fastest way to get an image of the ASA operating system is to copy it from an ASA you already own (that is, from the ASA installation CD or directly from an ASA device). Copying files from a Cisco ASA works the same way as copying files from a Cisco router: you can use FTP or TFTP. In this example, you'll use a TFTP server. There are plenty of free TFTP servers to choose from, so find one you like and install it on your PC.

After you have a TFTP server running on your network, log on to your physical ASA and copy your ASA image file to your PC. In the following listing, my ASA image file is named *asa824-k8.bin*, and my TFTP server is running on a PC at IP address 192.168.1.100:

```
ciscoasa# copy flash:asa824-k8.bin tftp
Address or name of remote host []? 192.168.1.100
```

After you have an ASA image file, you need to make some modifications to the file before you can use it with GNS3.

Prepping the ASA Image for GNS3

The Cisco ASA is really just a small Linux PC, and ASA image files like *asa824-k8.bin* contain a compact Linux operating system designed to run on ASA hardware.

The image file includes a Linux kernel and other support software for the appliance. To run the ASA software using GNS3, you have to unpack the *.bin* file, make some modifications, and repack it in a way that's suitable for QEMU. Fortunately, there are plenty of clever people in the Linux and Cisco communities who have written image unpacker software that does this for you. You can download Cisco Image Unpacker for Windows from the GNS3 website, or you can use a Linux shell script like *repack.v4.sh*. Regardless of which unpacker you choose, you'll need to find one designed for your version of ASA software. After running the script, you should be left with two files: *asa-vmlinuz* (a Linux kernel) and *asa-initrd.gz* (a RAM disk file). These are the files used by QEMU and GNS3.

If you don't want to modify your own ASA image file, a quick Internet search should turn up plenty of ready-to-use ASA files. These images usually come in a *.zip* file that contains the two files (*asa-vmlinux* and *asa-initrd.gz*).

Configuring GNS3 for ASA

Before configuring an ASA in GNS3, check that QEMU is installed and tested on your PC. (See the QEMU installation information for your particular operating system in Chapter 6.) Next, launch GNS3, select **Edit ▸ Preferences** on Linux and Windows or **GNS3 ▸ Preferences** on OS X, and choose **QEMU VMs** from the panel on the left, as shown in Figure 8-4.

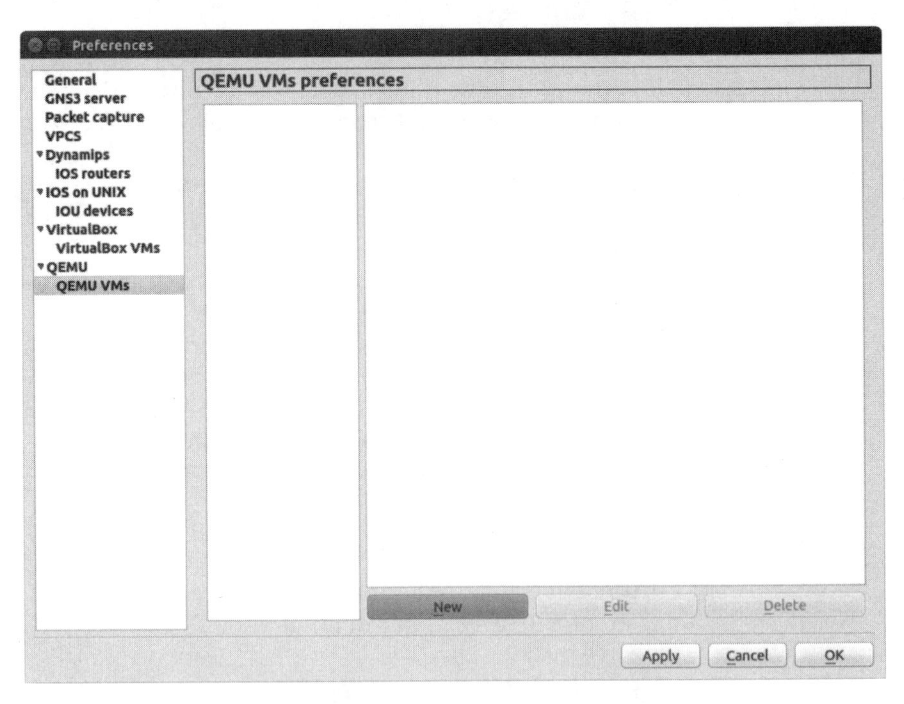

Figure 8-4: QEMU VMs preferences

To create a new ASA in GNS3, click **New** to start the New QEMU VM wizard. Select **ASA 8.4(2)** from the Type drop-down menu, as shown in Figure 8-5.

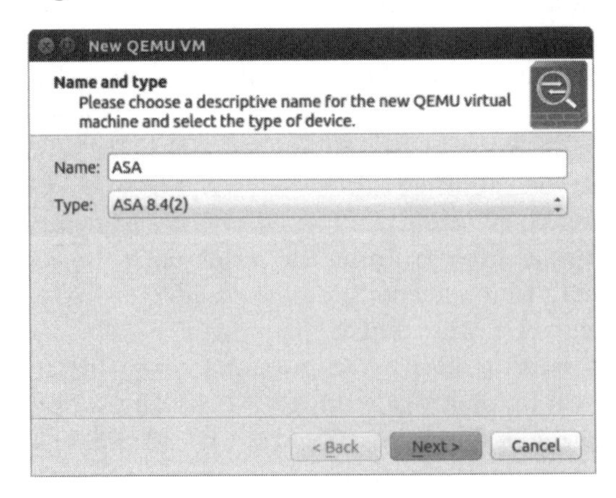

Figure 8-5: Creating a new QEMU virtual machine and setting Type to ASA 8.4(2)

By default your device is automatically named *ASA*, but you can rename it whatever you prefer. When you're done naming your ASA, click **Next** to continue.

The wizard should automatically locate and choose the correct QEMU binary file for your PC, as shown in Figure 8-6.

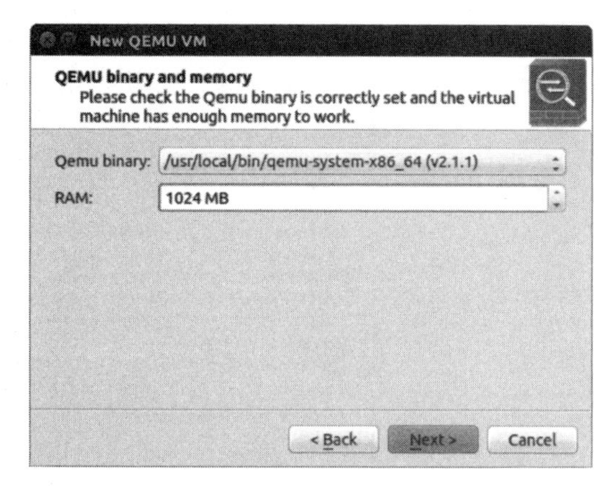

Figure 8-6: Selecting the ASA virtual machine's QEMU binary and memory

If it does not find a QEMU binary, verify that QEMU is installed correctly on your PC and try again. The default RAM value is 1024MB, but this is the minimum amount required to run the ASA image. You can increase the value by entering a new value in the field. When you're done, click **Next** to continue the wizard.

The last step is to browse and select your initial RAM disk and kernel image, as shown in Figure 8-7.

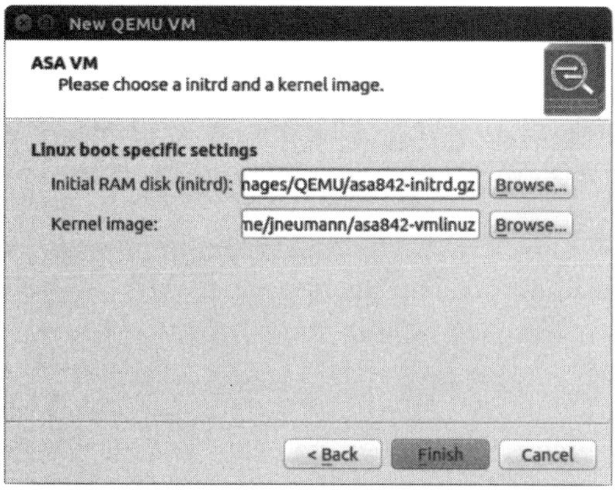

Figure 8-7: Linux boot-specific settings for an ASA virtual machine

Set Initial Ram disk (initrd) and Kernel image to the correct files for your computer; these are usually named *asa842-initrd.gz* and *asa842-vmlinuz*, respectively.

When you're done choosing the two images, click **Finish** to complete the installation. After successfully adding your ASA, the ASA device should be displayed in the QEMU VM Preferences window, as shown in Figure 8-8.

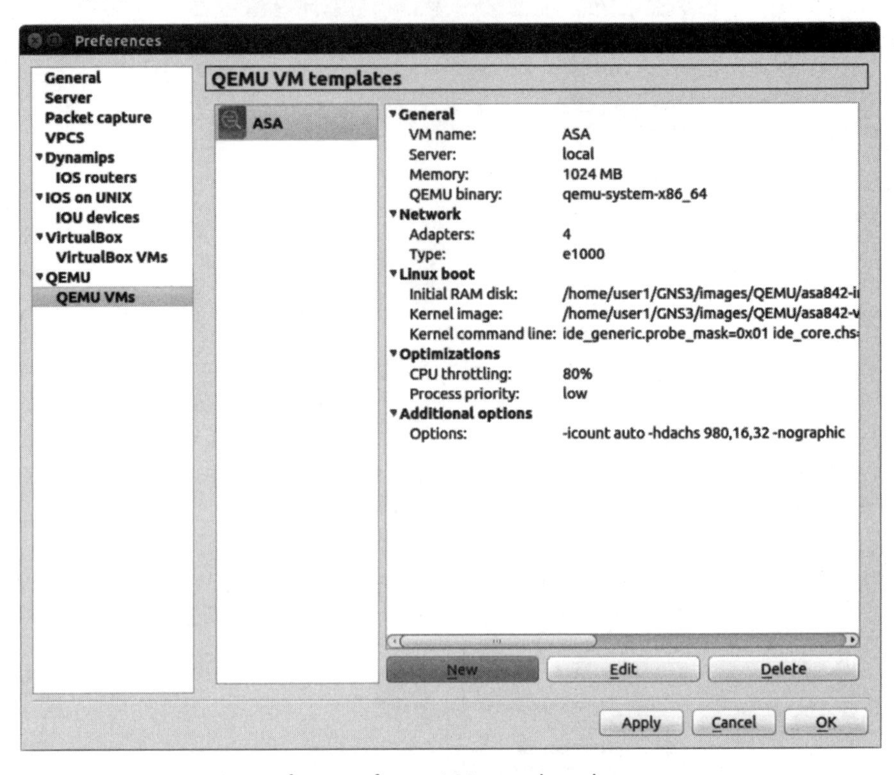

Figure 8-8: QEMU VMs preferences for an ASA virtual machine

The current settings of your ASA should be displayed in the panel on the right, and one setting you should note is CPU throttling (located under Optimizations).

Unlike Dynamips devices, the ASA does not have an Idle-PC option to control CPU consumption. This means that an ASA can consume your entire CPU, much like a Dynamips router does when no Idle-PC value has been set. To prevent this, GNS3 uses another open source application (cpulimit) to adjust the maximum amount of CPU that a QEMU/ASA instance can consume. The default value is 80 percent, which works well in most situations. You can edit your ASA settings and raise or lower the value, but be careful; using too little of your CPU, by decreasing the percentage, can result in poor ASA performance and frequent ASA crashes, and setting the percentage too high can result in slower overall PC performance.

Another setting to note under Optimizations is the Process priority. The default value in GNS3 is low, but it can be set to low, medium, or high. The Process priority determines when the QEMU/ASA instance gets CPU time.

Processes with a high priority gain access to the CPU before processes with a low priority. In general, changing the priority should have little or no effect on your system, but to be safe, keep it set to low to prevent your ASA from potentially overriding important system processes.

On Windows and OS X, the cpulimit program should have been installed with GNS3. On Ubuntu Linux you need to install cpulimit using the following command:

```
$ sudo apt-get install cpulimit
```

Now that your ASA virtual machine won't take over your system, let's log on to an ASA and perform a basic configuration.

Testing an ASA in GNS3

Drag an ASA firewall node from the Devices toolbar to your workspace. Your ASA should be located in the Security Devices section of the toolbar. Start the ASA and open a GNS3 console connection. While it loads, you should see standard ASA startup messages followed by the ASA command prompt:

```
ciscoasa>
```

A few error messages before the prompt are perfectly normal, but if your ASA fails to start or you see a lot of errors, check your settings or try a different ASA image file.

NOTE *It's not uncommon for an ASA in GNS3 to hang or stall during the boot cycle, especially on older hardware. If this happens, stop and restart the ASA. It may take a couple attempts before you get a successful boot.*

To test simple network connectivity, create a link from your ASA to another GNS3 device in your workspace. Next, open a console connection to the ASA and configure an interface with an IP address.

```
ciscoasa> enable
ciscoasa# configure terminal
ciscoasa(config)# interface GigabitEthernet0
ciscoasa(config-if)# ip address 10.10.10.1 255.255.255.0
ciscoasa(config-if)# nameif inside
ciscoasa(config-if)# no shutdown
```

After you've configured an interface, use a ping command to test connectivity from your ASA to other devices in your project.

WARNING *Even with CPU throttling enabled, ASA devices are processor intensive, so you may want to use them sparingly in your projects, especially if you have a low-end PC.*

After verifying that your ASA device is running properly, you're ready to begin adding them to your projects. This can be helpful for learning how to configure the ASA or to prepare for a Cisco certification exam.

ASDM Installation

Cisco's ASDM is similar to the CCP software that was covered in "Cisco Configuration Professional" on page 124, so many of the details are the same. Like CCP, ASDM provides a point-and-click Java-based web interface. The key difference between CCP and ASDM is that ASDM is designed to configure only the Cisco ASA, not other Cisco devices.

Before you install the ASDM software, create a project like the one in Figure 8-9. You'll use the Windows virtual machine to install and run the ASDM application, and then you'll launch ASDM and use it to take a look at the ASA.

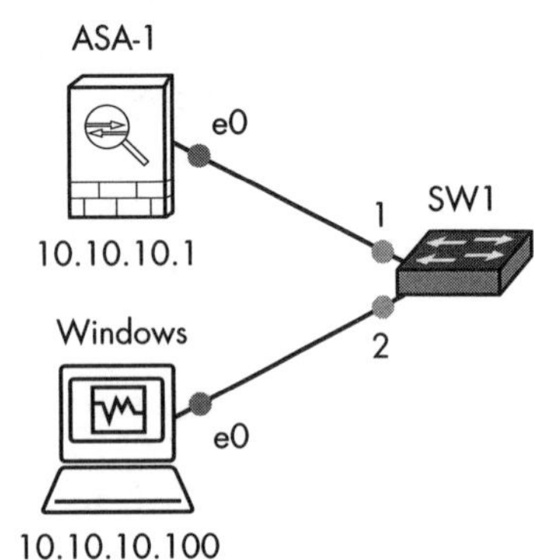

Figure 8-9: ASDM topology with an ASA firewall and Windows guest

There are two ways to acquire the ASDM software: copy it from the flash memory of a real ASA or find it online. After you have the ASDM software, it needs to be stored on your virtual ASA's flash drive; from there you'll install it on your Windows virtual machine PC using a web browser. I recommend Mozilla Firefox because I've found that it runs ASDM better than Internet Explorer. (Just be sure to disable any pop-up blockers and firewalls and install the latest version of Java.) You'll also need FTP or TFTP server software to copy the ASDM software from the GNS3 Windows virtual machine to your ASA.

After you have an ASDM image, there's some prep work to do on the ASA device so you can copy over the ASDM image. Enter these commands on the ASA:

```
  ciscoasa(config)# interface gigabitEthernet0
❶ ciscoasa(config-if)# ip address 10.10.10.1 255.255.255.0
  ciscoasa(config-if)# nameif inside
  ciscoasa(config-if)# no shutdown
  ciscoasa(config-if)# exit
❷ ciscoasa(config)# username admin password cisco privilege 15
❸ ciscoasa(config)# http server enable
  ciscoasa(config)# http 10.10.10.0 255.255.255.0 inside
```

Just like when you set up CCP, start by assigning an IP address to an inside interface ❶. Then, create a local user account ❷, and enable the HTTP server ❸.

After the ASA is configured and you have the ASDM software on your FTP or TFTP server, copy the software from your Windows virtual machine to the flash memory of the ASA.

```
ciscoasa# copy tftp flash
Source filename []? asdm-641.bin
Address or name of remote host []? 10.10.10.100
Destination filename [asdm-641.bin] <enter>
Accessing tftp://10.10.10.100/asdm-641.bin !!!!!!!!!!!
```

This example copies a file named *asdm-641.bin* from my GNS3 Windows virtual machine to my ASA device using TFTP.

After copying the ASDM file, you need to install the software on your Windows virtual machine. Launch your web browser and open an HTTP Secure (HTTPS) connection to the IP address of your ASA. You should be presented with a screen similar to Figure 8-10.

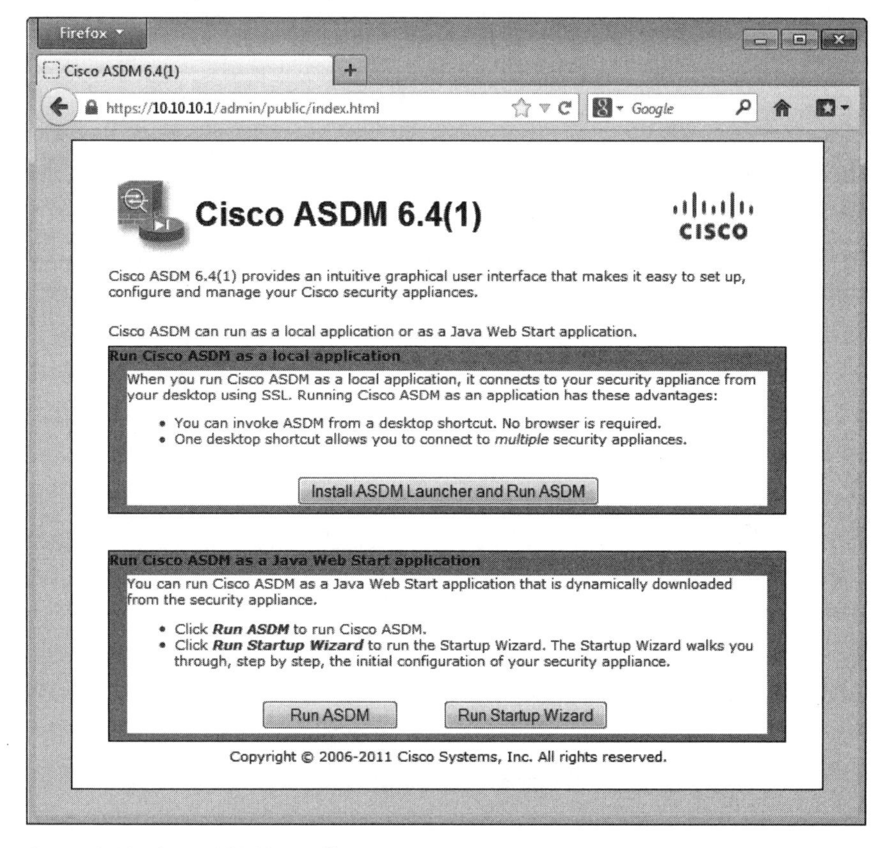

Figure 8-10: Cisco ASDM install screen

Because you'll be using the Java Web Start option, click **Run ASDM**. Your PC should download Java software and present you with a few security warnings, which you can safely click past until you see the Cisco ASDM-IDM Launcher, shown in Figure 8-11.

Figure 8-11: Windows ASDM-IDM Launcher

Enter your ASA username and password (**admin** and **cisco**) and select **OK** to log on to your ASA. After you have successfully logged on, you can begin configuring the system from the ASDM Device Dashboard, shown in Figure 8-12.

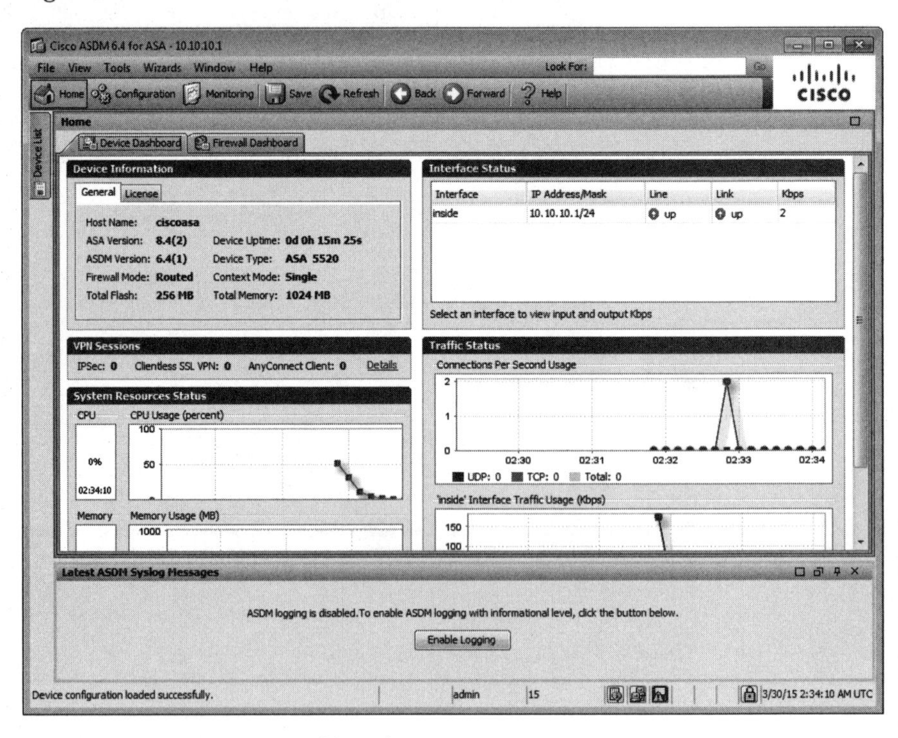

Figure 8-12: ASDM Device Dashboard

The ASDM Device Dashboard includes several wizards that provide guided setups for creating common network and virtual private network (VPN) configurations. It also provides many real-time statistics to assist you in monitoring your network performance. Although not necessarily useful in GNS3, this information could be invaluable for maintaining a healthy network in real life.

Cisco IDS/IPS

The Cisco IDS/IPS identifies and prevents malicious activity on a network. In the real world, an IDS/IPS can be a stand-alone Cisco device or a module that you plug into an ASA or integrated service router.

Creating an IDS/IPS virtual machine for GNS3 is a real pain compared to most tasks, so before you begin, you may want to set aside a couple of hours.

Acquiring an IDS/IPS Image

Like PIX and ASA, IDS/IPS runs on special Linux software. If you own a physical IDS/IPS appliance, then an upgrade/recovery CD containing the software should have come with your device.

To install IDS/IPS using a QEMU virtual machine, you need an ISO image of the CD. You can create your own ISO image file using your CD or find one on the Internet. In this example, I used an IOS image file named *IPS-K9-cd-1.1-a-6.0-6-E3.iso*. Other versions of the software may work fine, but this version has proven to work well for creating a GNS3-compatible IDS/IPS.

Creating a QEMU-Ready IDS/IPS System

IDS/IPS software runs using QEMU, so be sure you have installed it on your PC and have tested it with GNS3 before you begin. Then, create a build directory for your IDS/IPS and copy your ISO file to the directory. This is where you'll create the IDS/IPS virtual machine.

To install IDS/IPS software on a QEMU virtual machine, you have to create two QEMU virtual hard disk image files. Open a terminal window and enter the following commands to create the images:

```
$ qemu-img create ipsdisk1.img 512M
$ qemu-img create ipsdisk2.img 4000M
```

NOTE *On Windows and OS X you may need to set your system path to include the location of your QEMU installation. Please refer to "Installing QEMU on Windows and OS X" on page 63 for details.*

Now that you've created the virtual disks, enter the following command to boot your virtual machine from the ISO image file:

```
$ qemu-system-i386 -hda ipsdisk1.img -hdb ipsdisk2.img -m 1024 -cdrom IPS-K9
-cd-1.1-a-6.0-6-E3.iso -boot d
```

On Windows systems, replace `qemu-system-i386` in this command with `qemu-system-i386w`. After the system boots, you should see a screen similar to Figure 8-13.

```
QEMU
$Revision$ $Date$
Options: apmbios pcibios eltorito rombios32

ata0 master: QEMU HARDDISK ATA-7 Hard-Disk ( 512 MBytes)
ata0  slave: QEMU HARDDISK ATA-7 Hard-Disk (4000 MBytes)
ata1 master: QEMU DVD-ROM ATAPI-4 CD-Rom/DVD-Rom

Booting from CD-Rom...
24MB medium detected

ISOLINUX 2.08 2003-12-12  Copyright (C) 1994-2003 H. Peter Anvin

                   Cisco IPS 6.0(6)E3 Upgrade/Recovery CD!


 -   To recover the Cisco IPS 6.0(6)E3 Application using a local keyboard/monitor
,
     type: k <ENTER>.
     (WARNING: ALL DATA ON DISK 1 WILL BE LOST)

 -   To recover the Cisco IPS 6.0(6)E3 Application using a serial connection,
     type: s <ENTER>, or just press <ENTER>
     (WARNING: ALL DATA ON DISK 1 WILL BE LOST)

boot: _
```

Figure 8-13: IDS/IPS installation screen

At the `boot:` prompt, enter **`k`** to perform a full system recovery. During the recovery process, your QEMU virtual machine will boot Linux from the ISO image, install a GRUB boot loader, and install the IDS/IPS software. When the install finishes copying files, the virtual machine will reboot automatically and end with a "FATAL" boot error message, as shown in Figure 8-14.

```
QEMU
Plex86/Bochs VGABios (PCI) current-cvs 17 Dec 2008
This VGA/VBE Bios is released under the GNU LGPL

Please visit :
 . http://bochs.sourceforge.net
 . http://www.nongnu.org/vgabios

cirrus-compatible VGA is detected

QEMU BIOS - build: 07/11/09
$Revision$ $Date$
Options: apmbios pcibios eltorito rombios32

ata0 master: QEMU HARDDISK ATA-7 Hard-Disk ( 512 MBytes)
ata0  slave: QEMU HARDDISK ATA-7 Hard-Disk (4000 MBytes)
ata1 master: QEMU DVD-ROM ATAPI-4 CD-Rom/DVD-Rom

Booting from CD-Rom...
CDROM boot failure code : 0003
Boot failed: could not read the boot disk

FATAL: No bootable device.
_
```

Figure 8-14: FATAL: No bootable device

Don't worry, this error is perfectly normal and expected. Quit QEMU and enter the following command to boot the IDS/IPS again:

```
$ qemu-system-i386 -name IPS4215 -hda ipsdisk1.img -hdb ipsdisk2.img -m
1024 -smbios type=1,product=IDS-4215 -net nic,vlan=1,model=e1000 -net
nic,vlan=2,model=e1000
```

The IDS/IPS virtual machine will boot to a Linux GRUB boot menu. At the boot menu, enter **e** to edit an entry. Use the arrow key to move down to highlight the `kernel` entry and enter **e** again to edit this entry.

Use the back arrow key to locate and change **init=/loadrc** to **init=1**. Press ENTER to accept the change and press **b** to boot from the modified GRUB menu. The system should now boot, bypassing the IDS/IPS startup, and bring you to a Linux console. From the console command line, you'll use the vi editor to modify some IDS/IPS configuration files.

NOTE *You have to use the vi editor to modify files because no other editor is installed. If you are unfamiliar with vi, you'll want to brush up on it before you continue. Just search for* man vi *online or enter* `man vi` *at the command line to view the man page.*

After you're familiar with vi editing commands, you're ready to continue.

Hijacking the Hardware

First, you'll need to trick the IDS/IPS software into thinking your QEMU virtual machine is a real Cisco IDS-4215 Appliance Sensor. To fool the software, you have to modify two files: *ids_functions* and *interface.conf*. Modifying these files is pretty tedious, and the smallest mistake will prevent you from creating a working IDS/IPS device.

Start by entering the following commands from the shell prompt:

```
-sh-2.05b# /loadrc
-sh-2.05b# cd /etc/init.d
-sh-2.05b# ./rc.init
```

This will mount the Linux file systems used by the IDS/IPS and initialize the system. Next, use vi to open the *ids_functions* file.

```
-sh-2.05b# vi ids_functions
```

After opening the file, enter the command `/845` to have vi locate the following entry:

```
elif [[ `isCPU 845` -eq $TRUE && $NUM_OF_PROCS -eq 1 ]]; then
        MODEL=$IDS4215
        HTLBLOW=8
        MEM_PAGES=${HTLBLOW}
        DEFAULT_MGT_OS="fe0_0"
        DEFAULT_MGT_CIDS="FastEthernet0/0"
```

Next, edit the elif statement and DEFAULT_MGT statements so they read as follows:

```
elif [[ 1 -eq 1 ]]; then
        MODEL=$IDS4215
        HTLBLOW=8
        MEM_PAGES=${HTLBLOW}
        DEFAULT_MGT_OS="ma0_0"
        DEFAULT_MGTCIDS="Management0/0"
```

When you're finished editing and certain that you have made the correct changes, save the file and exit the vi editor.

Next, you'll edit the *interface.conf* file.

```
-sh-2.05b# cd /usr/cids/idsRoot/etc
-sh-2.05b# vi interface.conf
```

Use the arrow key to move down to the section that begins with `####### IDS-4215 ########`, modify each of the interface entries starting at `[models/IDS-4215/interfaces/1]` and ending with `[models/IDS-4215/interfaces/6]`. Each entry must look exactly like the following six entries:

```
[models/IDS-4215/interfaces/1]
name-template=Management0/0
port-number=0
pci-path=3.0
vendor-id=0x8086
device-id=0x100e
type=fe
mgmt-capable=yes
net-dev-only=yes
tcp-reset-capable=yes

[models/IDS-4215/interfaces/2]
name-template=FastEthernet0/0
port-number=1
pci-path=4.0
vendor-id=0x8086
device-id=0x100e
type=fe
sensing-capable=yes
tcp-reset-capable=yes

[models/IDS-4215/interfaces/3]
name-template=FastEthernet0/1
port-number=2
pci-path=5.0
vendor-id=0x8086
device-id=0x100e
type=fe
sensing-capable=yes
tcp-reset-capable=yes
```

```
[models/IDS-4215/interfaces/4]
 name-template=FastEthernet0/2
 port-number=3
 pci-path=6.0
 vendor-id=0x8086
 device-id=0x100e
 type=fe
 sensing-capable=yes
 tcp-reset-capable=yes

[models/IDS-4215/interfaces/5]
 name-template=FastEthernet0/3
 port-number=4
 pci-path=7.0
 vendor-id=0x8086
 device-id=0x100e
 type=fe
 sensing-capable=yes
 tcp-reset-capable=yes

[models/IDS-4215/interfaces/6]
 name-template=FastEthernet0/4
 port-number=5
 pci-path=8.0
 vendor-id=0x8086
 device-id=0x100e
 type=fe
 sensing-capable=yes
 tcp-reset-capable=yes
```

After you've finished editing the interfaces, scroll through the entries and verify that each interface is correctly configured. If you're certain everything is correct, save the file and quit vi. Reboot the IDS/IPS virtual machine using the `reboot` command.

```
-sh-2.05b# reboot
```

The system should boot, configure a few things, and reboot again automatically. After the automatic reboot, immediately quit QEMU when you see the GRUB boot manager, shown in Figure 8-15. If you fail to quit and relaunch QEMU without using the proper options, the install will fail, and you'll have to start over.

After quitting QEMU, restart your IDS/IPS virtual machine with the following command options:

```
$ qemu-system-i386 -name IPS4215 -hda ipsdisk1.img -hdb ipsdisk2.img -m
1024 -smbios type=1,product=IDS-4215 -net nic,vlan=1,model=e1000 -net
nic,vlan=2,model=e1000
```

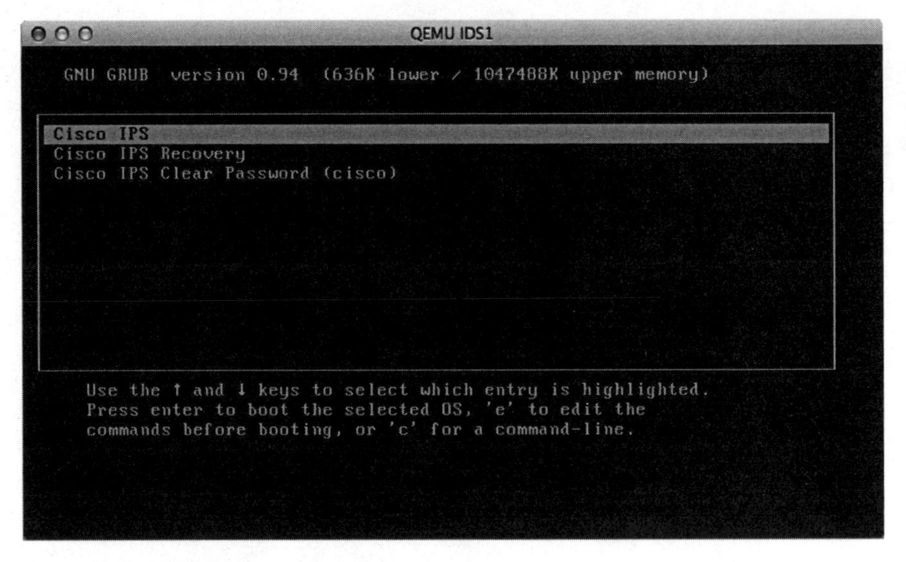

Figure 8-15: GRUB boot manager screen

Your IDS/IPS should now boot to the login prompt shown in Figure 8-16.

```
QEMU IPS4215
Create node:
ln: /etc/modprobe.conf: File exists
Shutting down network... ifconfig lo down
ifconfig lo down
done
Starting network... ifconfig lo 127.0.0.1 netmask 255.255.255.255 up
done
Creating boot.info[  OK  ]
Checking for system modifications since last boot            [WARNING]
Checking model identification[  OK  ]
Model: IDS-4215
Model=IDS-4215
interface type 0x8086:0x100e at pci address 0:3.0(0) is currently named eth0
Renaming eth0 --> ma0_0
interface type 0x8086:0x100e at pci address 0:4.0(0) is currently named eth1
Renaming eth1 --> fe0_0
Initializing access list

MGMT_INTFC_CIDS_NAME Management0/0
MGMT_INTFC_OS_NAME ma0_0
SYSTEM_PCI_IDS 0x0018
Starting CIDS:

sensor login: _
```

Figure 8-16: IDS/IPS login prompt

You're almost done! Log on to the system by entering the default username **cisco** and password **cisco**, and you should be directed to reset the password. If any part of the IDS/IPS setup has gone wrong, you may see the message "UNSUPPORTED HARDWARE DETECTED," as in Figure 8-17.

At this point, you could continue using the IDS/IPS virtual machine, or you could start over. I recommend you start over and create a new IDS/IPS until you can log on without errors. If you continue, the IDS/IPS system may produce further errors and not work as expected.

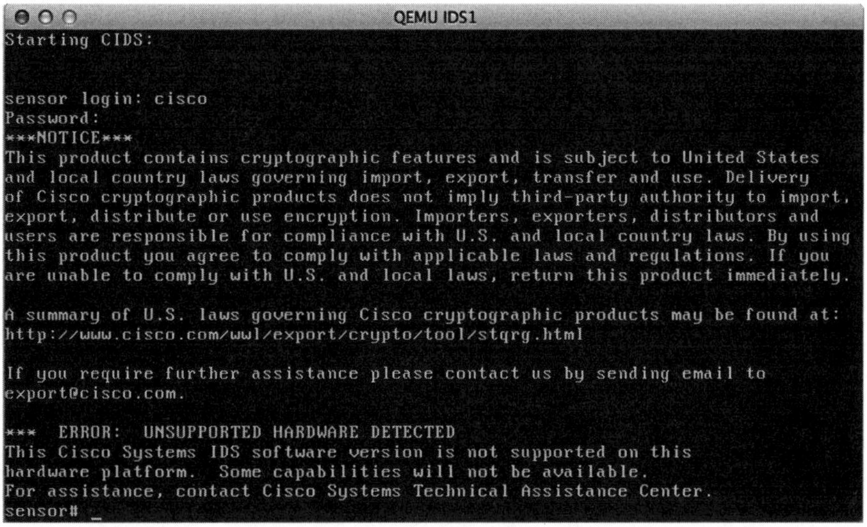

```
Starting CIDS:


sensor login: cisco
Password:
***NOTICE***
This product contains cryptographic features and is subject to United States
and local country laws governing import, export, transfer and use. Delivery
of Cisco cryptographic products does not imply third-party authority to import,
export, distribute or use encryption. Importers, exporters, distributors and
users are responsible for compliance with U.S. and local country laws. By using
this product you agree to comply with applicable laws and regulations. If you
are unable to comply with U.S. and local laws, return this product immediately.

A summary of U.S. laws governing Cisco cryptographic products may be found at:
http://www.cisco.com/wwl/export/crypto/tool/stqrg.html

If you require further assistance please contact us by sending email to
export@cisco.com.

***  ERROR:  UNSUPPORTED HARDWARE DETECTED
This Cisco Systems IDS software version is not supported on this
hardware platform.  Some capabilities will not be available.
For assistance, contact Cisco Systems Technical Assistance Center.
sensor# _
```

Figure 8-17: "UNSUPPORTED HARDWARE DETECTED" error

When you can log on without errors, you're ready to continue.

Testing IDS/IPS (or Patience Is a Virtue)

The first time you log on to the IDS/IPS virtual machine, you will have to wait approximately 20 minutes or so while the system rebuilds its regex cache tables. This is normal even for an actual IDS/IPS appliance, and you should not interrupt it. You can check the progress periodically using the `iplog-status` command.

```
sensor# iplog-status
```

If the status message reads "Error: getIpLogList : Analysis Engine is busy rebuilding regex tables. This may take a while." then the system is still working and should not be interrupted. After the rebuild is finished, you should instead see "No IP logs available."

When the rebuild is finished, enter the **reset** command to shut down and reboot the virtual machine. Unfortunately, there's no elegant way to shut down the system. To avoid file corruption, you should quit QEMU when the reboot reaches the GRUB boot menu.

Configuring GNS3 for IDS/IPS

Adding an IDS/IPS to GNS3 is similar to adding an ASA. To add an IDS/IPS device, launch GNS3, select **Edit ▸ Preferences** on Linux and Windows or **GNS3 ▸ Preferences** on OS X, and select **QEMU VMs** from the sidebar, as shown in Figure 8-18.

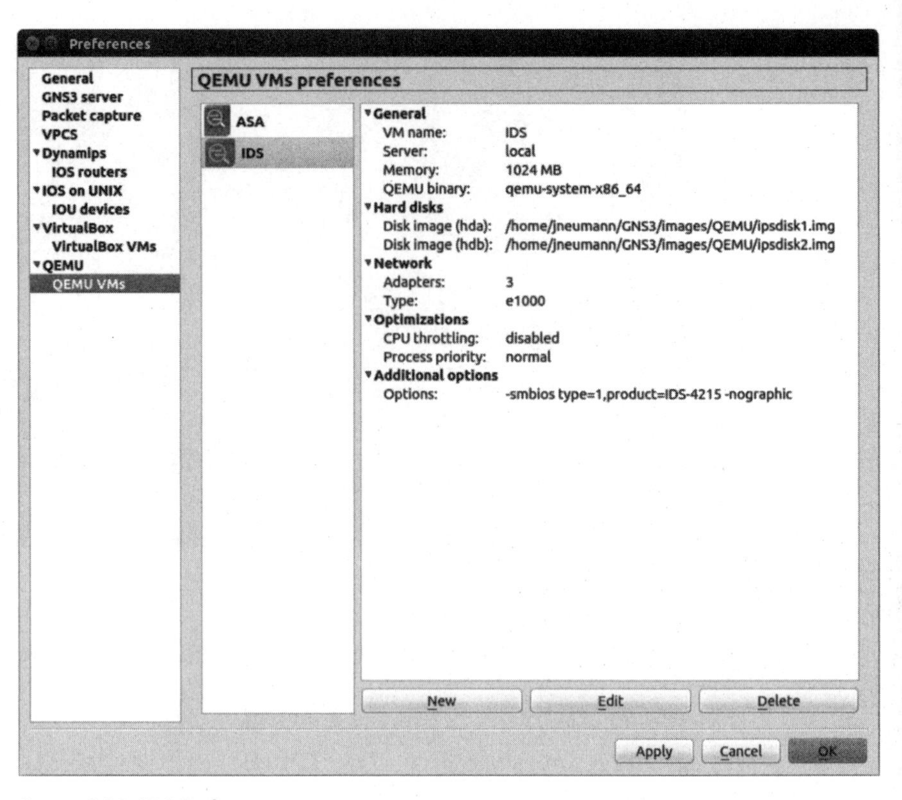

Figure 8-18: IDS Preferences

To create a new IDS/IPS in GNS3, click **New** to start the New QEMU VM wizard. Select **IDS** from the Type drop-down menu, as shown in Figure 8-19.

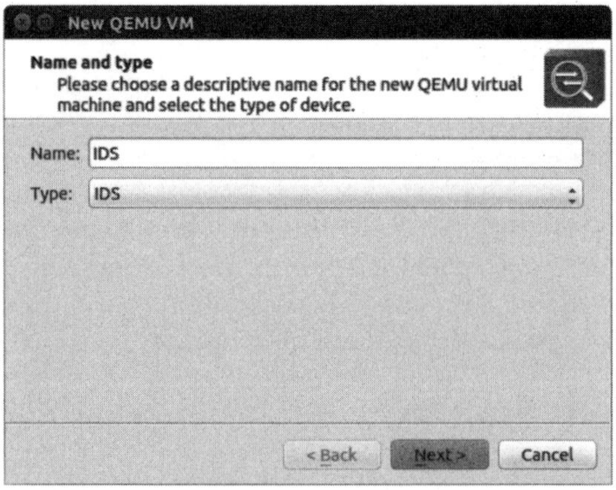

Figure 8-19: Selecting IDS in the New QEMU VM wizard

By default your device is automatically named *IDS*. Click **Next** to continue. GNS3 should automatically locate and choose the correct QEMU binary file for your PC, shown in Figure 8-20.

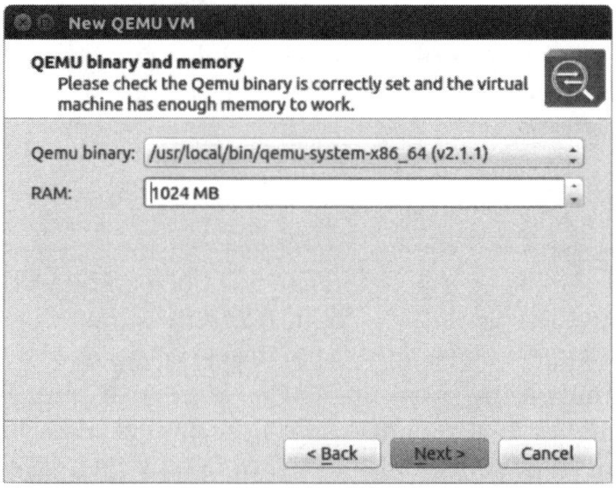

Figure 8-20: QEMU binary and memory screen

Set the RAM field to **1024 MB** or greater, and click **Next** to continue to the Disk image (hda) selection, shown in Figure 8-21.

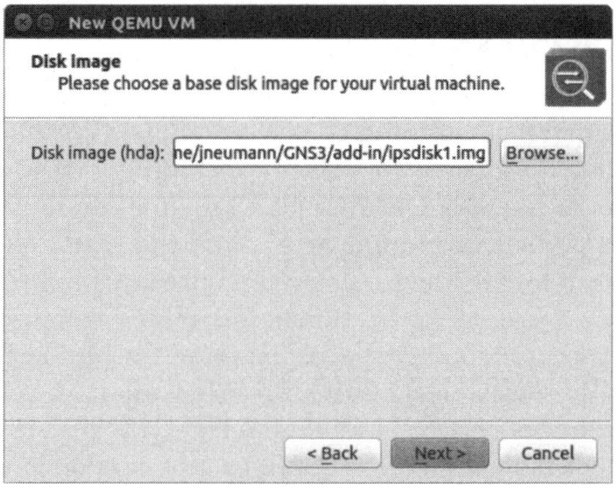

Figure 8-21: Chooseing a disk image

Browse and select the file named *ipsdisk1.img* that was created when you built your QEMU-ready IDS system. Click **Next** to continue to the Disk image (hdb) selection screen and choose *ipsdisk2.img*. Click **Finish** to complete the installation. You're now ready to test your IDS.

Verifying IDS/IPS in GNS3

To verify that your IDS/IPS is working, drag an IDS/IPS node to your workspace and start the device. GNS3 cannot open a console connection to an IDS/IPS device until after it has fully booted. This means you will not see any IDS/IPS messages prior to the login prompt. After the login prompt appears, you should be able to log in and configure the IDS/IPS. To prevent file corruption from occurring, use the reset command whenever you shut down the device.

After determining that your IDS/IPS is in good working order, you should make a backup copy of the QEMU disk image files. If something happens to your working IDS/IPS device, a backup copy of the files can save you hours of work later.

Cisco IOS-XRv

Cisco offers a version of IOS-XR in the form of a 32-bit virtual machine called IOS-XRv. The cool thing about IOS-XRv is that it's not an emulator like IOU or NX-OSv. Instead, it's a "hamstrung" version of IOS-XR that contains only a single route processor (RP). Network throughput is limited to 2Mbps, and there's a hard-coded AAA user named *cisco* with the password *cisco*, making it impossible to use in a production environment, unless you want a slow and insecure network. Despite these limitations, the operating system includes management features, routing, and forwarding capabilities.

The software is designed to run using VMware ESXi or QEMU, making it a breeze to use with GNS3. If you have a Cisco CCO account, you should be able to download the software from the Cisco file exchange.

Configuring GNS3 for IOS-XRv

Cisco IOS-XRv files come in two image formats; the first is an OVA, and the second is a Virtual Machine Disk (VMDK) file. The OVA image (ending in *.ova*) is suitable for use with VMware ESXi; the VMDK file (ending in *.vmdk*) is ready to use with QEMU, and it's the file you'll use in GNS3. In this example, I'll be using an image file named *iosxrv-k9-demo-5.2.2.vmdk*.

Adding an IOS-XRv device to GNS3 is pretty straightforward. You'll launch the New QEMU VM wizard and follow the prompts; then you'll edit the device, making a small change to increase the number of adapters. To add an IOS-XRv device, select **Edit ▸ Preferences** on Linux and Windows or **GNS3 ▸ Preferences** on OS X and then select **QEMU VMs** from the panel on the left. Click **New** to start the configuration and open the dialog in Figure 8-22.

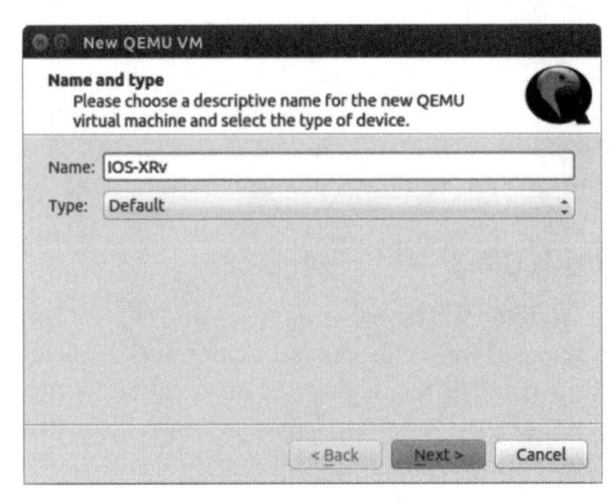

Figure 8-22: New QEMU VM wizard

Set Type to **Default** and enter a name for your device; I've entered **IOS-XRv**. When you're finished, click **Next** to proceed to the QEMU binary and memory settings, shown in Figure 8-23.

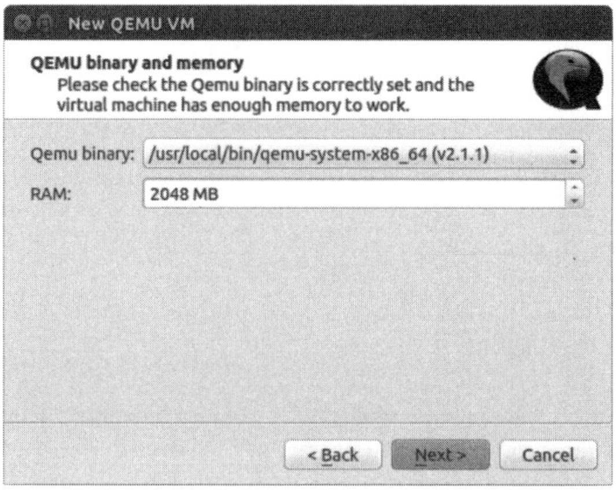

Figure 8-23: Configuring IOS-XRv for 64-bit systems

IOS-XRv can run using 32-bit or 64-bit QEMU hardware emulation. Because I'm running a 64-bit operating system on my PC, I've chosen to use a 64-bit QEMU binary, named *qemu-system-x86_64* (shown in Figure 8-23), and I've set RAM to **2048 MB**, which is the recommended amount. However, if you run a 32-bit operating system, such as Windows, you'll have to set the RAM to less than 2048MB. This is because the 32-bit QEMU program is unable to allocate that much memory to the IOS-XRv virtual machine. In this case, you should enter **1920 MB** and use the drop-down menu to choose the QEMU binary named *qemu-system-i386w.exe*, as shown in Figure 8-24.

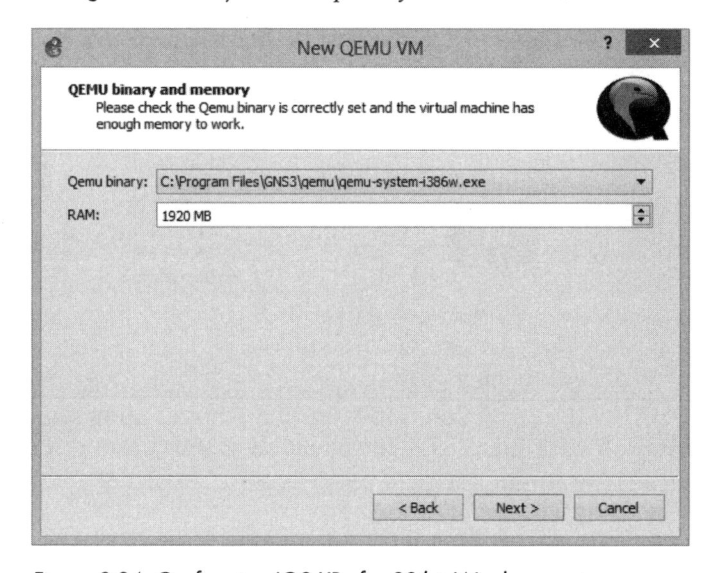

Figure 8-24: Configuring IOS-XRv for 32-bit Windows systems

After configuring your QEMU binary and RAM, click **Next** to proceed to the Disk Image selection screen in Figure 8-25.

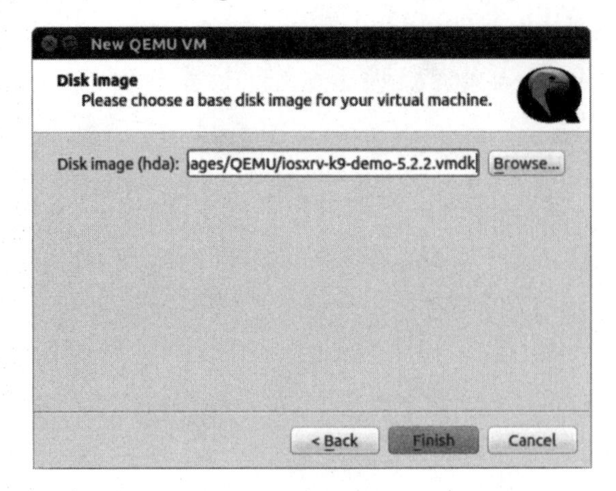

Figure 8-25: Selecting a disk image

Click the **Browse** button to locate and choose your IOS-XRv *.vmdk* image file. I've selected a disk image named *iosxrv-k9-demo-5.2.2.vmdk*.

When you're done selecting your image, click **Finish** to close the wizard. Next, select your newly created IOS-XRv device and click **Edit**. Select the **Network** tab and increase the number of adapters to **4**. Click **OK** to close the window and then click **Apply** and **OK** to commit the change. You can set the number of adapters to whatever best suits your needs, but four should be suitable for most GNS3 projects.

Creating a Simple IOS-XR Project

Cisco IOS-XR is very IOS-like, but it's not IOS. In this section, you'll configure a simple project using one Dynamips router and one IOS-XRv device, shown in Figure 8-26.

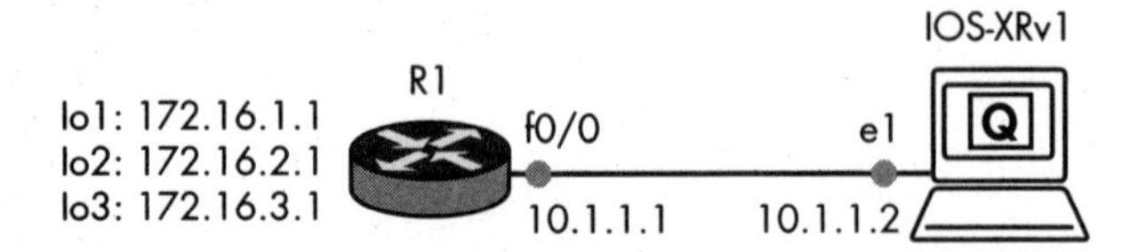

Figure 8-26: A simple IOS-XRv project

You'll use EIGRP to advertise three networks from router R1 to the IOS-XRv1 device. Finally, you'll verify the routes using some IOS-XR commands. This is only a basic introduction to IOS-XR. If you truly want to learn IOS-XR, you'll have to dig deep into Cisco's documentation.

Configuring the Router

Begin by configuring router R1. Configure an IP address on the Ethernet interface that's linked to IOS-XRv1.

```
R1# configure terminal
R1(config)# interface f0/0
R1(config-if)# ip address 10.1.1.1 255.255.255.0
R1(config-if)# no shutdown
```

Next, configure the three IP addresses on router R1's loopback interfaces.

```
R1(config-if)# interface loopback1
R1(config-if)# ip address 172.16.1.1 255.255.255.0
R1(config-if)# interface loopback2
R1(config-if)# ip address 172.16.2.1 255.255.255.0
R1(config-if)# interface loopback3
R1(config-if)# ip address 172.16.3.1 255.255.255.0
R1(config-if)# exit
```

These addresses will be advertised to your IOS-XRv1 device using EIGRP. Finally, configure EIGRP and advertise all the networks.

```
R1(config)# router eigrp 10
R1(config-router)# no auto-summary
R1(config-router)# network 10.0.0.0
R1(config-router)# network 172.16.0.0
```

After you've finished configuring router R1, configure the IOS-XR device.

Configuring the IOS-XR Device

Log on to IOS-XRv1 and create a similar configuration to the one you created on router R1. You'll configure an IP address and enable EIGRP to allow IOS-XRv1 and router R1 to exchange routing information.

```
❶ RP/0/0/CPU0:ios#
  RP/0/0/CPU0:ios# configure terminal
  RP/0/0/CPU0:ios(config)# interface GigabitEthernet 0/0/0/0
❷ RP/0/0/CPU0:ios(config-if)# ipv4 address 10.1.1.2/24
  RP/0/0/CPU0:ios(config-if)# no shutdown
  RP/0/0/CPU0:ios(config)# router eigrp 10
❸ RP/0/0/CPU0:ios(config-eigrp)# address-family ipv4
❹ RP/0/0/CPU0:ios(config-eigrp-af)# interface GigabitEthernet 0/0/0/0
❺ RP/0/0/CPU0:ios(config-eigrp-af)# commit
```

The first notable difference between IOS and IOS-RX is the command prompt. The IOS-XRv1 command prompt ❶ indicates that your context is the first route processor (RP/0/0/CPU0). Because this is a demo version of IOS-XRv, it's limited to this single route processor.

Next, when an IP address is configured on an Ethernet interface, you have to specify the family of the IP address you're using (IPv4 or IPv6), and the subnet mask is represented in CIDR notation (/24) ❷. Similarly, you have to specify IPv4 or IPv6 when configuring the EIGRP route process ❸. Lastly, you advertise networks by placing an IP-configured interface under the EIGRP route process ❹. When you're done, be sure to commit your changes ❺.

Once you've configured everything, enter the `show eigrp neighbors` command, and you should see this output:

```
RP/0/0/CPU0:ios# show eigrp neighbors
IPv4-EIGRP Neighbors for AS(10) VRF default

H   Address                 Interface        Hold Uptime   SRTT   RTO   Q   Seq
                                             (sec)         (ms)         Cnt Num
0  ❶10.1.1.1              ❷Gi0/0/0/0        13 00:28:09   19     200   0   3
```

In a correct configuration, an EIGRP neighbor adjacency will form with router R1 at IP address 10.1.1.1 ❶ from interface Gi0/0/0/0 ❷.

Now, verify that all the 172.16.0.0 networks have been advertised from router R1 to IOS-XRv1 using the `show route` command.

```
RP/0/0/CPU0:ios# show route
--snip--

C    10.1.1.0/24 is directly connected, 02:58:51, GigabitEthernet0/0/0/0
L    10.1.1.2/32 is directly connected, 02:58:51, GigabitEthernet0/0/0/0
D  ❶172.16.1.0/24 [90/2570240] via 10.1.1.1, 00:43:21, GigabitEthernet0/0/0/0
D  ❶172.16.2.0/24 [90/2570240] via 10.1.1.1, 00:43:21, GigabitEthernet0/0/0/0
D  ❶172.16.3.0/24 [90/2570240] via 10.1.1.1, 00:43:21, GigabitEthernet0/0/0/0
```

All of the 172.16.0.0 networks have been successfully added to the IOS-XR routing table ❶. You can test connectivity by pinging one of the addresses.

```
RP/0/0/CPU0:ios# ping 172.16.1.1
Thu Oct 16 03:20:27.508 UTC
Type escape sequence to abort.
Sending 5, 100-byte ICMP Echos to 172.16.1.1, timeout is 2 seconds:
!!!!!
❶ Success rate is 100 percent (5/5), round-trip min/avg/max = 9/19/49 ms
```

Here, the ping was 100 percent successful ❶. Now, save the configuration.

```
RP/0/0/CPU0:ios# copy running-config nvram:
Thu Oct 16 03:22:39.679 UTC
Destination file name (control-c to abort): [/running-config]? <enter>
Building configuration.
24 lines built in 1 second
[OK]
```

By now it should be obvious that IOS-XR is a little different from traditional IOS, but it's also similar. IOS-XRv is a reliable platform, and it's a lot of fun to play with in GNS3. Perhaps someday Cisco will port a version of IOS-XR from their carrier class routers down to their smaller commercial routers. If so, practicing with IOS-XRv in GNS3 will help prepare you for it.

Final Thoughts

Using GNS3, you can quickly become proficient at configuring and installing ASA firewalls. Having worked with Cisco gear for more than a decade, I've learned that ASAs are rock solid and work great for small network installations. Understanding how to configure the ASA is a must for anyone involved in small business networking. They're one of the few nonenterprise Cisco products that are reasonably priced, feature rich, and easy to install.

Using ASDM, you can quickly configure an ASA to allow remote users to connect to their corporate networks through an IPSec VPN. Several cross-platform VPN clients are compatible with Cisco ASAs and routers; OS X has a built-in Cisco VPN client. On Windows, you have to install the Cisco VPN Client or Cisco AnyConnect software. On Linux, you can use Virtual Private Network Connection (VPNC), which works great. I use VPNC on a daily basis with Linux to access VPNs all across the country.

In the next chapter, you'll look at Cisco IOU and learn how to integrate IOU devices into GNS3 projects. It's an exciting new advancement that broadens the future of GNS3.

9

CISCO IOS ON UNIX AND NX-OSV

In this chapter, I'll discuss strategies for installing and integrating Cisco IOU devices with GNS3. You'll also learn how to install and run Cisco's next-generation switch operating system (NX-OS) using VirtualBox and NX-OSv.

Cisco IOU

Cisco IOU is one of the cooler things to happen to the Cisco education community in a long time. IOU functions similarly to Dynamips but uses far fewer resources. Like Dynamips, IOU allows you to add routers and switches to your GNS3 projects. Unlike Dynamips, IOU images emulate the features of an IOS technology train rather than the hardware component of a particular Cisco model. Each IOU image file is a self-contained binary application that runs an instance of a device. There are images designed for routing, switching, voice over IP (VoIP), and Pagent (for generating IP traffic). IOU doesn't require a hypervisor to emulate Cisco hardware, often making IOU devices less memory hungry and CPU intensive than Dynamips devices. The obvious advantage here is that you can create larger topologies on a modestly configured PC.

In 2010, Cisco integrated IOU into the Cisco Learning Network to provide online virtual labs for CCNA and CCNP students. The labs are inexpensive and well designed. If you're interested in Cisco Learning Labs, you should check out the Cisco Learning Center (*http://learningnetwork.cisco.com/*).

As the name implies, IOS on Unix runs only on Unix-based systems. Sometimes referred to as IOS on Linux (IOL), it was developed on Solaris Unix and Linux.

What IOU Means to GNS3

After Cisco announced it was moving away from industry-standard hardware in favor of proprietary integrated service router (ISR) hardware, the GNS3 community wondered whether the end of Dynamips and GNS3 had arrived. Without access to the technical specifications for the new proprietary hardware, it would be impossible to create a new hypervisor required to run the latest IOS software. Eventually, the old Dynamips devices would stop getting IOS updates and become obsolete.

Cisco actually keeps IOS current for the 7200 series routers that GNS3 uses, but all other GNS3 routers stop cold at IOS release 12.4(15)T, which imposes limits on learning modern technologies such as VoIP. This is why IOU is exciting. It breathes new life into GNS3 by allowing you to integrate updated IOS technologies into your GNS3 projects—and that's pretty cool!

Switching, Switching, and More Switching!

One of the best reasons to integrate IOU into GNS3 is that you can use many of Cisco's advanced switching features, which are missing from the NM-16ESW module in Dynamips (refer to Appendix C). These features allow GNS3 to step up its game and become an all-inclusive training tool for more advanced certifications like CCIE.

With IOU, you no longer have to purchase physical switches and create a breakout switch or use funny little tricks like ISL bridging to access real switches. Using a GNS3 EtherSwitch router, it's now possible to create a regular 802.1Q trunk link from your Dynamips switches to an IOU switch block running on your PC. IOU switches are stable, run fast, and, unlike physical switches, are completely portable, which means they can travel with you on a laptop as part of your GNS3 projects.

IOU Images

IOU images are designed around IOS features, and their filenames often reveal what features they include, much like IOS image filenames. For example, let's break down the filename of an IOU switch named *I86BI_LINUXL2-UPK9-M-15.0.*

I86BI Indicates this is an Intel 32-bit binary image.

LINUX Indicates it runs on Linux.

L2 Indicates it's an L2/L3 switch.

UPK9 Indicates the image contains advanced cryptographic features such as 3DES/AES.

M Indicates it's a mainline IOS.

15.0 Specifies the IOS version the image is based on.

Using this information, you should be able to look at almost any IOU filename to quickly determine what features it includes.

Things to Know Before Installing IOU

By default, a standard GNS3 installation doesn't allow you to run IOU devices. IOU devices are Linux binary files, so they can be run using a Linux operating system only. Typically, images are 32-bit binary files, but with the proper library files, you can easily run them on 64-bit Linux systems. If you're running GNS3 on Windows or OS X, you have to install a virtualization program like VirtualBox and run your IOU devices using a Linux virtual machine. Fortunately, GNS3 provides an IOU virtual machine that you can download from the GNS3 website. The GNS3 IOU virtual machine is ready to run IOU images, provides an easy way for you to upload your images, and doesn't require that you know how to use Linux commands.

The upside to running GNS3 in Linux is that installing and configuring IOU is more straightforward, and everything should run seamlessly without extra configuration. The downside is that you have to know a little something about Linux, but in my opinion, that's a small price to pay. When you run GNS3 on Windows or OS X, you have to configure it to communicate with the Linux virtual machine over TCP/IP, which can be a pain to manage. If your workstation or IOU virtual machine's IP addresses change (which often happens), you'll have to reconfigure GNS3 to use the new IP addresses. Also, when you upgrade GNS3, you have to upgrade the GNS3 server software that runs on the IOU virtual machine. The version numbers must be identical, or IOU will not run. These steps are unnecessary when you run both GNS3 and IOU on Linux.

Setting Up IOU on a Linux PC

There are some distinct advantages to running GNS3 and IOU on a Linux PC. The big one is that you don't need to use an IOU virtual machine because on Linux IOU image files run natively. This means you don't have to give up precious resources, such as CPU cycles and memory, that would be taken by the IOU virtual machine. Another advantage is that you can use Wireshark to capture and monitor packets between two IOU devices, which you can't do when using the IOU virtual machine. This is because the *.pcap* capture file, which is created when you start a Wireshark capture, is saved on the IOU virtual machine and not locally, so Wireshark cannot access the file.

If you're running GNS3 on Linux, follow the instructions in this section to get IOU up and running. Otherwise, skip ahead to "Using the GNS3 IOU Virtual Machine on Windows and OS X" on page 160.

Installing IOU

When you run an IOU image, the image looks for the file *libcrypto.so.4* and won't run without it. Although a libcrypto library file may already be installed on your system, you should install *libssl1.0.0* because this version is proven to be stable with IOU images. Next, create a symbolic link (symlink) from *libcrypto.so.1.0.0* to *libcrypto.so.4*; a symlink is the Linux equivalent of a Windows shortcut. If you're using a 32-bit version of Ubuntu, install libcrypto using the following commands:

```
$ sudo apt-get install libssl1.0.0
$ sudo ln -s /lib/i386-linux-gnu/libcrypto.so.1.0.0 /lib/libcrypto.so.4
```

When running a 64-bit Ubuntu system, you'll need to install the 32-bit libssl package before you can configure libcrypto and run a 32-bit IOU image. If you have a 32-bit Ubuntu system, you can disregard the next commands.

```
$ sudo apt-get install libssl1.0.0:i386
$ sudo ln -s /lib/i386-linux-gnu/libcrypto.so.1.0.0 /lib/i386-linux-gnu/
libcrypto.so.4
```

If you're not running Ubuntu, then you may need to do a little research to configure libcrypto on your system because not all Linux systems use the same library files and versions or even store the files in the same directories as Ubuntu. The key is that the libcrypto file must be symlinked to *libcrypto.so.4*.

After you've configured *libcrypto.so.4*, copy one or more IOU image files to your Ubuntu system. You have to make the IOU files executable before they'll run; here's how:

```
$ sudo chmod 555 I86BI_LINUXL2-UPK9-M-15.0.bin
```

Next, install the dependencies for the GNS3 iouyap application. This program is responsible for setting up communication between IOU and other GNS3 devices, like Dynamips routers. Begin by installing bison and flex, two packages that are needed before iouyap can compile.

```
$ sudo apt-get install bison
$ sudo apt-get install flex
```

Now, install and compile the iniparser program using the following commands:

```
$ sudo apt-get install git
$ git clone http://github.com/ndevilla/iniparser.git
$ cd iniparser
$ make
$ sudo cp libiniparser.* /usr/lib/
$ sudo cp src/iniparser.h /usr/local/include
$ sudo cp src/dictionary.h /usr/local/include
```

A ZIP file containing iouyap should have been included in your GNS3 for Linux download. Unzip *iouyap-<x>.zip*, replacing *<x>* with the version you have, and compile the program using the following commands:

```
$ cd iouyap-x
$ sudo make
$ sudo make install
```

If necessary, copy the compiled application to the */usr/local/bin* directory.

```
$ sudo copy iouyap /usr/local/bin
```

Now that all the applications are installed, you need to do some configuration.

Creating a License File

Before running IOU, you have to create a license file that contains the hostname of your PC and a valid license key. The license key is generated from your Linux hostname, so make sure you're satisfied with your PC's hostname. If you change your hostname, you'll need to enter a new license key.

Once you have obtained a license key, use a text editor to create the license file. I usually name my file *.iourc*, but any name will do. The following is an example of a license file for a PC named Ubuntu using the license key 1234567812345678. The hostname is case sensitive, so take care when entering it in the license file.

```
[license]
Ubuntu = 1234567812345678
```

If you're unsure what your Linux host is named, you can use the `hostname` command from your terminal to display the name.

Configuring GNS3

Next, set the path to the iouyap application and your IOU license file in the IOS on UNIX preferences. The iouyap application is used to bridge Dynamips, and other GNS3 devices, with IOU devices so that all your devices can be seamlessly networked together. Select **Edit ▸ Preferences** and then select **IOS on UNIX** from the left menu, as shown in Figure 9-1.

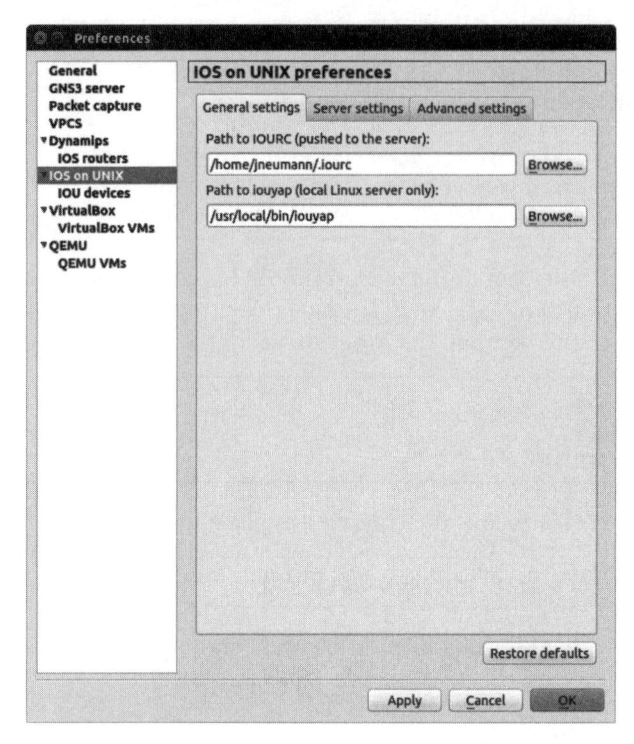

Figure 9-1: IOS on UNIX preferences, General settings tab

On the General settings tab, set the path and name of your license file in Path to IOURC. This refers to the IOU license file you created earlier. Also, set the file path to your *iouyap* file in Path to iouyap, typically */usr/local/bin/iouyap*. Next, go to the Server settings tab, shown in Figure 9-2.

Select the **Always use the local server (Linux only)** checkbox so that IOU uses the local PC for GNS3 and IOU integration. Then, go to the Advanced settings tab, shown in Figure 9-3.

Each IOU device is assigned a unique console port number within the defined range. Don't change these values unless the range conflicts with other IP-based applications running on your PC; the same is true for the UDP tunneling port range. UDP ports are used to set up network communication between IOU and other GNS3 devices.

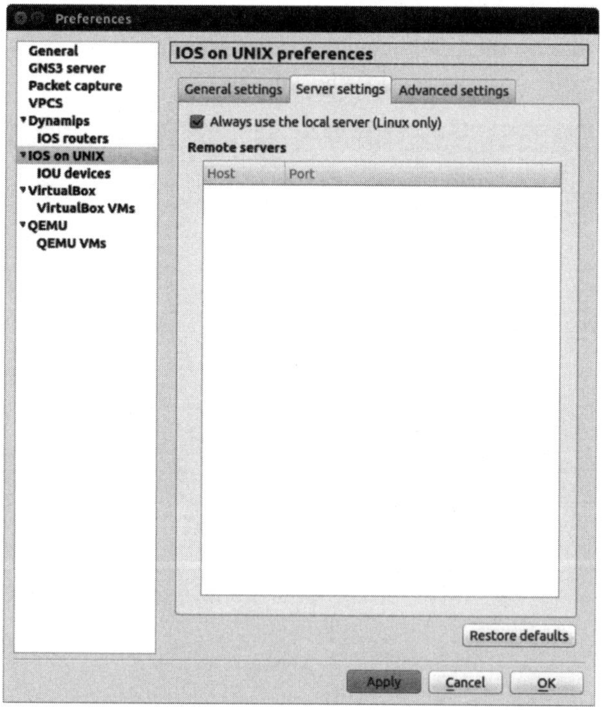

Figure 9-2: IOS on UNIX preferences, Server settings tab

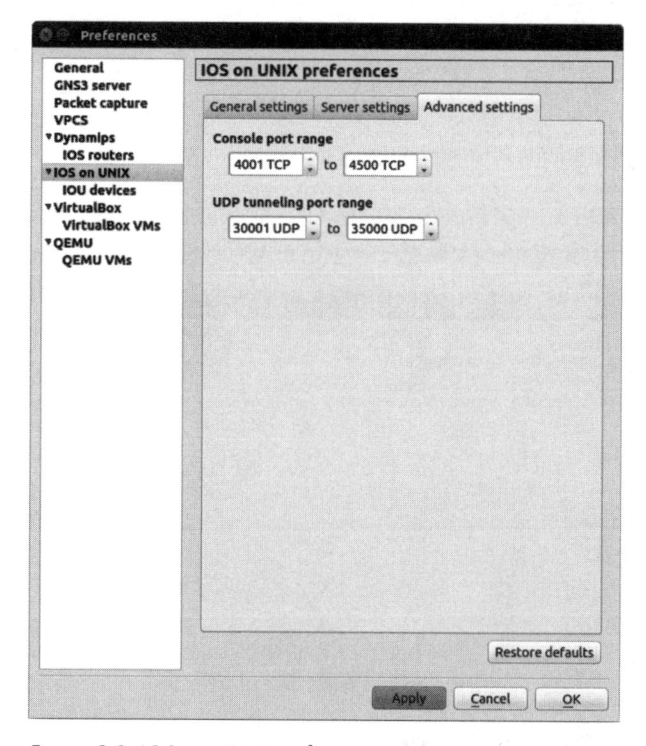

Figure 9-3: IOS on UNIX preferences, Advanced settings tab

Finally, expand **IOS on UNIX** in the left menu of the Preferences window to display the IOU devices section, shown in Figure 9-4. From here, you can add one or more IOU image files to GNS3.

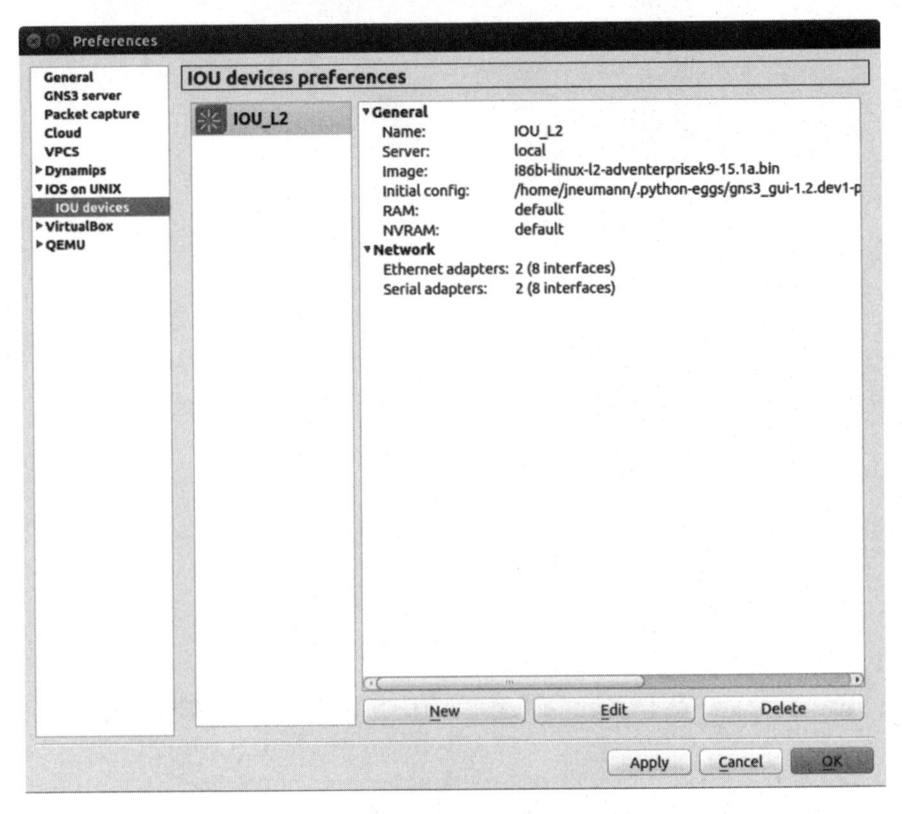

Figure 9-4: Adding IOU images to GNS3

To add an IOU image file to GNS3, click the **New** button to start the New IOU device wizard, shown in Figure 9-5.

Figure 9-5: New IOU device wizard

Enter a name for your new device (*IOU_L2* in this example); then click the **Browse** button to locate and select your IOU image file. When you're done, click **Finish** to complete the wizard. Once added, your IOU image file should be copied to your GNS3 user directory under *GNS3/images/IOU.*

To configure an IOU device, drag an IOU device icon from the Devices toolbar to your workspace. Right-click the device and choose **Configure** to open the Node configurator (shown in Figure 9-6).

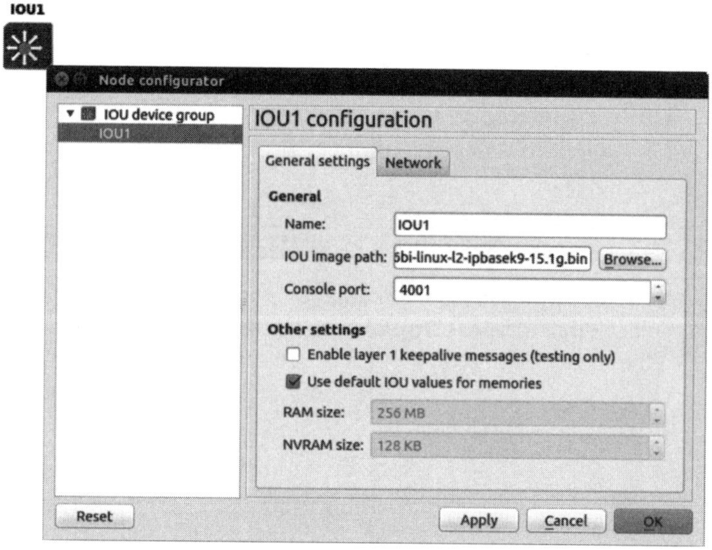

Figure 9-6: IOU Node configurator

The options on the General settings tab allow you to rename your device and change the IOU image file, console port number, and default RAM and NVRAM values.

You can change the number of Ethernet and serial adapters installed by adjusting the values on the Network tab. The default is two of each adapter, but they provide four interfaces each, giving you a total of eight Ethernet and eight serial interfaces. This should be plenty for most projects, but you can easily adjust the quantity to meet your needs. The total combined number of adapters (Ethernet and serial) can't exceed 16, for a total of 64 interfaces per IOU device.

An IOU device can be linked to any other GNS3 device, just as you would a standard Dynamips router or switch. You can even *hot-link* them to devices, meaning links can be formed between the devices after they're started.

To export an IOU configuration, enter **`copy running-config unix:initial-config.cfg`** from the IOU console and then right-click the IOU device in your workspace and select **Export config**. You will then be prompted for a filename and location, where the file will be saved. You can import a configuration by selecting **Import config** instead.

If you want to run IOU in Windows or OS X, read the next section. If not, you can skip ahead to "NX-OSv" on page 168.

Using the GNS3 IOU Virtual Machine on Windows and OS X

As I mentioned in "Things to Know Before Installing IOU" on page 153, Windows and OS X systems can run IOU only using a Linux virtual machine. If you haven't done so already, download and install VirtualBox (*https://www.virtualbox.org/*). Accepting the default installation settings should provide everything you need for running an IOU virtual machine.

After installing VirtualBox, visit the GNS3 website (*http://www.gns3.com/*) and download the OVA file named *GNS3 IOU VM.ova*. This is a Linux virtual machine that's been preconfigured with all the tools you need to run IOU, but it doesn't include any IOU image files. Instead, it provides a web-based utility that allows you to easily upload your image files to the appliance, but you'll need to import the appliance into VirtualBox before you can use it.

Importing the GNS3 IOU Virtual Machine into VirtualBox

Start by launching the VirtualBox application. After the application loads, select **File ▸ Import Appliance**. You should be presented with the Import Virtual Appliance dialog, shown in Figure 9-7.

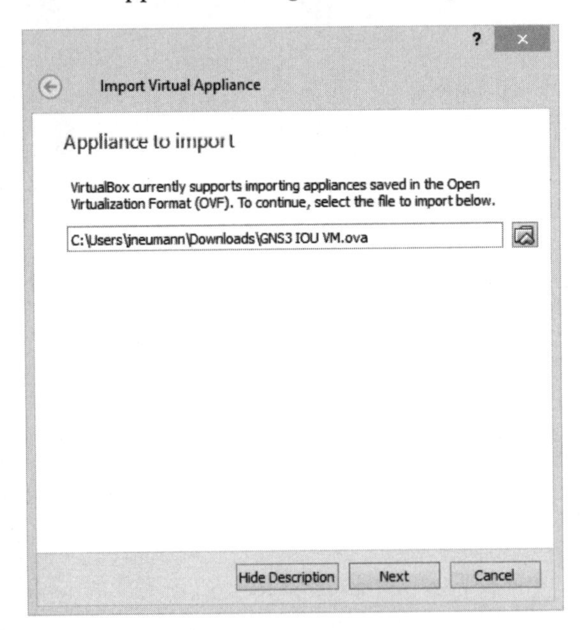

Figure 9-7: Select the virtual appliance.

Use the browse icon to locate and select the *GNS3 IOU VM.ova* file. In Figure 9-7, my virtual machine is located in my *Downloads* directory, *C:\Users\jneumann\Downloads*. Once you select the file, click **Next** and verify the appliance settings. They should look similar to Figure 9-8.

Import Virtual Appliance

Appliance settings

These are the virtual machines contained in the appliance and the suggested settings of the imported VirtualBox machines. You can change many of the properties shown by double-clicking on the items and disable others using the check boxes below.

Description	Configuration
Virtual System 1	
Name	GNS3 IOU VM
Description	VM for GNS3 (development)
Guest OS Type	Debian (32 bit)
CPU	1
RAM	2048 MB
DVD	☑

☐ Reinitialize the MAC address of all network cards

Restore Defaults | Import | Cancel

Figure 9-8: Virtual Appliance settings

You should be able to accept the suggested appliance settings. Notice that the default RAM setting is 2048MB. I've found that the RAM can be reduced to 1024MB if you're using only a couple of IOU devices in your projects. Doing so reduces the overall amount of memory used in your PC and may help GNS3 perform better if you're strapped for resources. If you're unsure, then just accept the defaults and click **Import** to complete the import. You can always modify the settings later.

After importing the virtual machine, click **Settings** and then click **Network** to access the Network pane, shown in Figure 9-9.

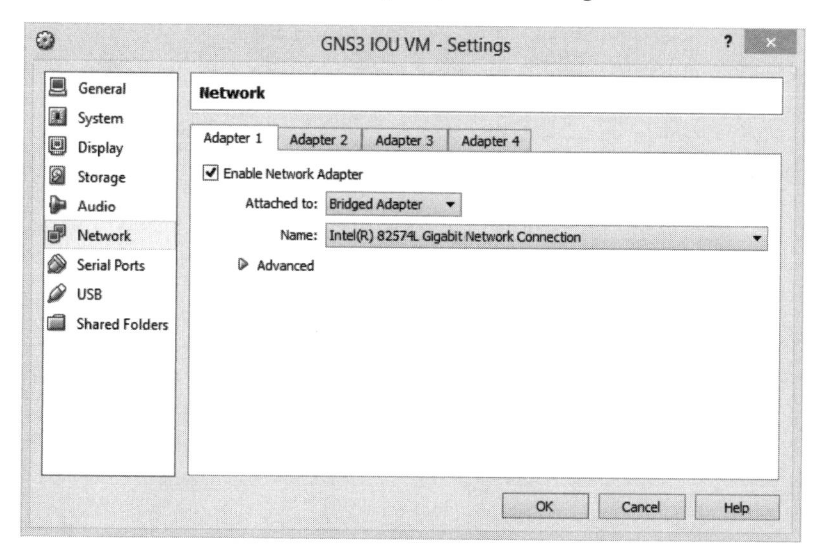

Figure 9-9: Bridge the network adapter to your PC.

From the Adapter 1 tab, select the **Enable Network Adapter** option. Then, choose **Bridged Adapter** next to the Attached to field. When you're finished, click **OK**. This bridges your virtual machine's Ethernet adapter to your PC and allows it to access the Internet so you can install additional packages, if needed.

Uploading IOU Image Files

Now that you've imported the GNS3 IOU virtual machine, you should be able to run the virtual machine and upload your IOU image files. To power on the virtual machine, select **GNS3 IOU VM**, as in Figure 9-10, and click **Start**.

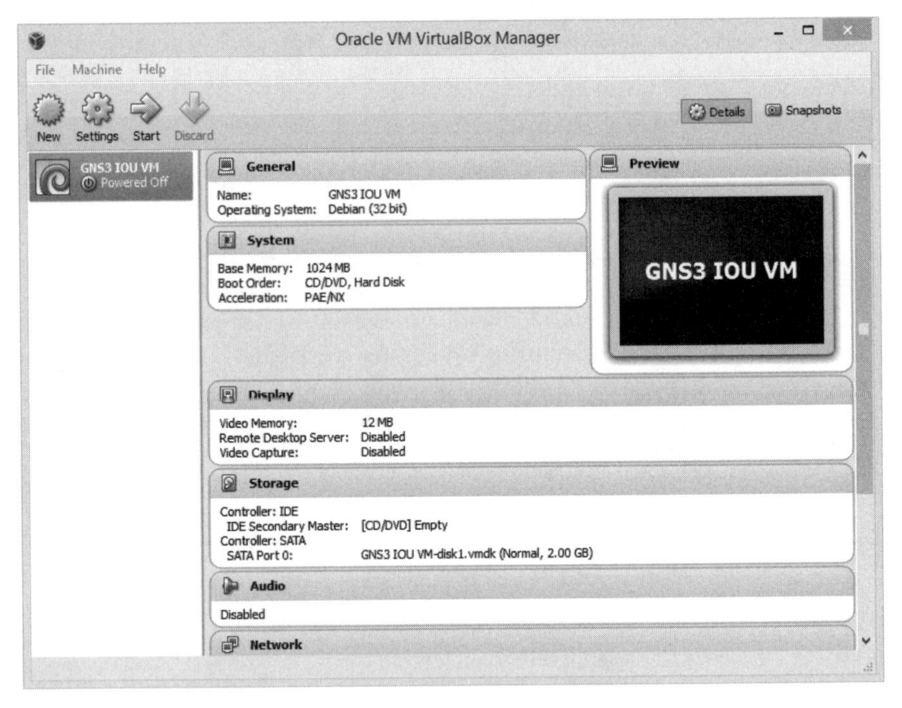

Figure 9-10: Select and start your GNS3 IOU virtual machine.

It's normal for the virtual machine to take a minute or two to start because it's booting a fully functional Linux OS. After the virtual machine is up and running, a console message similar to the following should be displayed on the screen:

```
Welcome to GNS3 IOU appliance
Use 172.16.231.204 to configure a remote server in GNS3 Preferences
Use your browser with http://172.16.231.204:8000/upload to upload IOS images

gns3-iouvm login:
```

Notice that the screen instructs you to use your PC's web browser to upload IOU image files to the appliance. For this to work, your PC and the GNS3 IOU virtual machine must each have an IP address assigned from your local network. In this example, my virtual machine's IP address is 172.16.231.204.

NOTE *Sometimes the IOU virtual machine may not display the IP address. In that case, log on to the virtual machine using the username* root *and the password* cisco. *Then enter* **`ifconfig eth0`** *to display the IP address of your virtual machine's Ethernet interface.*

To upload an IOU image file, open your web browser and browse to the IP address, using port 8000 as instructed. After entering the URL (*http://172.16.231.204:8000/upload* in this example), you should be presented with a web page like the one in Figure 9-11.

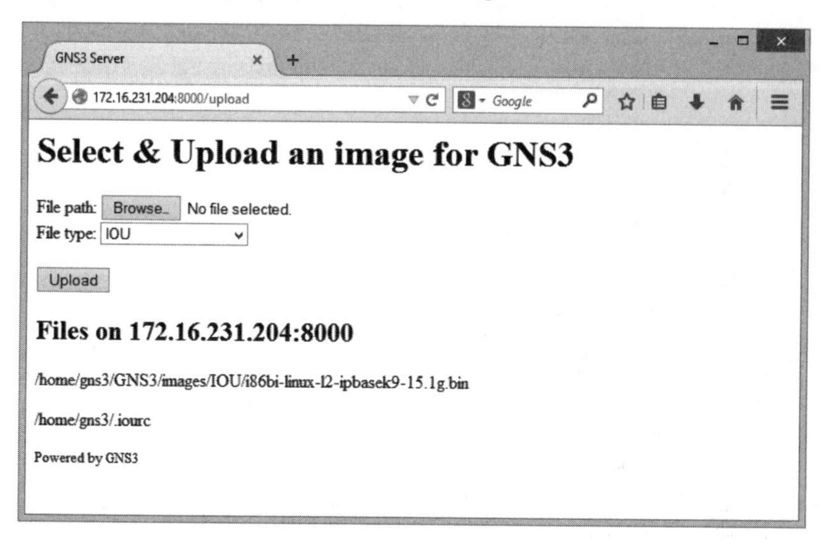

Figure 9-11: Select and upload your IOU image files.

Use the **Browse...** button to select an IOU image file from your PC. Once selected, click **upload** to complete the process. Repeat this step for each image you want to use with GNS3 and your IOU license file. Images are stored on the IOU virtual machine under */home/gns3/GNS3/images*, and the path is displayed on the web page for later reference. You'll need this information when you configure your IOU images in GNS3, so it's a good idea to highlight and copy the full path and filename now. That way, you won't have to type it later.

Configuring GNS3 for IOU

Now that IOU is ready, you just have to prepare GNS3. First, create a plain-text license file on your PC using the hostname *gns3-iouvm*, as in the following example. Replace 1234567812345678 with your license number.

```
[license]
gns3-iouvm = 1234567812345678
```

A common name that's often used for the IOU license file is *.iourc*, but you can use any name that makes sense to you (for example, you might call it *iou-license.txt*), and the license file can be stored anywhere on your system.

After you've created the license file, you're ready to configure the GNS3 preferences for IOU. Launch GNS3, select **Edit ▸ Preferences** on Windows or **GNS3 ▸ Preferences** on OS X, and select **GNS3 server**, as shown in Figure 9-12.

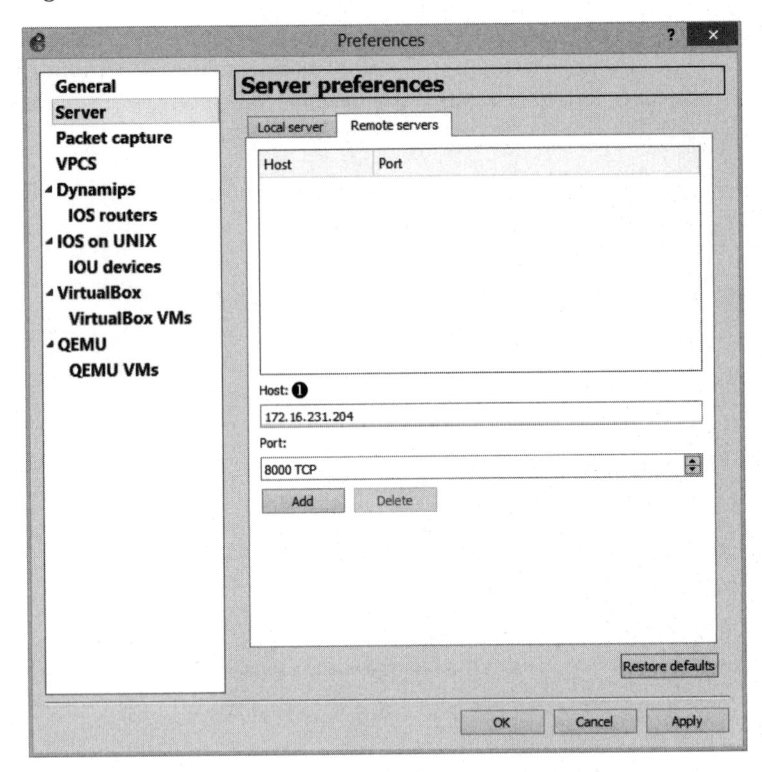

Figure 9-12: GNS3 server preferences, Remote servers tab

Select the Remote servers tab. Under Host ❶ enter the IP address of your GNS3 IOU virtual machine, click **Add**, and then click **Apply**. In this example, the IP address of my GNS3 IOU virtual machine is 172.16.231.204.

Next, tell GNS3 where to find the IOU license file. Click **IOS on UNIX** from the pane on the left and select the General settings tab, shown in Figure 9-13.

Click the **Browse...** button to the right of the Path to IOURC field to locate your license file. Select the file and then click **Add** and **Apply**. In this example, the path to my license file is *C:\Users\jneumann\GNS3\iourc_license.txt*.

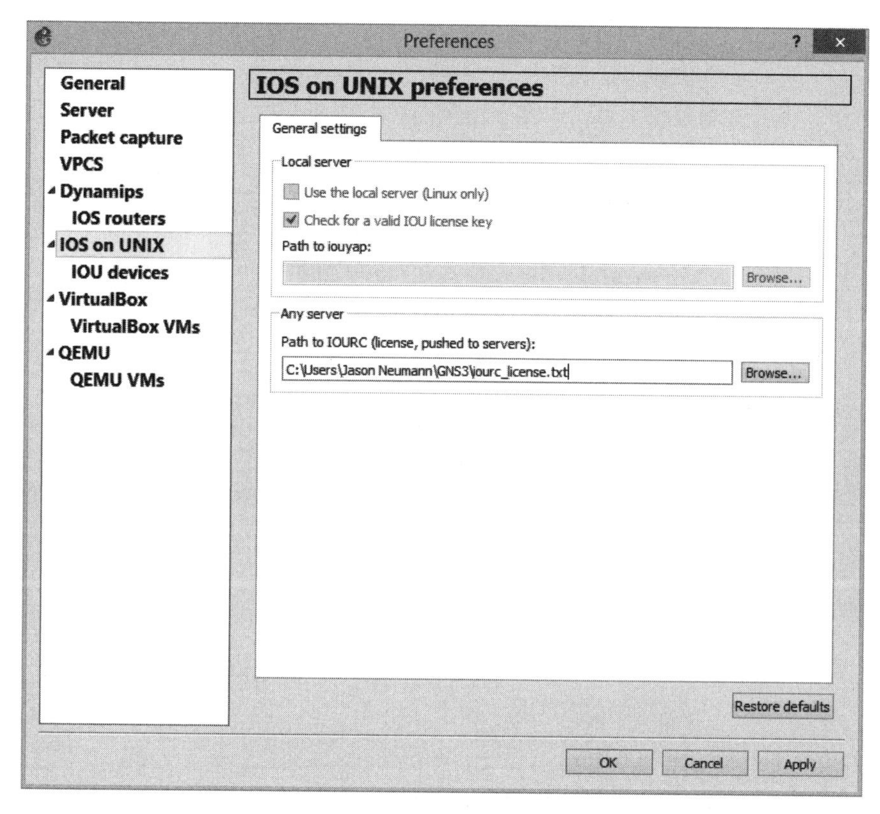

Figure 9-13: IOS on UNIX preferences, General settings tab

Next, expand **IOS on UNIX** in the pane on the left to display IOU devices, as shown in Figure 9-14.

The final configuration step is to add the path to an IOU image file. Select the **IOS devices** preference and click **New** to start the wizard. Under Server type, make sure there's a check next to **Remote** and click **Next**. A message about choosing a path to your image should appear; click **OK**, and you should see the New IOU device window, shown in Figure 9-15.

Enter a name for your IOU device (*IOU_L2*, for example) and then enter the IOU image path. Because IOU images are installed on the Linux virtual machine, you'll have to enter the "Linux pathname" to your image file. That path is */home/gns3/GNS3/images/<image_name>*. In this example I've entered */home/gns3/GNS3/images/i86bi-linux-l2-adventerprisek9-15.1a.bin*. You can find this information on the IOU web page that you used to upload your image files (refer to Figure 9-11). Be careful to enter the path and filename correctly; otherwise, IOU won't work. I recommend copying and pasting the information directly from the IOU virtual machine web page to avoid any confusion.

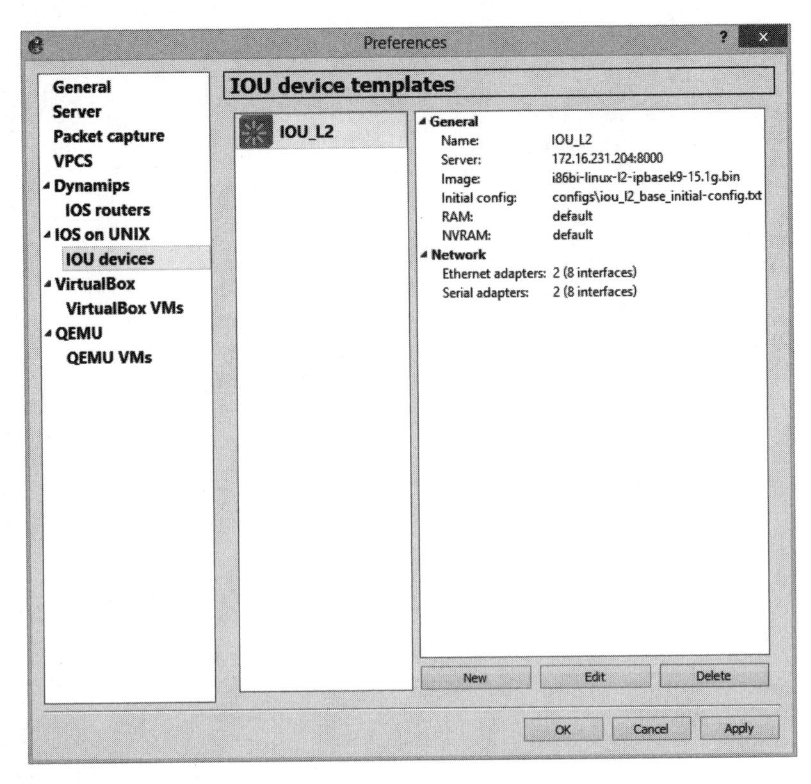

Figure 9-14: IOU devices preferences

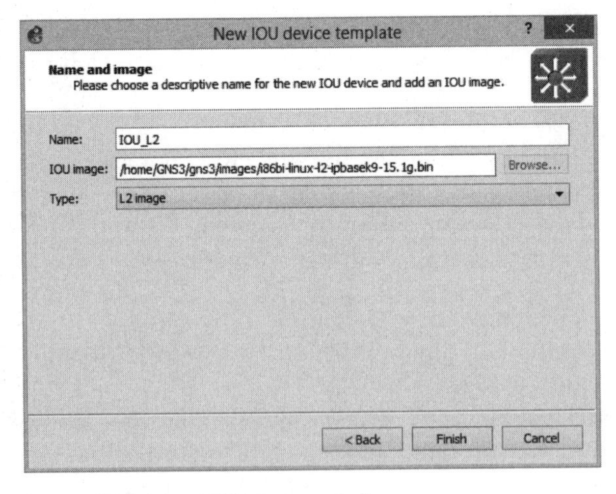

Figure 9-15: New IOU device window

When you're finished, click **Finish** to close the wizard and then click **Apply** and **OK** to complete the configuration. Once you've added an IOU image, you're ready to start using IOU devices in your projects.

If you upgrade GNS3 to a new version, you also have to upgrade the server on your GNS3 IOU virtual machine to the same version, or it won't work. To upgrade the server, log on to the GNS3 IOU virtual machine and enter the following commands, replacing *version* with your version of GNS3:

```
Login: root
Password: cisco
# pip3 install gns3-server==version
```

IOU in Action

Now let's create a simple project that allows an IOU switch to route TCP/IP traffic between two VLANs. Start by creating the project shown in Figure 9-16.

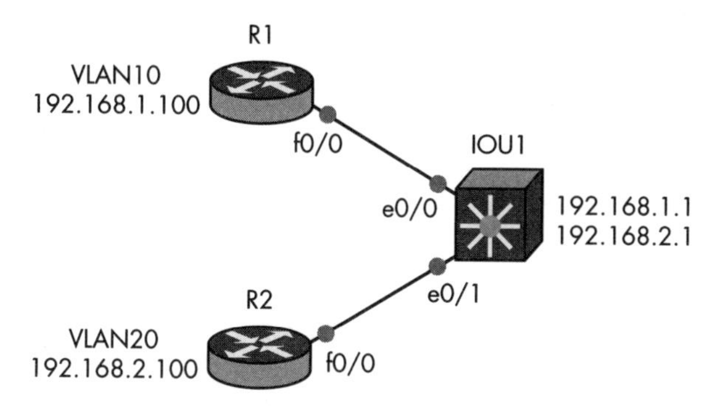

Figure 9-16: VLAN routing using an IOU switch

In this project, you'll configure an IOU L2 switch with two VLANs (VLAN 10 and VLAN 20). Then you'll assign router R1 to VLAN 10 and router R2 to VLAN 20. In this lab, the IOU switch will route packets between the two VLANs so that R1 and R2 can ping each other. Start by configuring the IOU1 switch as follows:

```
  IOU1# configure terminal
❶ IOU1(config)# ip routing
❷ IOU1(config)# vlan 10
  IOU1(config-vlan)# vlan 20
❸ IOU1(config-vlan)# interface vlan 10
❹ IOU1(config-if)# ip address 192.168.1.1 255.255.255.0
❺ IOU1(config-if)# no shutdown
  IOU1(config-if)# interface vlan 20
  IOU1(config-if)# ip address 192.168.2.1 255.255.255.0
  IOU1(config-if)# no shutdown
❻ IOU1(config)# interface Ethernet 0/0
❼ IOU1(config-if)# switchport mode access
❽ IOU1(config-if)# switchport access vlan 10
  IOU1(config-if)# no shutdown
```

```
IOU1(config-if)# interface Ethernet 0/1
IOU1(config-if)# switchport mode access
IOU1(config-if)# switchport access vlan 20
IOU1(config-if)# no shutdown
```

Enable IP routing ❶ and then create the two VLANs (10 and 20) using the vlan command ❷. Next, create a switched virtual interface (SVI) ❸ for each VLAN and assign each SVI an IP address ❹. Use the no shutdown command ❺ to bring up the interface. Now go under the physical interfaces ❻ that are connected to R1 and R2, make them access ports ❼, and assign them to the appropriate VLAN ❽.

Next, configure an IP address on router R1.

```
R1(config)# interface f0/0
R1(config-if)# ip address 192.168.1.100 255.255.255.0
R1(config-if)# no shutdown
R1(config-if)# ip route 0.0.0.0 0.0.0.0 192.168.1.1
```

After assigning the IP address to F0/0 on R1, set the default gateway address to 192.168.1.1 so that the router will use IOU1 for its gateway. Finally, configure R2 in a similar manner.

```
R2(config)# interface f0/0
R2(config-if)# ip address 192.168.2.100 255.255.255.0
R2(config-if)# no shutdown
R2(config-if)# ip route 0.0.0.0 0.0.0.0 192.168.2.1
```

After configuring the project, you can test VLAN routing using the ping command. Router R1 should be able to ping router R2 through the IOU1 switch, as in the following:

```
R1# ping 192.168.2.100

Type escape sequence to abort.
Sending 5, 100-byte ICMP Echos to 192.168.1.100, timeout is 2 seconds:
!!!!!
Success rate is 100 percent (5/5), round-trip min/avg/max = 16/24/32 ms
```

That's all it takes to get IOU devices up and running with GNS3. Now let's take a look at Cisco's newest operating system, NX-OS.

NX-OSv

Cisco NX-OS runs on a data-center class of switches known as Nexus. Though similar to IOS, NX-OS is not IOS and uses a different set of configuration commands. NX-OSv, sometimes called Titanium, is a Linux virtual machine that runs an NX-OS simulator using virtualization software, like

VirtualBox. NX-OSv is not a complete OS simulation, and it's missing a lot of functionality. It provides just enough features and commands to give you a feel for how NX-OS works, and it can be networked to GNS3 devices. After you've acquired an NX-OSv image, make a copy and keep it in a safe place in case your working copy gets corrupted in some way.

Create a directory for NX-OSv under your GNS3 directory and copy the NX-OSv image file there. You should have a file named *N7K.vmdk*. Your filename may be different depending on your version of NX-OSv. With your image file in place, it's time to get NX-OSv wired up in VirtualBox.

Importing NX-OSv into VirtualBox

NX-OSv usually comes ready to run in the form of a single virtual machine hard disk file (*.vmdk* file), and you can run it using VMware, VirtualBox, or QEMU. VirtualBox is free and runs NX-OSv reliably, even on PCs with older processors such as the Core 2 Duo, so I'll cover VirtualBox here. Configuration consists of importing the hard disk image file into a custom Linux virtual machine and adjusting a couple of settings. If you don't have VirtualBox installed on your PC, download and install it now.

Launch VirtualBox and click **New** to create a new virtual machine. You should be presented with the Create Virtual Machine wizard, shown in Figure 9-17.

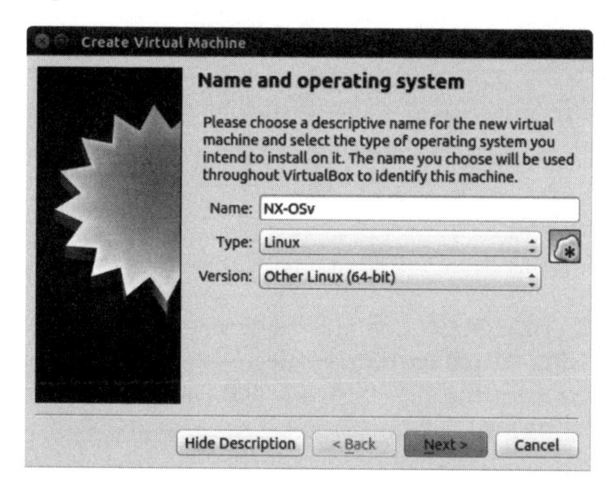

Figure 9-17: Create Virtual Machine wizard, Name and operating system window

Enter a name for the device, set Type to **Linux** and Version to **Other Linux (64-bit)**, and then click **Next** to continue. You should be presented with the Memory size window, shown in Figure 9-18.

To adjust the memory size, use the slider or enter the amount in the field provided. NX-OSv runs best with 2048MB of RAM. When you're done, click **Next** to configure the hard drive settings, shown in Figure 9-19.

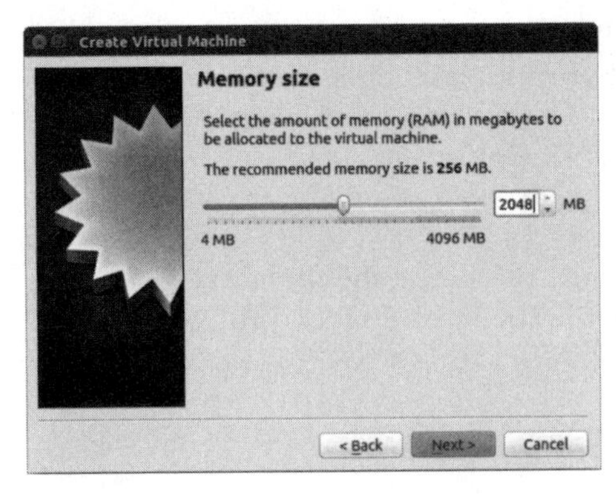

Figure 9-18: Create Virtual Machine wizard, Memory size window

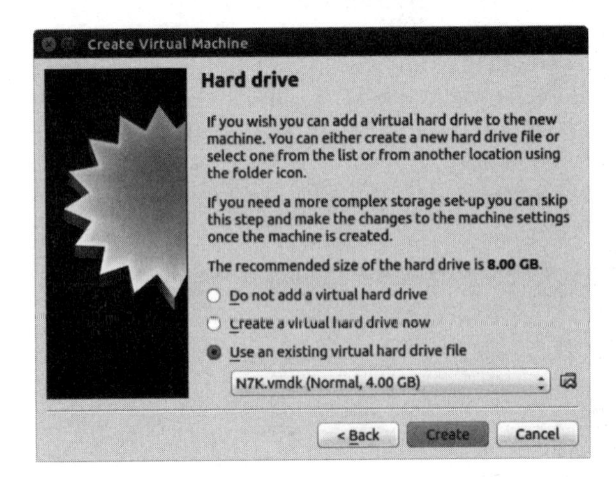

Figure 9-19: Create Virtual Machine wizard, Hard drive window

To attach the NX-OS virtual hard drive to your virtual machine, select **Use an existing virtual hard drive file** and click the browse icon to locate your NX-OSv *.vmdk* file. Select the file and click **Create** to finish creating the virtual machine.

Configuring GNS3 for NX-OSv

Start GNS3 and add the NX-OSv virtual machine to your virtual machine library. Select **Edit ▸ Preferences** and expand **VirtualBox** to show VirtualBox virtual machines, as shown in Figure 9-20. From here you can add VirtualBox virtual machines to GNS3, which is the last step before you can use NX-OSv.

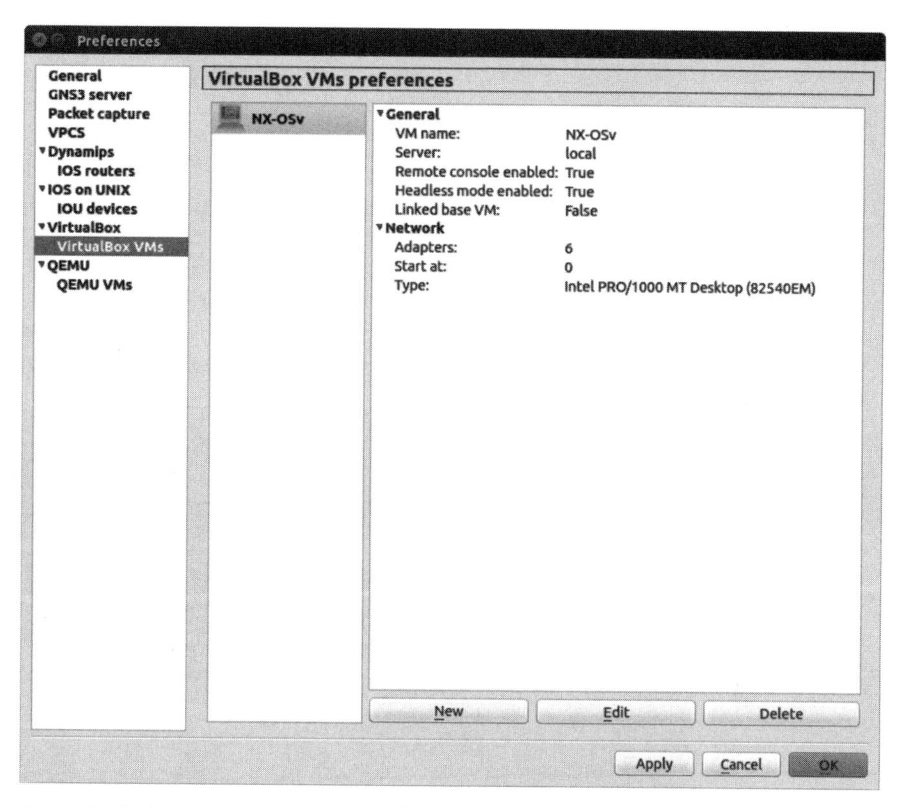

Figure 9-20: Adding the NX-OSv VirtualBox virtual machine to GNS3

Click **New** to start the VirtualBox wizard, select your NX-OSv virtual machine from the virtual machine name drop-down menu, and click **Finish**. Now click **Edit** and navigate to the General settings tab. Select the **Enable remote console** and **Start VM in headless mode** boxes and click **Apply**. Under the Network tab, change the number of interfaces from 1 to 6, and click **Apply** to close the window. Then click **Apply** and **OK** to complete the installation. To use a NX-OSv virtual machine in your projects, drag your NX-OSv virtual machine from the End devices toolbar to your workspace.

NX-OSv in Action

Now that you have the NX-OSv device added to GNS3, let's use it in a project. Create a topology that includes one NX-OSv device and one IOS router, as shown in Figure 9-21. This project will advertise all 172.16.0.0 networks from R1 to NX-OSv using Cisco EIGRP.

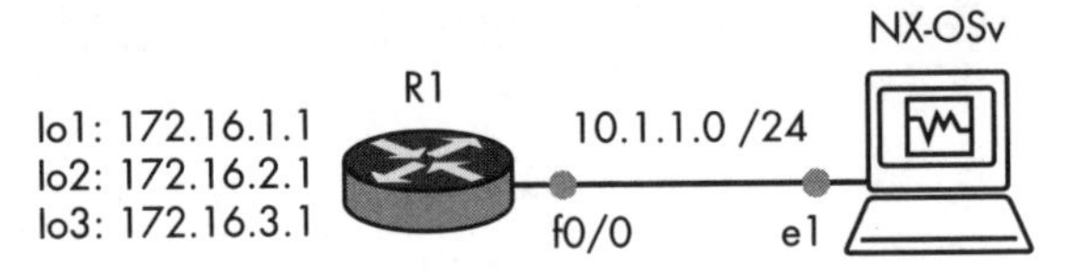

Figure 9-21: Simple topology using NX-OSv

After you create the project, start all your devices and open a console connection to NX-OSv. NX-OS running on a PC takes a long time to boot and often hangs for a minute at the `SCSI disk detected` message, displayed in Figure 9-22. This is normal, so be patient while it starts.

```
NX-OSv
Auto booting bootflash:/titanium-d1-kickstart.7.0.1.ZD.0.216.bin bootflash:/tit
anium-d1.7.0.1.ZD.0.216.bin...
Booting kickstart image: bootflash:/titanium-d1-kickstart.7.0.1.ZD.0.216.bin...
.
.........................................................................
...................Image verification OK

[    0.000000] Unknown boot option `ide_generic.probe_mask=0x0': ignoring
INIT: version 2.86 booting
SCSI disk detected.
```

Figure 9-22: Booting NX-OSv

If you don't see the boot messages, you may have misconfigured something. Go back and check all your settings in VirtualBox and GNS3. If you continue to have problems, there may be something wrong with your *N7K.vmdk* image file.

After the system starts, you should be presented with a login prompt, like the one shown here:

```
User Access verification
vNX-OS-01 login:
```

The default login and password should be `admin` and `admin`. Use these credentials to log on to NX-OSv. This is a good time to enter a few commands. I would start with `show run`, `show version`, and `show interface brief`, but you can try any IOS commands you're familiar with. Some will be the same on NX-OS; others will not. You can use the question mark (?) to display a complete list.

Now that you've taken a peek at NX-OSv, you can configure your project. First, you'll configure router R1. Open a console on router R1 and enter the following commands to configure all the IP addresses for the project:

```
R1# configure terminal
R1(config)# interface f0/0
R1(config-if)# no shutdown
R1(config-if)# ip address 10.1.1.1 255.255.255.0
R1(config-if)# interface loopback1
R1(config-if)# ip address 172.16.1.1 255.255.255.0
R1(config-if)# interface loopback2
R1(config-if)# ip address 172.16.2.1 255.255.255.0
R1(config-if)# interface loopback3
R1(config-if)# ip address 172.16.3.1 255.255.255.0
```

Next, enable EIGRP and advertise all the IP networks.

```
R1(config-if)# router eigrp 10
R1(config-router)# no auto-summary
R1(config-router)# network 10.0.0.0
R1(config-router)# network 172.16.0.0
```

Now log on to NX-OSv and configure an IP address from the same subnet as R1's interface f0/0.

```
vNX-OS-01# configure terminal
vNX-OS-01(config)# interface ethernet 2/1
vNX-OS-01(config-if)# ip address 10.1.1.2/24
vNX-OS-01(config-if)# no shutdown
```

The first thing you should notice is that NX-OS only accepts IP addresses using CIDR notation, so here, the subnet mask is entered as `/24` and not `255.255.255.0` as commonly used in IOS. Now use the `ping` command to test connectivity from NX-OSv to router R1 and exit to configuration mode.

```
vNX-OS-01(config-if)# do ping 10.1.1.1
PING 192.168.1.1 (110.1.1.1): 56 data bytes
64 bytes from 10.1.1.1: icmp_seq=0 ttl=254 time=19.494 ms
64 bytes from 10.1.1.1: icmp_seq=1 ttl=254 time=7.849 ms
64 bytes from 10.1.1.1: icmp_seq=2 ttl=254 time=7.511 ms
64 bytes from 10.1.1.1: icmp_seq=3 ttl=254 time=20.637 ms
64 bytes from 10.1.1.1: icmp_seq=4 ttl=254 time=8.524 ms

--- 10.1.1.1 ping statistics ---
5 packets transmitted, 5 packets received, 0.00% packet loss
round-trip min/avg/max = 7.511/12.803/20.637 ms
vNX-OS-01(config-if)# exit
```

Now let's configure NX-OSv so that it can exchange EIGRP advertised routes with router R1. Note that NX-OS allows you to run EIGRP only for a grace period of 120 days, unless you have a feature license. Enter the `license grace-period` command to start the grace period.

```
vNX-OS-01(config)# license grace-period
vNX-OS-01(config)# feature eigrp
vNX-OS-01(config)# router eigrp 10
vNX-OS-01(config)# network 10.0.0.0/8
vNX-OS-01(config)# exit
```

You can verify that routes from R1 are being advertised to NX-OSv using the `show ip route` command.

```
vNX-OS-01# show ip route
IP Route Table for VRF "default"
'*' denotes best ucast next-hop
'**' denotes best mcast next-hop
'[x/y]' denotes [preference/metric]
'%<string>' in via output denotes VRF <string>

10.1.1.0/24, ubest/mbest: 1/0, attached
    *via 10.1.1.2, Eth2/1, [0/0], 00:49:54, direct
10.1.1.2/32, ubest/mbest: 1/0, attached
    *via 10.1.1.2, Eth2/1, [0/0], 00:49:54, local
172.16.1.0/24, ubest/mbest: 1/0
    *via 10.1.1.1, Eth2/1, [90/130816], 00:32:04, eigrp-10, internal
172.16.2.0/24, ubest/mbest: 1/0
    *via 10.1.1.1, Eth2/1, [90/130816], 00:32:04, eigrp-10, internal
172.16.3.0/24, ubest/mbest: 1/0
    *via 10.1.1.1, Eth2/1, [90/130816], 00:32:04, eigrp-10, internal
```

In the previous lines, notice that the output from this command is different from IOS, but all the pertinent information is there. In this example, all of the 172.16.0.0 routes have been advertised from R1 to NX-OSv via EIGRP, so you should be able to ping any of those addresses. Try that now.

```
NX-OSv-01# ping 172.16.2.1
PING 172.16.2.1 (172.16.2.1): 56 data bytes
64 bytes from 172.16.2.1: icmp_seq=0 ttl=254 time=20 ms
64 bytes from 172.16.2.1: icmp_seq=1 ttl=254 time=10 ms
64 bytes from 172.16.2.1: icmp_seq=2 ttl=254 time=20 ms
64 bytes from 172.16.2.1: icmp_seq=3 ttl=254 time=10 ms
64 bytes from 172.16.2.1: icmp_seq=4 ttl=254 time=20 ms

--- 172.16.2.1 ping statistics ---
5 packets transmitted, 5 packets received, 0.00% packet loss
round-trip min/avg/max = 10/16/20 ms
```

Finally, save your configuration. The command itself is the same as IOS, but it provides different output.

```
vNX-OS-01# copy running-config startup-config
[########################################] 100%
Copy complete.
vNX-OS-01#
```

Now that you've created a simple project, you can begin experimenting with NX-OSv on your own. Keep in mind that some functions will definitely be missing. In my version, for example, none of the L2 switch functionality works, only layer 3 routing. Another item to be aware of is tab completion; it works only on some commands, so don't assume a command doesn't work just because NX-OSv doesn't provide tab completion on the command line.

In spite of these limitations, I still find it fun to add NX-OS devices to my projects, and I'm sure you will too. To learn more about Cisco Nexus and NX-OS, visit *http://www.cisco.com/en/US/products/ps9402/index.html.*

Final Thoughts

In this chapter, you explored IOS on Unix and learned how to leverage IOU to add nearly full-featured switching capabilities to GNS3 without using physical switches. Although not required for CCNA-level certifications, IOU switching is highly useful for CCNP and CCIE certifications.

Next, you installed NX-OSv, a virtual machine that simulates a Cisco Nexus switch running NX-OS. NX-OSv can be networked to GNS3 devices using protocols such as OSPF and EIGRP, and it's fun to play with, but it lacks much of the functionality you'd find using a real Nexus switch.

In the next chapter, I'll show you a few fun things you can do with GNS3, such as creating a simulated access server to manage your routers.

10

COOL THINGS TO DO ON A RAINY DAY

Now that you've seen GNS3's most commonly used features, let's explore some fun tricks you can do with your GNS3 projects. First, you'll create a simulated Cisco access server that functions like its real Cisco counterpart. Next, I'll show you how to move your GNS3 projects from one operating system to another and how to copy your GNS3 virtual router configurations from GNS3 to real Cisco routers. Finally, you'll look at sharing a project's resource load using multiple PCs, create some nerdy labs, and simulate a few real network scenarios.

Managing Devices from an Access Server

An *access server* allows you to manage all network devices from a central console so you can concurrently log on to multiple device consoles and easily switch between them. It's an efficient way to manage devices on large Cisco networks, and with only a little effort you can create a fully functional virtual Cisco access server (sometimes called a *terminal* or *comm server*) to manage your GNS3 devices. I find that using a virtual access server is a fast way to manage and configure devices in GNS3, and you can also do it to learn the commands and keystrokes of a real access server.

A GNS3 virtual access server has two components. The first is a Cloud node configured with a virtual interface; you'll use a Loopback Adapter driver in Windows and a TAP adapter in Linux. The second is a Cisco Dynamips router that acts as the management console. Configuring the virtual access server itself varies slightly depending on your operating system. I'll cover Windows and Ubuntu Linux, but the concepts apply to other Linux operating systems. Unfortunately, OS X is not supported at the time of writing.

Installing the Virtual Interface

Whether you use Windows or Linux, you'll need to install a virtual network adapter and assign it an IP address. On Windows, you'll install a Loopback Adapter driver, and on Unix-based systems like Linux, you'll install a TAP driver. If you're a Linux user, you can skip to "Configuring a TAP Adapter in Linux" on page 179.

Configuring a Loopback Adapter in Windows

If you haven't done so already, install the Microsoft Loopback Adapter driver. (Refer to "Using a Loopback Adapter on Windows" on page 106.) After you've installed the adapter, assign it an IP address. The IP address and subnet mask you choose must be unique from any network adapters already configured on your PC and from any IP addresses that you plan to use in your GNS3 network topology.

To configure the adapter, open the Windows **Control Panel** and select **Network and Sharing Center**. Next, select **Change Adapter Settings** to display a list of available adapters, as shown in Figure 10-1.

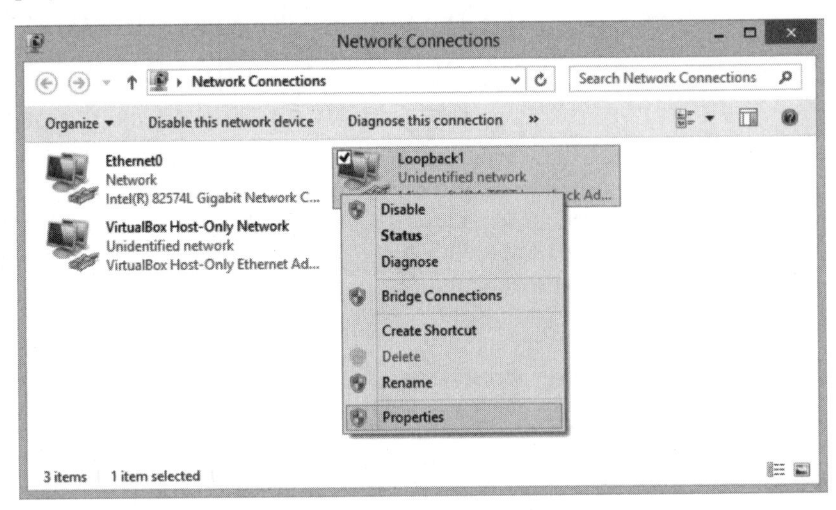

Figure 10-1: Selecting Properties to configure the Microsoft Loopback Adapter driver

Right-click the Microsoft Loopback Adapter driver and select **Properties**. From the Properties window, select **Internet Protocol Version 4 (TCP/IPv4)** and then click the **Properties** button to display the IP address settings, shown in Figure 10-2.

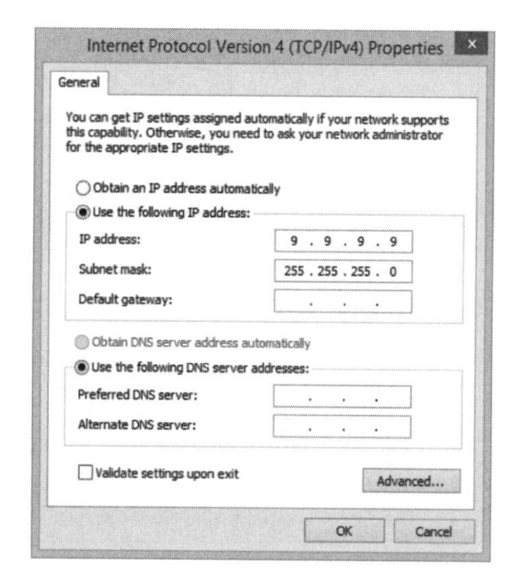

Figure 10-2: Configuring your Loopback Adapter driver with an IP address

Select **Use the following IP address** and enter a unique IP address and subnet mask. I've chosen 9.9.9.9 and 255.255.255.0, but any address and mask will work, as long as they're unique from any addresses assigned to any Ethernet adapters in your PC, and from any addresses that you plan to use in your GNS3 network topology. There's no need to include a default gateway address or provide any DNS servers because they won't be used by the access server. When you're finished, click **OK** to complete the configuration. Now close any open windows and launch GNS3. If you're a Linux user, read on; otherwise, you can skip to "Preparing the GNS3 Server" on page 180.

Configuring a TAP Adapter in Linux

On Ubuntu Linux, you'll use a virtual TAP adapter for the access server. Open a terminal and enter the following command to install the drivers:

```
$ sudo apt-get install uml-utilities
```

To enable tap0, enter the following command, replacing *jneumann* with your Linux username:

```
$ sudo tunctl -u jneumann -t tap0
```

Next, assign a unique IP address to the tap0 interface. The IP address and subnet mask you choose must be unique from any network adapters configured on your PC and from any IP addresses that you plan to use in your GNS3 network topology.

```
$ sudo ifconfig tap0 9.9.9.9 netmask 255.255.255.0 up
```

To ensure the tap0 interface maintains its IP address and is available after a reboot, you'll need to change your Linux network settings.

Open the *interfaces* file under */etc/networks/* in a text editor like pico or vi. You'll need administrator privileges to make changes to the file, so log in as *root* or run the editor with the `sudo` command, as in `sudo pico interfaces`. Then, append the following to the end of the file:

```
auto tap0
iface tap0 inet static
        pre-up tunctl -t tap0
        up ifconfig tap0 up
        down ifconfig tap0 down
        address 9.9.9.9
        netmask 255.255.255.0
```

With these commands in place, save the *interfaces* file, close it, and reboot. When Ubuntu restarts, the TAP driver should automatically load, and interface tap0 should be ready to use.

WARNING *Use caution when editing the* /etc/networks/interfaces *file. Entering a typo here can prevent Ubuntu from booting properly.*

Enter the `ifconfig` command to verify the tap0 settings:

```
$ ifconfig
--snip--
❶ tap0      Link encap:Ethernet  HWaddr 16:81:25:c1:cc:8c
❷           inet addr:9.9.9.9  Bcast:9.9.9.9.255  Mask:255.255.255.0
            UP BROADCAST MULTICAST  MTU:1500  Metric:1
            RX packets:0 errors:0 dropped:0 overruns:0 frame:0
            TX packets:0 errors:0 dropped:0 overruns:0 carrier:0
            collisions:0 txqueuelen:500
            RX bytes:0 (0.0 B)  TX bytes:0 (0.0 B)
```

The output from `ifconfig` should show that the tap0 adapter is enabled ❶ and configured with an IP address ❷. After you've installed and configured a virtual adapter, you'll need to set up the GNS3 server.

Preparing the GNS3 Server

On Windows, run GNS3 as administrator. Begin by binding the GNS3 server to the IP address of your virtual interface; otherwise, your access server will not work. Click **Edit ▸ Preferences** and choose **GNS3 server** from the left column. Select the **Host binding** drop-down menu and then select the IP address you assigned to the virtual interface, as shown in Figure 10-3.

In Figure 10-3, the IP address is 9.9.9.9 ❶. Click **Apply** and **OK**, and the GNS3 server should restart with the new host binding.

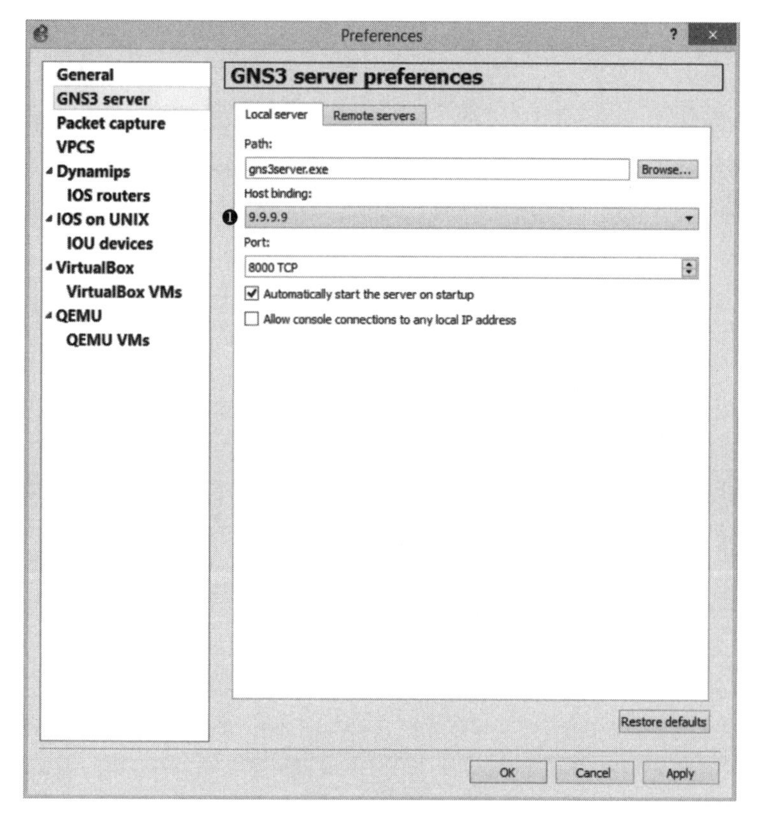

Figure 10-3: Changing the GNS3 server host binding

Creating a Virtual Access Server in GNS3

With your GNS3 server bound to the virtual adapter's IP address, you can create the virtual access server. The access server is created using two devices: a Cloud node and a Dynamips IOS router.

Configuring the Cloud Node

Begin a project by adding a Cloud node to your workspace. Right-click the Cloud node and select **Configure**. If you're running Windows, select the **NIO Ethernet** tab (shown in Figure 10-4).

Click the drop-down menu under Generic Ethernet NIO and select your Microsoft Loopback Adapter driver (**Loopback1** in this example); then click **Add**, **Apply**, and **OK** to complete the configuration.

If you're running GNS3 on Ubuntu Linux, configure the Cloud node using tap0. Instead of NIO Ethernet, select the **NIO TAP** tab and enter **tap0** in the TAP interface field, as in Figure 10-5.

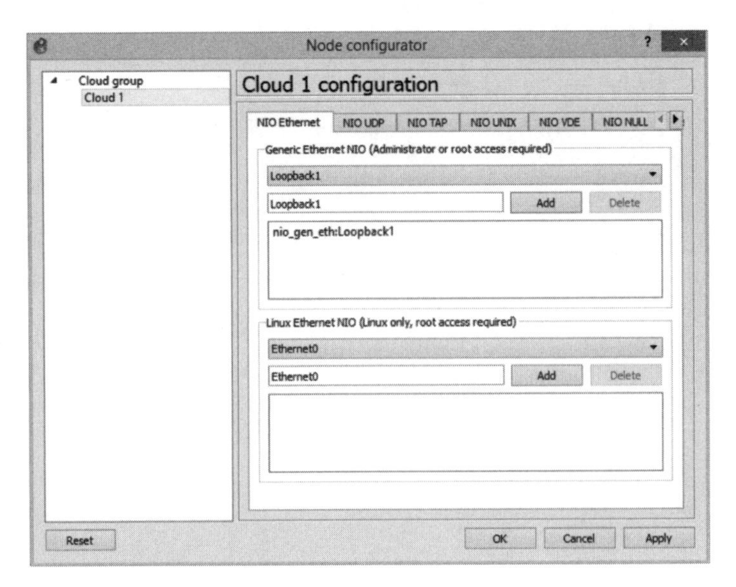

Figure 10-4: Configuring the Cloud node with a Loopback Adapter driver in Windows

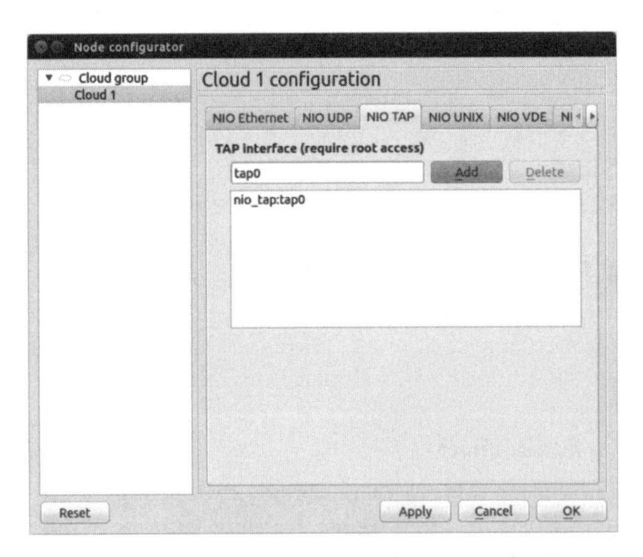

Figure 10-5: Configuring NIO TAP with tap0 on Ubuntu Linux

When you're finished, click **Add**, **Apply**, and **OK** to complete the Cloud node configuration.

Configuring the Access Server Router

After configuring the Cloud node, add a Dynamips router to your workspace and create a link from the router to the Cloud node. Together, these two devices comprise the virtual access server, shown in Figure 10-6. They will not be linked to any other devices in your GNS3 project.

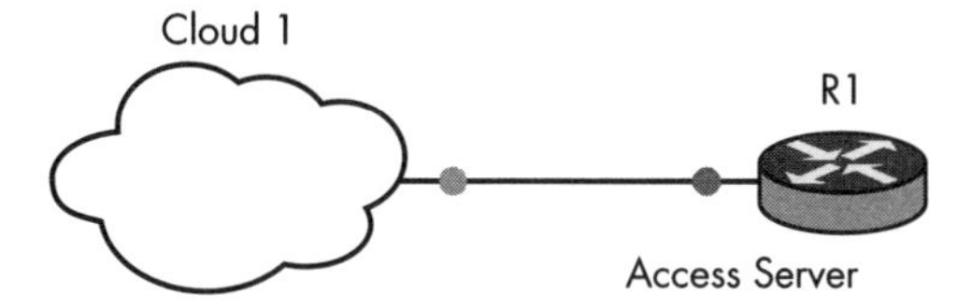

Figure 10-6: Virtual access server

After linking the virtual access server components together, add more routers to your workspace to create a simple three-router network, as shown in Figure 10-7. This is the network topology that will be managed using the virtual access server.

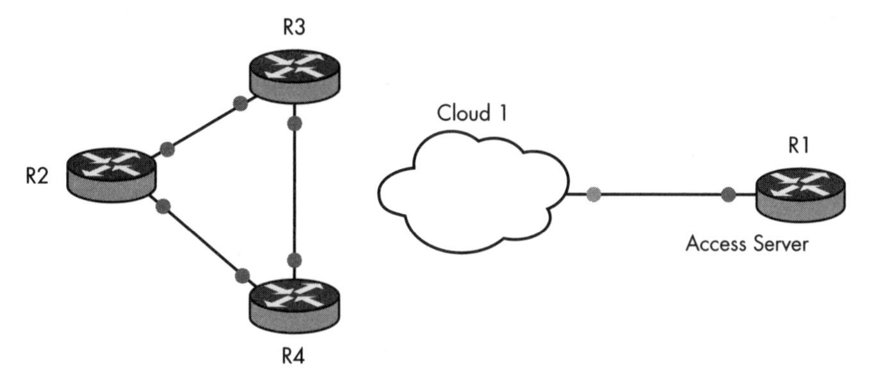

Figure 10-7: Network configured with a virtual Cisco access server

Figure 10-7 shows that you have created a virtual access server using router R1 and a Cloud node (Cloud 1), and you have created a network topology that's made up of three routers, named R2, R3, and R4.

Now that you've created both the access server and a GNS3 network topology, you can configure the access server router. Assign router R1 an IP address from the same network as your PC's virtual adapter, and test connectivity from R1 to the virtual adapter interface. For example, if you assigned the virtual adapter the IP address 9.9.9.9 255.255.255.0 as I have, you could assign the access server router R1 any IP address in that network range. I use the IP address 9.9.9.8 and the subnet mask 255.255.255.0.

To configure the address on interface f0/0, open a console connection to router R1 and enter the following commands:

```
R1>enable
R1#configure terminal
R1(config)#interface f0/0
R1(config-if)#ip address 9.9.9.8 255.255.255.0
R1(config-if)#no shutdown
R1(config-if)#exit
R1(config)#exit
R1#ping 9.9.9.9
```

```
Type escape sequence to abort.
Sending 5, 100-byte ICMP Echos to 9.9.9.9, timeout is 2 seconds:
!!!!!
Success rate is 100 percent (5/5), round-trip min/avg/max = 1/1/4 ms
```

In this configuration, router R1's interface f0/0 is linked to the Cloud node and configured with IP address 9.9.9.8 255.255.255.0. Test the connection between R1 and the virtual interface using a `ping` command. If the ping test is successful, you're ready to move on. If the ping test is unsuccessful, verify that all your interfaces are enabled and that the virtual interface (loopback or TAP) is configured with the proper IP address and subnet mask.

Configuring a Cisco IP Hostname Table

After configuring an IP address on the virtual access server (R1), you're ready to configure an IP hostname table using information gathered from the devices that the access server will manage. In this project, the devices are routers R2, R3, and R4. Using Cisco IOS commands, you'll create an IP hostname table using the IP address of the virtual interface (9.9.9.9) and the console port numbers that GNS3 has assigned to the routers used in your network topology. A Cisco IP hostname table works much like a Unix hosts file, except that you'll also include port numbers in the table. You'll create an entry for each device in the topology that you want to manage.

Begin by finding the console port numbers for routers that the access server will manage. In this project, you're interested only in the console port numbers for routers R2, R3, and R4. You can quickly find any device's console port number by hovering your mouse over the device, as shown in Figure 10-8.

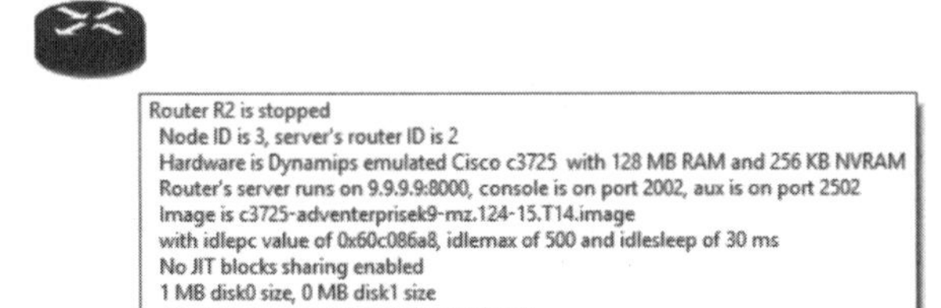

Figure 10-8: Displaying device information

Router R2's console is on port 2002. Because console port numbers are assigned sequentially as devices are added to a project, routers R2, R3, and R4 should have been assigned the console port numbers 2002, 2003, and 2004, respectively. If you're unsure, hover your mouse over each device icon to verify the information.

NOTE *If you add multiple routers at the same time, instead of one at a time, the console port numbers may not be assigned in sequential order.*

To create the IP hostname table, open a console on router R1 (the access server) and enter the following commands:

```
R1#configure terminal
R1(config)#ip host R2 2002 9.9.9.9
R1(config)#ip host R3 2003 9.9.9.9
R1(config)#ip host R4 2004 9.9.9.9
R1(config)#exit
R1#
```

Notice the host port numbers correspond with the unique console port numbers from the three routers you want to manage, but the IP address is always the same; it is the IP address assigned to the virtual adapter (9.9.9.9). That's because when the virtual access server opens a console to one of the lab routers, GNS3 creates a telnet session from the access server to the routers using the virtual adapter's IP address. From there, it connects to the individual console port number that you assigned. For example, when the access server opens a console connection to router R2, GNS3 telnets to IP address 9.9.9.9 using port number 2002. This is similar to how an actual Cisco access server works.

Now, verify which hosts are configured on your virtual access server with the `show hosts` command.

```
R1>show hosts
Default domain is not set
Name/address lookup uses static mappings

Codes: UN - unknown, EX - expired, OK - OK, ?? - revalidate
       temp - temporary, perm - permanent
       NA - Not Applicable None - Not defined

 Host❶                      Port❷ Flags        Age Type  Address(es)❸
 R2                         2002  (perm, OK)  0   IP     9.9.9.9
 R3                         2003  (perm, OK)  0   IP     9.9.9.9
 R4                         2004  (perm, OK)  1   IP     9.9.9.9
```

This command displays the hostname ❶, port number ❷, and IP address ❸ for each host configured on the access server.

VIRTUAL ACCESS SERVER LIMITATIONS

There are limitations as to what devices can be managed by the virtual access server. Because the GNS3 server is bound to a virtual adapter and runs "locally" on your PC, the virtual access server can manage only local devices.

On a Windows PC, you cannot manage VirtualBox virtual machines, including IOU, though you can manage QEMU devices, like Junos. On Ubuntu Linux, you can manage all devices, including Dynamips, IOU, QEMU, and VirtualBox, as long they're running locally on your Linux PC.

To learn more about configuring and using a real Cisco access server, visit the Cisco website (*http://www.cisco.com/*) and search for *configuring a comm server*. For now, you should know all you need to try your virtual access server.

Seeing the Virtual Access Server in Action

After you've fully configured the access server and started your project routers, you should be able to manage those routers using the access server. You can open a console connection to several routers, and easily switch between them.

Opening Consoles

Begin by opening a console connection to R1. Right-click router R1 and choose **Console**. Next, type the name of a host you want to manage and press ENTER. The hostnames are case sensitive, so be sure to use the correct case.

```
R1>R2
Translating "R2"
Trying R2 (9.9.9.9❶, 2002❷)... Open
Connected to Dynamips VM "R2" (ID 1, type c3600) - Console port
Press ENTER to get the prompt.

R2>❸
```

In this example, I open a session with router R2 by entering **R2** from the access server command line. The output shows that a session is established using IP address 9.9.9.9 ❶ and port number 2002 ❷, and the prompt ❸ has changed to the router being managed (R2 in this example). After the session is open, you can configure the router as though you opened a console directly from GNS3.

When you're finished configuring the router, return to the access server console; just press SHIFT-CTRL-6 and then press the **X** key. (Cisco calls this combination of actions an *escape sequence*.) After returning to the access server console, enter the name of another router in your project to open a console on it. Try entering **R3** now, and configure the router however you'd like. When you're done, use the escape sequence again to return to the access server.

Even though you're currently logged on to the access server console, the sessions on the other two routers remain open. To display a list of open sessions and their corresponding connection numbers, enter the `show sessions` command.

```
R1>show sessions
Conn Host                Address             Byte  Idle Conn Name
     1 R2                 9.9.9.9              0     0   R2
  ❶* 2 R3                 9.9.9.9              0     0   R3
```

You should see two active connections (1 and 2). The asterisk ❶ next to Conn 2 indicates that router R3 was the last session used. To return to the last session, press ENTER. To return to a different session, type a connection number and press ENTER; for example, you'd enter `1` to return to router R2.

Closing Consoles

When you're ready to disconnect from an open connection, enter the `disconnect` command followed by the connection number; then press ENTER to confirm closing the session.

```
R1>disconnect 2
Closing connection to R3 [confirm]
R1>
```

In this example, I've disconnected from router R3 (connection 2). After disconnecting a session, you will have to enter the hostname again to reconnect to the device.

Setting Connection Timeouts

You may want to adjust the timeout setting (via the console `exec-timeout` parameter) on your routers and access server to ensure that you're not logged out automatically during idle times, such as when you're not actively configuring a router. The default value is ten minutes, but it can be set higher, lower, or changed to infinite.

The following commands set the console timeout to zero minutes and zero seconds (infinite):

```
R1>enable
R1#configure terminal
R1(config)#line console 0
R1(config-line)#exec-timeout 0 0
```

GNS3's default *startup-config* should have already done this for you, but know that from a security standpoint, never allowing the router to time out is a bad idea in production environments. It is, however, highly convenient in lab environments such as GNS3.

Deploying Configurations to Real Hardware

One of the benefits of GNS3 is that it allows you to create and test network configurations that can later be used on real equipment. You simply export a router configuration in GNS3 and load it on a real Cisco IOS router.

Exporting GNS3 Configurations to Cisco Routers

After thoroughly testing a router configuration inside GNS3, you're ready to export it and load it on a real Cisco router. You can export all the routers in your project, or you can export the configuration of an individual device.

Before exporting a GNS3 IOS router configuration, log in to that router and save its *running-config* file to the *startup-config* file. The saved *startup-config* is the configuration that will be exported by GNS3.

```
R1#copy running-config startup-config
```

If you have any IOU devices in your project, you'll need to make copies of their *running-config* files, too. Just log in to the device and enter the following command to create a text file of the IOU configuration:

```
IOU#copy running-config unix:initial-config.cfg
```

After you've saved a *running-config* file, you can export all device configurations at the same time by selecting **File ▸ Import/Export device configs**. GNS3 should then show the dialog in Figure 10-9.

Figure 10-9: Import/export tool for configuration files

Select **Export configs to a directory** from the drop-down menu, click **OK**, browse to the location where you want to save your configuration files, and click **Open** to save the configurations. The exported configuration files will be named after the devices in your workspace, like *R1_startup-config.cfg* and *IOU1_initial-config.cfg*. For each IOS device, you'll also see a *private config* file that's used only by GNS3 and contains SSH crypto keys. You don't need to upload this to your real Cisco router. This export method is an all-or-nothing procedure that exports all the device configurations in your project. To export the configuration of a single device, save the configuration, right-click the device in your project, and select **Export config**. The saved file will be named using the device name.

Importing Cisco Router Configurations into GNS3

Now, let's look at how to import a live Cisco router configuration into GNS3. Begin by logging on to your real Cisco router and saving its configuration to your PC, using FTP or TFTP. Use a text editor to clean up any interface name discrepancies. Next, append the name of the exported file with `.cfg` to ensure that GNS3 can recognize the file. If you haven't done so already, save your GNS3 project and stop the GNS3 router that is the target for the import. Finally, right-click the GNS3 router and choose **Import config**. Browse to the directory where you saved the *.cfg* file, and select the file to import it into the router. When you restart your GNS3 router, it should load and run the IOS configuration that you copied from the live Cisco router.

NOTE *When moving configurations back and forth between real routers and GNS3, you may have to perform some IOS configuration cleanup. For example, your GNS3 router may have an interface named* FastEthernet 0/0 *while your real Cisco router has an interface named* FastEthernet 0 *instead. In this case, use a text editor and modify the file before importing it into GNS3.*

Copying GNS3 Projects Between Platforms

Someday you may want to have your projects run on a PC that uses a different operating system than your existing PC. If your GNS3 projects include only Dynamips IOS routers and switches, you can copy them between different platforms such as Windows and Linux with minimal effort. But if they're made up of other device types such as IOU, QEMU, or VirtualBox, the process can get complicated. Either way, moving a project between platforms is mostly a matter of copying one or more projects from your old GNS3 projects folder to the projects folder on a new PC.

IOS-Only Projects

If your project consists of only Dynamips routers, then almost no additional configuration is necessary, as long as the target computer has compatible image files. If the target PC is configured with different IOS image files or the images are stored in a different directory, GNS3 should prompt you to substitute the original image file with one that's already configured on the target computer, as shown in Figure 10-10.

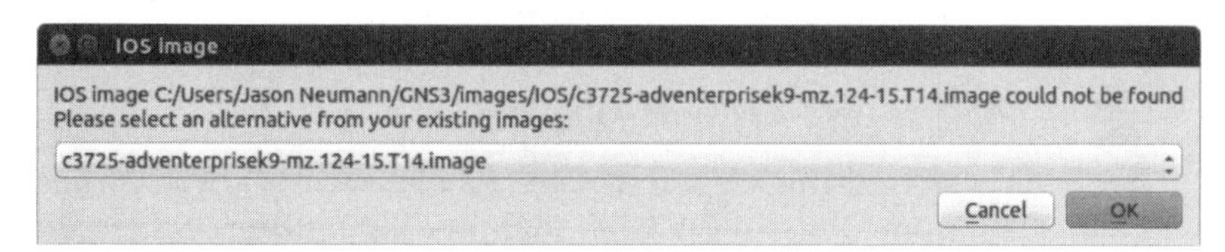

Figure 10-10: Substituting an IOS image file

In this example, you're moving a project from a Windows PC to a Linux host. Even though the *c3725-adventerprisek9-mz-124-15.T14.image* file is configured on the Linux host in Figure 10-10, GNS3 was unable to locate it because Windows stores IOS image files using a different path than Linux.

In this case, GNS3 should display a list of configured IOS images and allow you to choose one. Use the drop-down menu to select an image and click **OK**. After selecting the image, GNS3 should update the path information in the project file on the target PC. To make the change permanent, you have to save your project. All of the original IOS configurations should remain intact, and your project should run as expected. If it doesn't, start again and try using a different image file.

Projects with IOU Devices

Copying projects that contain IOU devices can be a bit more involved. The easiest method is to re-create the IOU devices in the project on the target PC and then upload the original IOU configuration. Before copying the project to a new platform, follow these steps:

1. Log on to each IOU device in the project and copy the running configuration to the *unix:initial-config.cfg* file. Right-click an IOU device

and choose **Export config** to save the configuration. Be sure to copy the exported configuration file to the new system when you copy your project.

2. Open the project on the target PC and resolve any IOS image file substitution issues (refer to Figure 10-10).
3. On the target PC, delete the IOU device from your project, add a new one, and link the IOU device to other project devices using the same interfaces as the original project.

To import the configuration, follow these steps:

1. Right-click the IOU device on the target PC and click **Import config**.
2. Browse to the directory where the IOU configuration is saved and select the file. Do this for each IOU device in your project.
3. When you're finished, start all the devices in your new project and verify that everything works as expected. Log on to each IOU device and examine its configuration. If everything looks good, save your updated project.

Finally, let's look at transferring projects that use VirtualBox.

Projects with VirtualBox Devices

If you're using a VirtualBox device in your original project, you'll have to export it to an OVA file. Launch VirtualBox and choose **File ▸ Export Appliance** to save the device file. With the OVA prepared, follow these steps:

1. Copy the OVA file to the new PC, launch VirtualBox, and choose **File ▸ Import Appliance** to import the file.
2. Launch GNS3 and add the VirtualBox virtual machine under Preferences, as discussed in "Importing Appliances" on page 51.
3. Add the device to your GNS3 project and link it to other devices, selecting the same interfaces that were used in the original project.

When you start your project on the new PC, your VirtualBox devices should have the same configuration they had on the old PC.

Exploring the GNS3 Console

The GNS3 management console provides a command line interface that you can use to control project devices. Based on the original Dynagen console that was written for Dynamips, the management console has been adapted and updated for GNS3. I won't cover every aspect of the console here, but I will show you some more useful things you can do with it.

By default, the management console should be visible when you launch GNS3. If not, select **View ▸ Docks ▸ Console** to display the console window.

From the management prompt (=>), enter help or a question mark (?) to see a list of commands. As you can see from the following listing, you can perform familiar tasks from the CLI, such as starting and stopping devices:

```
=> ?

Documented commands (type help <topic>):
========================================
console  debug  help  reload  show  start  stop  suspend  version
```

To display the details and syntax of a specific command, enter help followed by a command name, as shown here:

```
=> help show
   Show detail information about every device in current lab:
    show device

    Show detail information about a device:
    show device <device_name>

    Show the whole topology:
    show run

    Show topology info of a device:
    show run <device_name>
```

The show command offers a lot of different options to display information about your hypervisors, devices, and configurations. For example, the show run command displays the entire contents of your project configuration file.

Two commands that are useful for testing networks are suspend and start. Together they can be used to simulate a router failure and recovery. Another helpful command is the debug command. It can provide useful information when a project isn't running properly.

Creating Projects Using Multiple PCs

You can run devices using multiple PCs, allowing you to distribute the resource load across multiple computers. Sharing resources lets you use one PC to design your projects while running the devices themselves on one or more other PCs. This means you can create and manage your GNS3 project using a low-end workstation (such as an old laptop) while actually running the devices on a high-end server. If you use multiple servers, you could build a GNS3 uberlab!

In this section, I'll show you how to share resources in a basic client/server setup and cover strategies for creating an uberlab. Disable the firewalls on all PCs before you begin configuring client/server (or multiserver) load sharing, and let's get started.

A Dynamips Client/Server Setup

In this scenario, you operate GNS3 on one computer, while another GNS3 server runs on another PC. If you're running GNS3 on OS X or Windows, this may sound familiar because that's how the IOU virtual machine works. The IOU virtual machine runs on a virtual computer rather than on a separate PC, but otherwise, the concept is the same.

Preparing Your Workstations

In this example, I will use Windows for the client PC and Ubuntu Linux for the server PC. Begin by installing GNS3 on the two workstations. One workstation will be the client, where you configure and manage your projects, and the other is the server. The server will run only Dynamips routers, and it should have the better hardware because it will do most of the work. The more processing power and memory the server has, the better your devices will perform.

Launch GNS3 on each computer and configure an IOS image file. This lets you run both local and remote Dynamips routers at the same time and network them together using GNS3 from the client PC. When configuring GNS3 on the server PC, be sure to record the path and filename of your IOS image file. On my Ubuntu server, my image file path is */home/jneumann/GNS3/images/IOS/c3725-adventerprisek9-mz.124-15.T14.image*. You need this information to configure the remote Dynamips router on the client PC.

Next, find the IP address of each of your GNS3 PCs. In this example, my client PC is configured with the IP address 172.16.231.202, and my server PC is configured with the IP address 172.16.231.205. After configuring GNS3 and recording the IP and image path information, you should be ready to begin.

Running gns3server

You must run the `gns3server` program from its install directory. Log on to the remote server PC and open a terminal window on Linux and OS X or a command prompt if you're running Windows. On Windows, go to the *C:\Program Files\GNS3* directory, and on OS X go to the */Applications/GNS3.app/Contents/Resources/Server/Contents/MacOS* directory.

When starting the server program, you have to specify the IP address of your server PC and the port number that the server will listen on; enter the command `gns3server --host server-ip --port port-number`. If you don't know the IP address of your server PC, you can be lazy and use 0.0.0.0 and `gns3server` will listen on all configured interfaces. In the following example, I've started the `gns3server` program on Ubuntu Linux from the */usr/local/bin/* directory.

```
$ gns3server --host 172.16.231.205 --port 8000
2015-06-06 18:32:45 INFO main.py:145 GNS3 server version x.x
2015-06-06 18:32:45 INFO main.py:147 Copyright (c) 2007-2015 GNS3 Technologies
Inc.
2015-06-06 18:32:45 INFO main.py:150 Config file /home/jneumann/.config/GNS3/
gns3_server.conf loaded
```

```
2015-06-06 18:32:45 INFO main.py:163 Running with Python 3.4.2 and has PID 3436
2015-06-06 18:32:45 INFO main.py:72 Current locale is en_US.UTF-8
2015-06-06 18:32:45 WARNING project.py:397 Purge old temporary project f3b11fb8
-82ed-42c1-b66a-226198ce6189
2015-06-06 18:32:45 INFO server.py:214 ❶ Starting server on 172.16.231.205:8000
```

After starting the server, you should see similar output, and if all goes well, the server will start on 172.16.231.205:8000 ❶, shown on the last line of the output. This indicates the server program is listening on IP address 172.16.231.205 using port number 8000.

NOTE *If you want the GNS3 server to listen on some other port number, say 8001, you can enter* `gns3server --host 172.16.231.205 --port 8001` *instead. To see a complete list of server options, enter* `gns3server --help` *from the command line.*

Configuring the Client

That's all there is to configuring the server, so you can turn your attention to the GNS3 client, a Windows PC in this example. In GNS3, select **Edit ▸ Preferences** and select **GNS3 Server**, as shown in Figure 10-11.

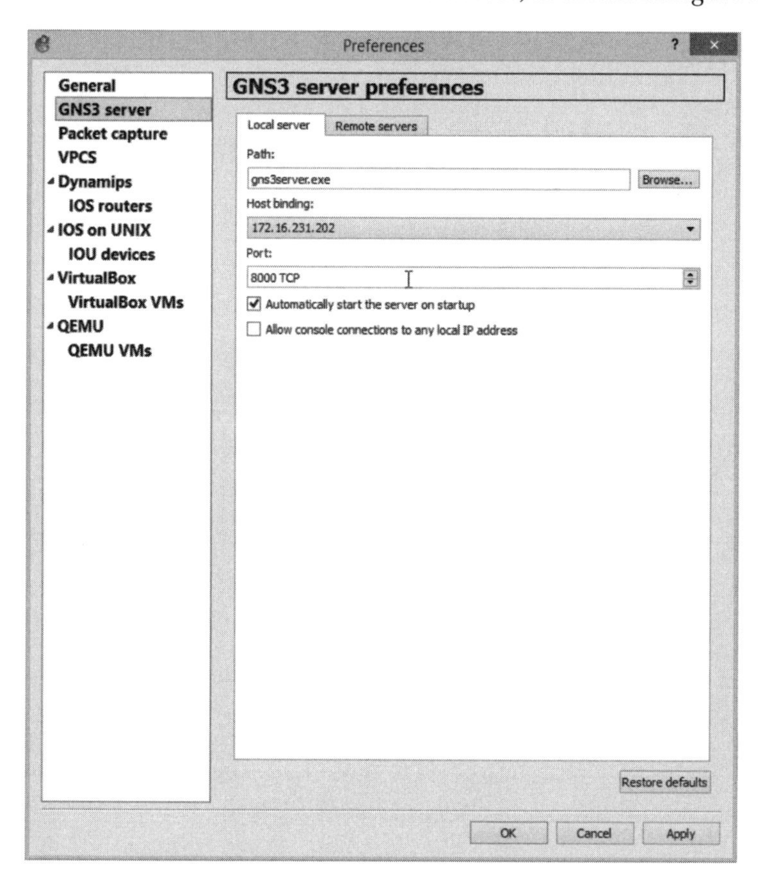

Figure 10-11: Setting the host binding to the IP address of the Ethernet adapter

Click the **Host binding** drop-down menu and select the IP address of your Ethernet interface. On this PC, the address is 172.16.231.202. Click **Apply** to complete the configuration.

Next, add the remote GNS3 server's IP address to the remote server list on the client. Click the **Remote Servers** tab, as shown in Figure 10-12.

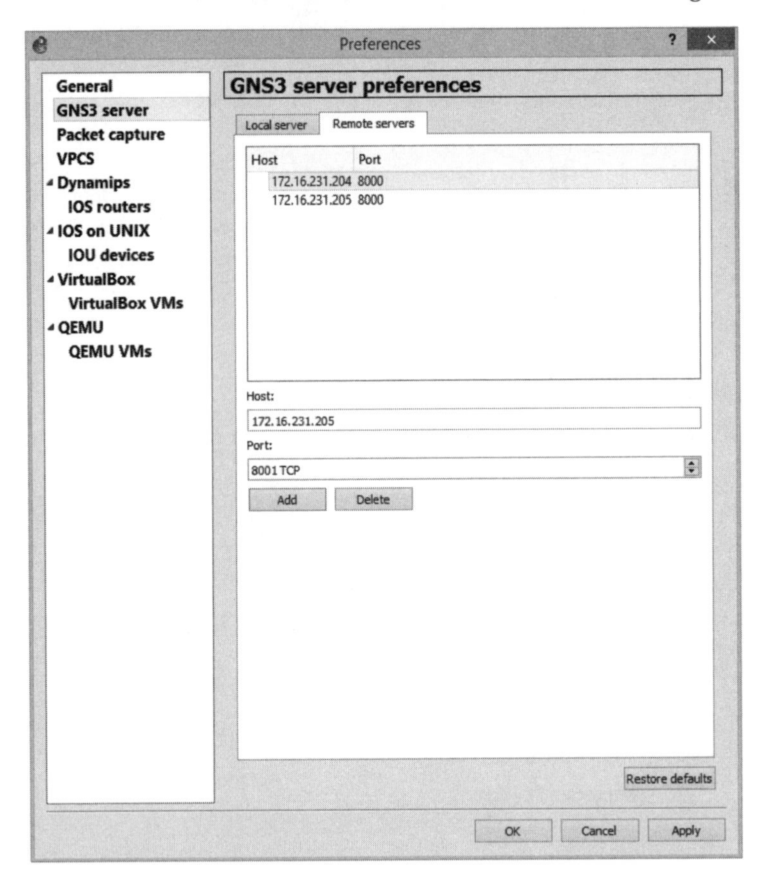

Figure 10-12: Configuring the remote server IP on the client host

In the Host field, enter the IP address of the remote GNS3 server. In this example, that IP address is 172.16.231.205. The default port number should be 8000, but you can change it if you've chosen some other port number on the remote PC. After adding the remote server, click **Apply** to save the settings.

Next, select **Dynamips** from the side menu and click the **General settings** tab, as shown in Figure 10-13.

Uncheck the **Use the local server** setting and click **Apply**. This ensures that you have the option to select a remote server when you configure a Dynamips router. Next, click **IOS routers**, as shown in Figure 10-14.

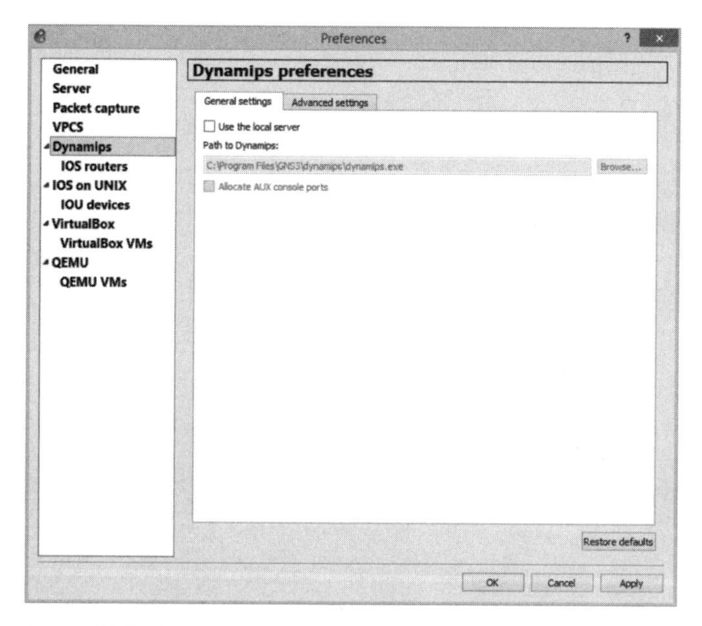

Figure 10-13: Dynamips server settings

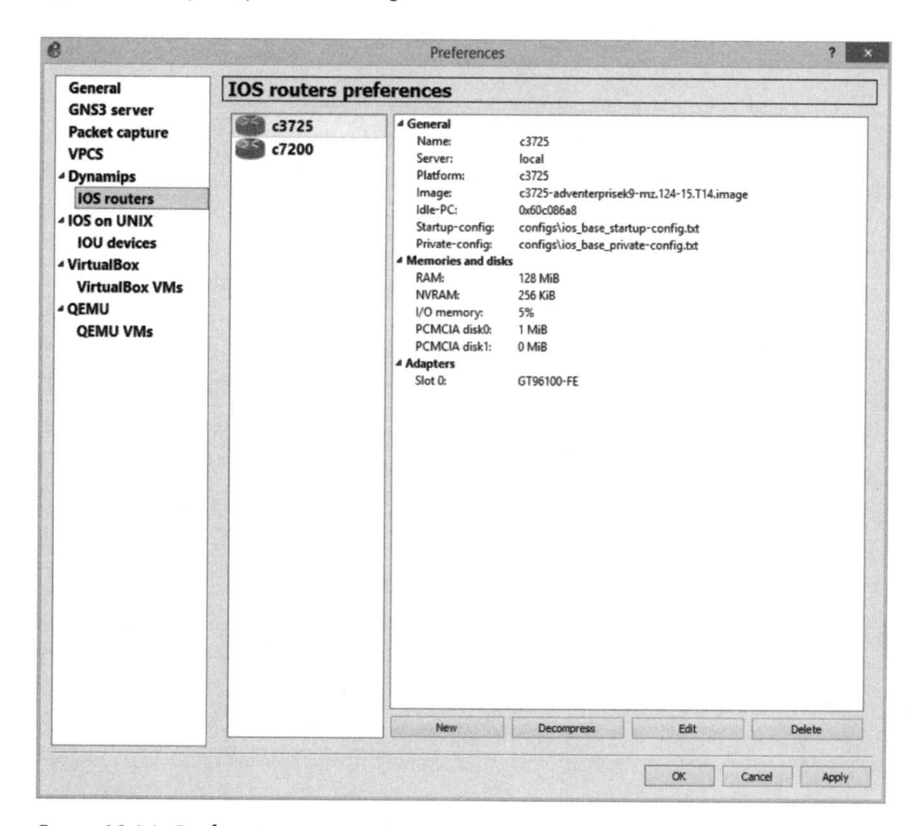

Figure 10-14: Configuring a remote Dynamips router

Click **New** to add a remote IOS router to your client PC, as shown in Figure 10-15.

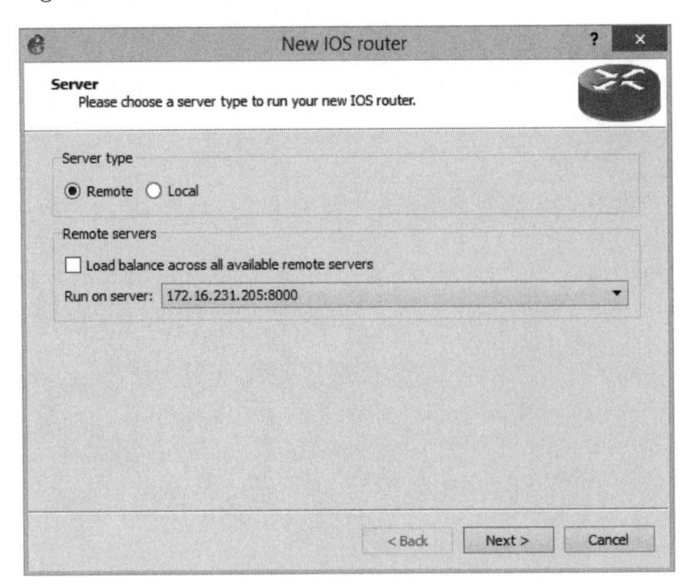

Figure 10-15: Selecting the Remote server type

Under Server type, select **Remote** and uncheck **Load balance across all available remote servers**. Click the **Run on Server** drop-down menu, select your remote server's IP address from the list, and click **Next** to continue. Enter the path and IOS image name that you recorded from the remote server, as shown in Figure 10-16.

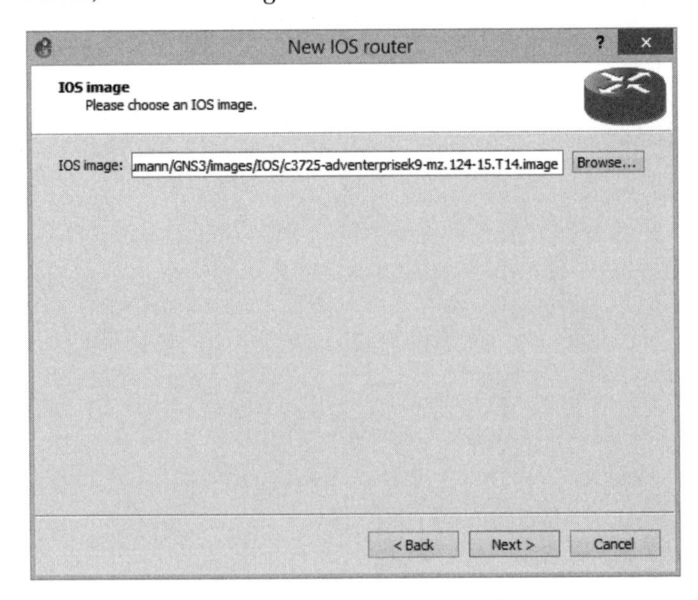

Figure 10-16: Entering the remote IOS image path

After entering the path and filename, click **Next** to continue. Enter a name in the Name field for your router, as shown in Figure 10-17.

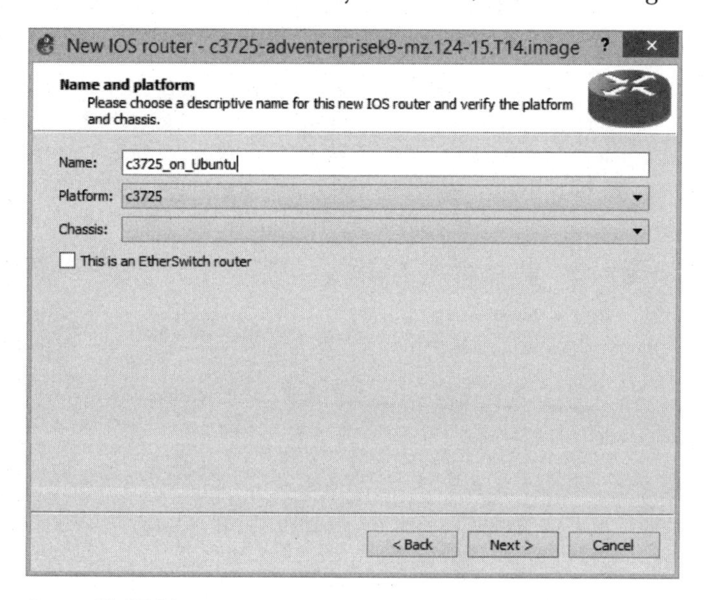

Figure 10-17: Naming your router

I've named my router *c3725_on_Ubuntu* so that I can easily identify the router in the Devices toolbar, and I know from the name that it's configured to run on a remote server.

At this point, you can click through the remaining options as if you're configuring a local Dynamips router. Be sure to enter an Idle-PC value when asked, or calculate one if you haven't already done so. Remember, Idle-PC values are calculated on a per-image basis, so the same value can be used on any PC that's using the same IOS image file.

When you're finished adding the router, it should be displayed in the Routers section of the Devices toolbar, as shown in Figure 10-18.

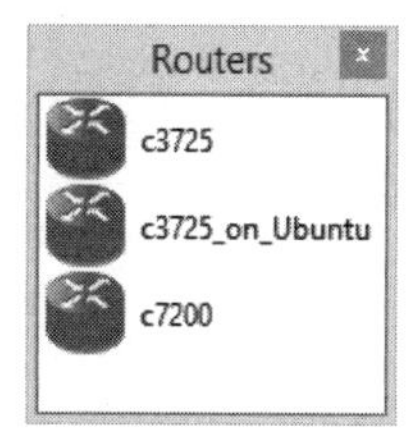

Figure 10-18: Routers section of the Devices toolbar

This example has two c3725 routers; one is a local router installed on the Windows PC, and the other is installed on the remote Ubuntu server. When you create a project, you can use both routers in the same project, reducing the CPU and memory consumption on the client PC by half.

Now that you know how to set up GNS3 using multiple PCs, you can leverage the ability to create large GNS3 projects.

RUNNING QEMU ON A REMOTE SERVER

In addition to running IOU and IOS routers on a remote server, you can also run QEMU on a remote server. Just be sure to install QEMU on the server PC before you begin. The process of setting up a remote QEMU device on the client PC is almost the same as any other remote device. However, during the New QEMU VM wizard, you will need to select the QEMU binary file for the virtual machine, shown in Figure 10-19.

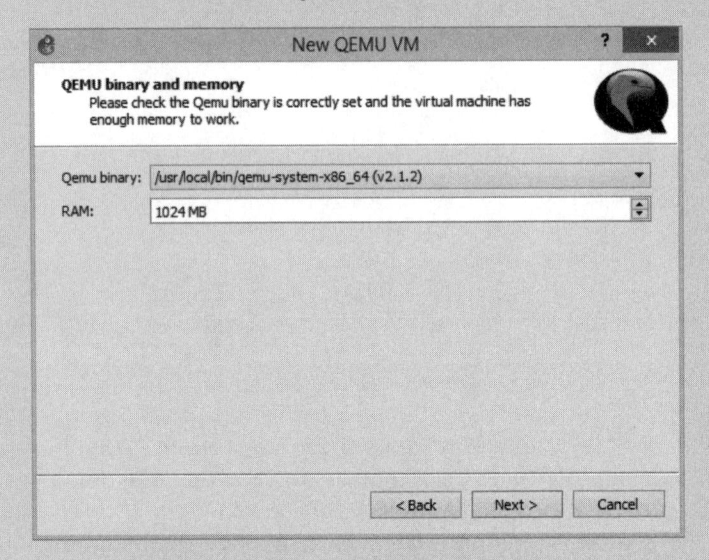

Figure 10-19: Configuring the QEMU binary

GNS3 should query the remote server for a list of installed QEMU binary files, and the virtual machine that you create should run on the remote server using the binary file that you select. Use the drop-down menu to select a binary file for your virtual machine, usually *qemu-system-i386* or *qemu-system-x86_64*. Adjust the RAM size and click **Next**. Configure the remaining options as if the virtual machine were a local device.

Creating a GNS3 Uberlab

GNS3 is all about scalability, and you can use it to create really large projects with dozens of switches and routers. One of the best ways to create an uberlab is to use multiple GNS3 servers. But what if you have one really fast computer and a few others that don't perform as well? In that case, you may want to run more devices on one machine than the other. For example, you might run most of your routers on the high-end server and run fewer devices on the less powerful machines.

An uberlab doesn't need to be confined to computers running on your local area network. If you're using GNS3 on a corporate network with multiple sites connected by a VPN, you can use the client/server model to run a variety of hypervisors from across town or even across the country! All you have to do is start the `gns3server` application on a remote computer (over the VPN) and configure your local client using the IP address of the remote PC. The only difference between this and a regular client/server setup is that packets will be sent through the VPN to the remote server.

Nerdy Labs for Fun and Profit

You've explored the tools you need to configure all sorts of projects in GNS3, but what should you do with this newfound knowledge? You could study for certifications or just have some fun! In this section, I discuss both. Many of these projects are intended for advanced users, but feel free to modify them to create projects and challenges that are better suited for your skill level.

Preparing for Cisco Exams

GNS3 is an amazing tool for education and certification, and it has everything you need to get Juniper or Cisco certified, starting at the entry-level JNCIA or CCNA all the way up to the crown jewel of Cisco certifications, the CCIE.

For entry-level exams such as CCNA or CCNP, start by searching online to find all sorts of network examples. You may even want to use the CBT Nuggets or Bryant Advantage videos with GNS3. Their videos are a good way to get started, and GNS3 is a great tool for experimenting with the concepts they introduce. If you're studying for CCIE, you may want to use something like the INE workbooks (*http://www.ine.com/*). They've proven themselves as leaders in CCIE lab preparation.

Securing Your Networks

These days, just about everyone stores confidential information on some sort of network server, so having a secure network infrastructure isn't just a good idea, it's a way of preventing substantial financial losses, unwanted lawsuits, and entanglements with your firm's errors and omissions (E&O) insurance carrier.

In this section, I outline a few security-related challenges that can be fun and educational, and prevent data theft or loss.

The "Hack My Rack" Challenge

Host a security competition with your friends! Each challenger creates a GNS3 project on their PC and applies as much security as they can to their devices. The challenge is for each user to crack the other users' security.

After each user creates their own network on their PC, they're allowed to install one VirtualBox virtual machine on their friend's PC with any system-cracking tools they want to use. When the challengers are done creating their networks, they swap computers and start the clock. Now the Battle Royale begins! Use your VirtualBox virtual machine to crack into another challenger's GNS3 network.

Creating Cisco VPNs

Create a Cisco site-to-site VPN or multisite VPN using Cisco routers and ASA devices. Try your hand at configuring a multihomed Cisco router with VPN failover. In this scenario, your WAN edge routers might have two or more interfaces configured with BGP to simulate WAN links to an Internet service provider. Someday you may want one of your own, or a client might need one. Learning how to do it in GNS3 is better than figuring it out on your client's time!

Practicing Real-World Scenarios

The following project ideas are designed to get you thinking about life outside of the GNS3 sandbox. As a network administrator or engineer, you'll need to understand the interworkings of multihomed networks, switch block design, and multiserver integration, just to name a few. Designing, running, and troubleshooting these types of networks in GNS3 is great preparation for the real world.

Cisco Switch Block Design

Understanding switching is an important part of managing networks. Although the GNS3 EtherSwitch router and IOU have restricted functionality, they're useful for configuring and testing redundant switch blocks with protocols such as HSRP, VRRP, and GLBP. Try your hand at creating a fully redundant Cisco campus model switch block with Internet access.

Multihomed Networks

Although many small businesses connect to the Internet using a single static IP address, larger companies need more static IPs and BGP links to maintain their presence on the Internet. Using a few GNS3 routers and BGP, you can simulate a multihomed network connected to multiple Internet service providers. Add additional routers to your bogus ISP to simulate sites such as *http://www.google.com/* or *http://www.gns3.com/*. Then ping the bogus sites from your multihomed network.

Multiple Vendor Integration

Create a project using Cisco, Juniper, Arista, Linux, or any other routable device you can think of. Configure the devices using open standards such as RIP, OSPF, BGP, or other open standards that are supported by all the vendors or use route redistribution to translate routes from one vendor device to another. The idea is to learn as much as you can about multi-vendor integration.

Use Everything, Including the "Kitchen Sink"

This project involves *everything*! It's simple: build the biggest, most badass project you can imagine. Use as many remote PCs as you can and run everything GNS3 has to offer: Cisco routers, switches, ASAs, IDSs/IPSs, Juniper, Firefly, Vyatta, Arista, and anything else you can think of. Apply every routing and switching protocol, and test end-to-end connectivity using `ping` or `traceroute`. Be sure to set up at least one ATM switch, a Frame Relay cloud, and a VPN or two.

How Many Routers Does It Take to Blow Out a Lightbulb?

Here's a fun way to earn bragging rights. Challenge a friend to see whose PC can run the most routers in GNS3. With the right Idle-PC value, you may find that you can run more than 100 before Dynamips crashes or GNS3 starts to slow down too much to use. One trick is to run GNS3 on Linux because Dynamips seems to scale better on Linux than it does on Windows or OS X.

Routers Gone Rogue

This "fly in the ointment" challenge is another way to have fun with a friend. Each challenger builds a complex network using as many routers as they want. The more the better! The networks are then configured and thoroughly tested. Once both challengers are happy that their networks are running properly, they swap computers and break each other's networks by changing a few configuration settings (dropping a fly in the ointment).

A break could be as simple as shutting down an interface or as complex as filtering BGP routes. It all depends on the skills of the individuals and the complexity of their networks. Once the networks are broken, the competitors swap computers again, and each tries to be the first to analyze and repair their original network.

Final Thoughts

A virtual Cisco access server takes some work to set up, but once configured, it's an easy way to manage your devices. If you have a small project that uses only a few routers, then it may not be necessary. But if you have to manage a few dozen devices, it quickly becomes an invaluable tool.

GNS3 runs on multiple PC operating systems, but you're not stuck with the one you're currently using. Moving projects between systems is fairly straightforward, so don't be afraid to try something new. GNS3 was designed using Linux and ported to Windows and OS X, so it runs great on Linux and generally uses fewer resources than it does running on Windows.

If you don't have the newest PC hardware, you can load-balance hypervisors across multiple PCs and create large projects that run better than they will on a single PC. This is also a great way to repurpose those old PCs you have lying around your home or office.

But the most important thing to remember about GNS3 is that it's fun to use because you get to create networks that otherwise may be out of your reach. So be creative, and have fun!

HELP! I'VE FALLEN AND I CAN'T GET UP

GNS3 is a complex program, and like anything complex, it will occasionally behave in unexpected ways. I've already included troubleshooting tips throughout the book, so in this appendix I won't provide a lot of break-fix information. Instead, I will provide you with basic strategies for solving problems, and I'll cover a few common problems and possible solutions.

Identifying the Problem

GNS3 problems broadly fall into two categories.

Sudden Problems Problems that occur with a previously working project.

Feature Problems Problems that occur when implementing a new feature.

Sudden problems appear out of nowhere. Your project may have been running fine for weeks, and then all of a sudden it won't open, or when it does open, devices refuse to start. Feature problems typically occur when creating a new project or implementing a new feature in an existing project. Both problem types can be frustrating, and if you use GNS3 for any length of time, you're likely to encounter at least one of them.

Sudden Problems

When a project has been running well and suddenly develops a problem, it usually indicates that something has changed. Something could have changed on your PC, within GNS3, or in the project itself. For GNS3's part, it could be that you inadvertently changed a setting or made changes to a helper application such as Dynamips, QEMU, or VirtualBox. It could also mean that you upgraded to a problematic version of GNS3. Whenever a new version of GNS3 is released, it's always a good idea to test it using a spare PC or virtual machine before you upgrade your production environment. This section provides tips to help correct a few sudden problems.

Stopping Dynamips Crashes

An unstable Dynamips program can result in lost connections to devices. In this case, you may see a GNS3 console error message indicating that Dynamips has stopped running, as shown in Figure A-1.

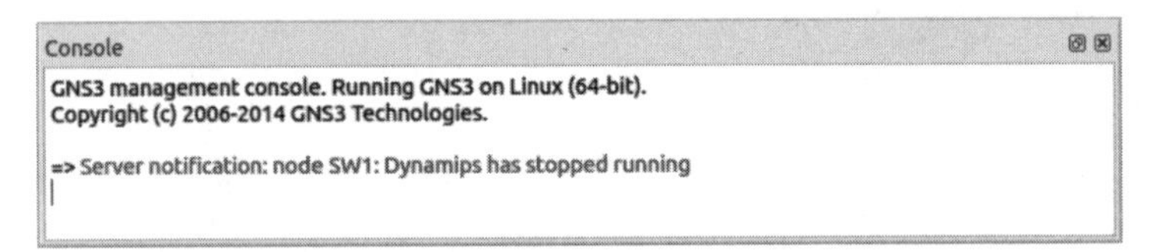

Figure A-1: Communication failure with Dynamips

This message may indicate that you're running software in your PC that conflicts with Dynamips, that you have an unstable Dynamips build, or that you don't have enough free PC resources, such as memory or CPU cycles. Try closing any nonessential applications, rebooting your PC, disabling all antivirus/antispam software, and disabling your firewall. If Dynamips continues to crash, you may have to re-install or restore Dynamips or GNS3 from a backup.

When IOS Images Fail to Load

Router memory is a common problem that can cause Dynamips routers to misbehave. When a router refuses to start, check the Cisco RAM requirements for the exact version of the IOS image you're using—you may have assigned it too much memory or not enough. To verify the requirements, visit the Cisco Feature Navigator website; browse to *http://tools.cisco.com/ITDIT/CFN/jsp/index.jsp*. From here, you can use the Search by Software feature to enter the details of your IOS, and the navigator will provide you with the requirements.

If the RAM setting of an IOS router is set too low, the router may either fail to start or crash upon starting, and the GNS3 Console window may display an error message, like the one shown in Figure A-2.

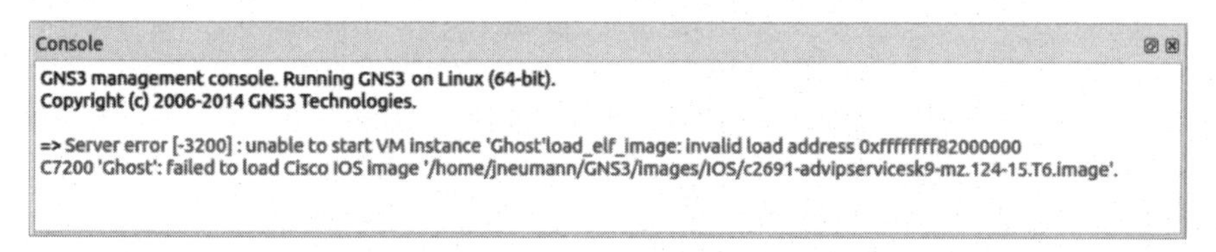

Figure A-2: Failed to load Cisco IOS image error message

In this case, you should reconfigure the router and assign it more memory. Right-click the router and select **Configure** to bring up the GNS3 Node Configurator. Choose your router name from the pane on the left and click the **Memories and disks** tab to display the RAM setting.

If you increase the memory and the router still refuses to start, you may have a corrupted IOS image file and should try a different one.

When you have a corrupt IOS image file, it may not display any error messages in the GNS3 Console window. Instead, the router console may be unresponsive or display information that may provide a clue about the problem, as in Figure A-3.

```
R1
        PC = 0x8024ed44, Cause = 0x0000000c, Status Reg = 0x34400002

                                                            *** TLB (Sto
re) Exception ***
                 PC = 0x8024ed44, Cause = 0x0000000c, Status Reg = 0x34400002

                                                                     ***
 TLB (Store) Exception ***
                          PC = 0x8024ed44, Cause = 0x0000000c, Status Reg = 0x34
400002

     *** TLB (Store) Exception ***
                                   PC = 0x8024ed44, Cause = 0x0000000c, Status R
eg = 0x34400002

              *** TLB (Store) Exception ***
                                            PC = 0x8024ed44, Cause = 0x0000000c,
 Status Reg = 0x34400002

                       *** TLB (Store) Exception ***
                                                     PC = 0x8024ed44, Cause = 0x
0000000c, Status Reg = 0x34400002

                                *** TLB (Store) Exception *
```

Figure A-3: IOS image fails to load

The console output shows that IOS is flinging exception errors at an alarming rate. This can indicate that the IOS image file is corrupt or that it's been misconfigured in GNS3. Verify and correct the image settings using the Cisco Feature Navigator or replace the image file if necessary.

Resolving IOS Memory Errors

Adding too much memory to a Dynamips router can prevent a router from booting properly. For instance, the maximum RAM handled by a c7200 with NPE-400 is 512MB. If you add more, say 1024MB, you may see an error message in the GNS3 Console window or the following message displayed in the router console:

```
Cisco IOS Software, 7200 Software (C7200-ADVENTERPRISEK9-M), Version 15.2(4)
S2, RELEASE SOFTWARE (fc1)
Technical Support: http://www.cisco.com/techsupport
Copyright (c) 1986-2012 by Cisco Systems, Inc.
Compiled Tue 11-Dec-12 13:32 by prod_rel_team

!!! WARNING - VM is not running, will be unresponsive (status=1) !!!
```

The router console message, `!!! WARNING - VM is not running, will be unresponsive (status=1) !!!`, is a clear indication that this router has crashed on startup. In this case, stop the device and check its configuration. The issue indicated here is that the device has been assigned too much memory. To correct the problem, reduce the amount of memory assigned to the device or replace the IOS image file with a different version.

Even when a router appears to run properly, you may encounter errors while configuring IOS. Here is an interesting situation where a router boots successfully even though it's low on memory but displays error messages while being configured:

```
R1(config-if)#ip nat inside
% NBAR ERROR: parsing stopped
% NBAR Error : Activation failed due to insufficient dynamic memory
% NBAR Error: Stile could not add protocol node
%NAT: Error activating CNBAR on the interface Vlan1
R1(config-if)#
*Mar  1 00:00:57.127: %LINEPROTO-5-UPDOWN: Line protocol on Interface NVI0,
changed state to up
*Mar  1 00:00:57.251: %SYS-2-MALLOCFAIL: Memory allocation of 10260 bytes
failed from 0x62915CD4, alignment 0
Pool: Processor  Free: 18968  Cause: Memory fragmentation
Alternate Pool: None  Free: 0  Cause: No Alternate pool
 -Process= "Exec", ipl= 0, pid= 195,  -Traceback= 0x6148BFF8 0x60016604
0x6001C564 0x6001CBBC 0x636756E4 0x62915CDC 0x628F468C 0x628F88C4 0x628F5968
0x628F87A0 0x628F5968 0x628F8344 0x628F5968 0x628F5B2C 0x62928FBC 0x62933A20
R1(config-if)#
```

```
*Mar  1 00:00:57.275: %NBAR-2-NOMEMORY: No memory available for StILE lmalloc,
-Traceback= 0x6148BFF8 0x62915CF8 0x628F468C 0x628F88C4 0x628F5968 0x628F87A0
0x628F5968 0x628F8344 0x628F5968 0x628F5B2C 0x62928FBC 0x62933A20 0x62920BD0
0x6293DF70 0x6293E2F0 0x61C77C70
R1(config-if)#
```

In this example, router R1 was running fine until I attempted to configure network address translation. Because this router is low on memory, Cisco IOS immediately displays memory allocation error messages. Assigning more memory to the router in GNS3 should correct the problem.

Resolving NIO Errors

NIO errors occur most often when you're attempting to link a GNS3 device to a physical Ethernet adapter in your PC using the Cloud node. If you're having trouble linking devices to each other or to a Cloud node or if you receive an NIO error message like the one shown in Figure A-4, you may have a permissions problem.

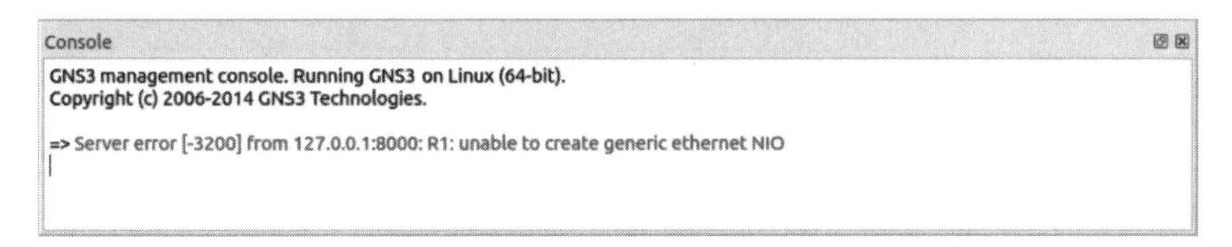

Figure A-4: Unable to create generic Ethernet NIO error message

In this case, you may need to assign yourself elevated privileges. If you're running GNS3 on Windows, launch GNS3 using the administrator account: right-click the GNS3 icon, and select **Run as Administrator**. If you're using OS X, you may need to assign ownership permissions to the */dev/tap* or */dev/bpf* device files, as in the following example:

```
$ sudo chown $(id -un):$(id -gn) /dev/bpf*
$ sudo chown $(id -un):$(id -gn) /dev/tap*
```

These commands will assign the currently logged-in user's user ID to the device files, allowing your user account to use the files while running GNS3. You will have to set these permissions each time you reboot your Mac because OS X resets all device file permissions at startup.

For a high degree of security, use the setcap command to elevate the capabilities of the *dynamips* file. On Ubuntu, you may need to install libcap2 before entering the setcap command.

```
$ sudo apt-get install libcap2
$ sudo setcap cap_net_raw,cap_net_admin+eip /usr/local/bin/dynamips
```

LINUX SECURITY CONSIDERATIONS

If you're running Linux, you may need to run Dynamips with elevated permissions. For this, there are two methods to choose from depending on your Linux distribution.

You can use the Linux chown and chmod commands, or you can use the setcap command. Both methods should resolve a permissions issue, but the chmod/chown method is less secure because it gives the Dynamips application the ability to run with full root-level permissions. If malicious code were to get into Dynamips, your entire Linux security could be compromised. The Linux setcap command allows you to assign root-like capabilities to a file, without actually giving the file root-level permissions. This gives Dynamips the permissions it needs, without compromising Linux security by over-subscribing root-level permissions. Therefore, it's the preferred method to fix GNS3 NIO errors.

Unfortunately, setcap is not available across all Linux platforms, but it is supported on Ubuntu and most Debian-based systems.

If you're unable to use the setcap command, instead use the chown and chmod commands to elevate Dynamips with root-level privileges.

```
$ sudo chown root /usr/local/bin/dynamips
$ sudo chmod 4755 /usr/local/bin/dynamips
```

If you're unable to connect an IOU device to a physical adapter or a virtual TAP adapter on Linux, try applying the setcap commands to the iouyap application. This works because iouyap is the GNS3 software that bridges IOU devices to other GNS3 devices, as well as virtual and physical interfaces. Here, you give iouyap the same elevated capabilities that you just gave Dynamips:

```
$ sudo setcap cap_net_raw,cap_net_admin+eip /usr/local/bin/iouyap
```

Another possible NIO problem is the method you choose for connecting GNS3 to your physical Ethernet adapter. This is especially true on Windows PCs. If you're using Windows 7, when attempting to connect GNS3 to the Internet, create a bridge using your physical Ethernet adapter and a loopback adapter (described in "Connecting GNS3 Devices to the Internet" on page 120). If you're running Windows 8, you may get better results if you connect the Cloud node directly to your physical Ethernet adapter or use Internet Connection Sharing.

Correcting Console Problems

Console problems could prevent a console from opening, cause it to open and immediately close, or cause it to act sluggish or unresponsive when configuring a device. There are a number of reasons why a console connection might misbehave. Most often the problem occurs because of improperly configured settings in GNS3, such as QEMU device settings or VirtualBox settings, but it could also be a problem with a device image, such as a corrupt IOU or ASA image file.

When a console won't open, first check the GNS3 Console Application preference. Open **Preferences**, select **General** from the pane on the left, click the **Console Applications** tab, and make sure the terminal type listed under Preconfigured terminal commands matches your operating system's terminal program. If not, use the drop-down menu to select your terminal; then click **Set**, **Apply**, and **OK** to save the configuration.

If you find that you are immediately disconnected after you open a console, then your firewall may be blocking the network connection from the console application to your GNS3 device. If the device is a QEMU device, the problem is often related to the QEMU virtual machine itself or its configuration. First, verify that you've assigned the correct amount of memory to the QEMU virtual machine. You can visit the GNS3 Jungle forums or a third-party vendor website to verify the requirements for the device. If the memory allocation is correct and the problem persists, check the QEMU virtual machine device properties. Go to **Preferences** and select **QEMU VMs** from the pane on the left. Select your QEMU device from the list, click **Edit**, and click the **Advanced settings** tab. Verify that the options under Additional Settings are correct. If they're not, fix the entry and try again.

Similarly, you can troubleshoot your VirtualBox virtual machines by examining the virtual machine's settings. Go to **Preferences** and select **VirtualBox VMs** from the pane on the left. Select your VirtualBox device from the list, click **Edit**, and click the **General settings** tab. Verify the Enable Remote Console and Start VM in Headless Mode options are configured correctly for your VirtualBox virtual machine.

If your console is sluggish when you start a Dynamips router, the router may not have been assigned an optimal Idle-PC value. A poorly chosen Idle-PC value can be just as devastating on your CPU as having no value set at all. To verify or set your Idle-PC value, right-click the router, select **Configure** to open the Node Configurator, and check your Idle-PC value on the **Advanced** tab. If the router has been assigned an Idle-PC value and the device is consuming a lot of CPU, then you may need to recalculate the value. (See "Setting a Manual Idle-PC Value" on page 28.)

Your console may also be sluggish if you've changed any of the Dynamips advanced optimization settings, such as Idlemax or Idlesleep. Idlemax and Idlesleep are used in conjunction with the Idle-PC value; Idlemax determines how often to sleep while executing idle loops in the router code, and the Idlesleep value determines how long to sleep. Try resetting them to their default values by clicking the **Reset** button, as shown in Figure A-5.

The GNS3 development team has determined that the default values of Idlemax and Idlesleep are optimal for most users, but you may be able to squeeze out a little better CPU performance by altering them as described in "Conserving Resources" on page 214.

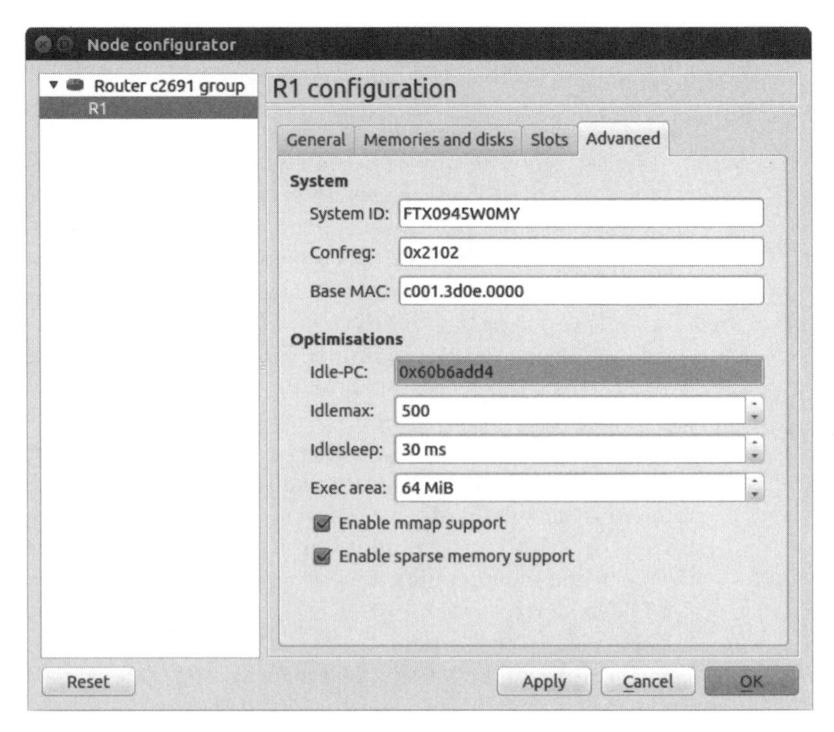

Figure A-5: Advanced router configuration

If the sluggish console is an IOU device and you're using the IOU virtual machine (required for Windows and OS X), try assigning more memory to the IOU virtual machine in VirtualBox.

Feature Problems

Feature problems occur when you try to implement a feature of GNS3 that you haven't used before, and they usually result from some sort of user error. GNS3 has a lot of features and options, and projects can get complicated rather quickly, particularly when you run GNS3 using multiple PCs or when you add QEMU and VirtualBox virtual machines to your projects. Feature problems may also lie within the configuration of your devices.

Configuration Issues

If you're experiencing a network routing problem inside a project, it may be that you've made a mistake configuring your device's network operating system; after all, GNS3 is a learning tool, and you're going to make mistakes along the way. When configuring features using operating systems such as Arista, IOS, and Junos OS, it's easy to make a mistake that could break your network. Check your device configurations and make sure you haven't assigned the wrong subnet mask to an IP address or forgotten to bring up an interface. One way to prevent these sorts of problems is to configure your GNS3 project devices just as you would an actual network. Start with a few devices, configure and test them, and then keep adding and testing devices until you've created a fully functional project.

Using Unsupported IOS Images

In short, don't try to use unsupported images. Dynamips supports a limited number of Cisco routers (see Appendix B for a complete list). If you see an unsupported image error, as shown in Figure A-6, when attempting to install an image file, it's because the image file is not supported by GNS3.

Figure A-6: Unsupported IOS image error

In Figure A-6, I tried to use an image file from a Cisco c850 router platform not supported by GNS3. The only option when you see this error message is to discard the file and replace it with one that is supported by GNS3.

The Nuclear Option

If you continue to encounter problems with GNS3 after trying the actions discussed so far, you can take the nuclear option as a last resort and clear the GNS3 settings file. Once you nuke the file, you'll lose all of your GNS3 settings, and you'll have to reconfigure GNS3 as though it's a newly installed system.

NOTE *None of your saved projects should be affected by clearing the GNS3 settings file, nor should VirtualBox or QEMU devices in those projects.*

Before you begin, back up your existing configuration file. This will give you the option of returning to the old settings if you need to do so. Go to **Preferences** and choose the **General** preference; then, in the new window select the **General** tab, as shown in Figure A-7.

The GNS3 settings file is displayed under Configuration file ❶. To back up the file, click the **Export** ❸ button. Choose a name and a location to save the file. Note the location of the original file (in this example, it's */home/jneumann/.config/GNS3/gns3_gui.conf*), and once the export is complete, close GNS3 and delete or rename this original file. Now when you reopen GNS3, all the preferences will be cleared as though you have installed it for the first time. If you decide that clearing the file was a mistake, you can use **Import** ❷ to reinstate the original GNS3 settings file.

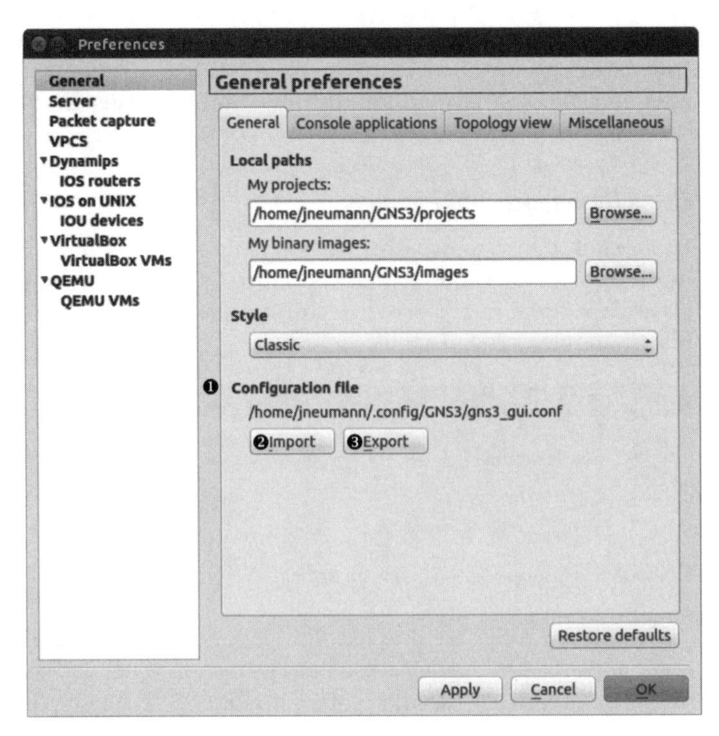

Figure A-7: Exporting and clearing the GNS3 configuration file

NOTE *On rare occasions, the GNS3 settings file can become corrupted. Keep a current backup of your* GNS3 settings *file at all times so you can revert to a working version if needed.*

Overburdened Hardware

When GNS3 is running slow and devices are crashing, it may be a clue that you're overburdening your PC's processor with too many devices; this will certainly slow down console response and can cause Dynamips to crash. If that's the case, consider trimming down your project, upgrading your PC, or using multiple PCs with GNS3. A great way to create large projects without overworking your CPU is to load share your hypervisors across multiple PCs, as described in "Creating Projects Using Multiple PCs" on page 191.

Resolving Port Number Conflicts

At some point, other software on your computer will probably conflict with GNS3. This often happens when the software is using a port number that GNS3 needs. If the port number used is the same as your GNS3 server application, GNS3 will load, but the server should select another port number.

When this happens, investigate the problem using the `netstat` command, which should be included on both Windows and Unix-based systems such as Linux and OS X.

```
$ netstat -an|more

Active Internet connections (servers and established)
Proto Recv-Q Send-Q Local Address           Foreign Address         State
tcp        0      0 127.0.1.1:53            0.0.0.0:*               LISTEN
tcp        0      0 127.0.0.1:631           0.0.0.0:*               LISTEN
tcp        0      0 0.0.0.0:8000            0.0.0.0:*               LISTEN
tcp        0      0 127.0.0.1:39191         127.0.0.1:8000❶         TIME_WAIT
tcp6       0      0 ::1:631                 :::*                    LISTEN
tcp6       1      0 ::1:53974               ::1:631                 CLOSE_WAIT
udp        0      0 0.0.0.0:59759           0.0.0.0:*
udp        0      0 0.0.0.0:39309           0.0.0.0:*
udp        0      0 127.0.1.1:53            0.0.0.0:*
udp        0      0 0.0.0.0:68              0.0.0.0:*
udp        0      0 0.0.0.0:631             0.0.0.0:*
udp        0      0 0.0.0.0:5353            0.0.0.0:*
udp6       0      0 :::57463                :::*
udp6       0      0 :::45876                :::*
udp6       0      0 :::5353                 :::*
```

TCP port number 8000 ❶ is the default port number reserved for the GNS3 server program, but the `netstat` output shows that another application is using this port. To solve this problem, find the offending application and close it or change the default port number used by GNS3. To change the port number, go to **Preferences ▸ Servers ▸ Local Server Port** and set the port number to something other than 8000, such as 8001.

Troubleshooting an ASA

When you install an ASA in GNS3, make sure you select **ASA 8.4(2)** from the **Type** drop-down menu during the installation wizard. The GNS3 wizard should then autofill the required fields with the correct information.

If your ASA is configured correctly but it locks up or runs poorly, the ASA may be causing high CPU usage, which in turn causes your PC's overall performance to suffer. You can greatly reduce the CPU usage by adjusting the CPU limit percentage for your ASA. Go to **Preferences**, select your ASA, click **Edit**, and enable **CPU throttling**. Be careful, though, because limiting the ASA CPU usage too much can also cause an ASA to become unresponsive. For the best results, try adjusting the setting until you find a sweet spot that reduces CPU usage without negatively impacting performance.

Conserving Resources

On the whole, GNS3 does a good job of handling projects of almost any size, provided you have the proper hardware resources, but the larger your project becomes, the more likely you are to encounter problems. The best way to avoid these problems is to take a minimalist approach when creating a project and avoid adding unnecessary complexity to your designs.

Select Devices Carefully

In GNS3, always choose devices that use the least amount of RAM and CPU consumption. For example, avoid using a c7200 router, which requires 512MB of RAM, if you can get by using a c3700 router that uses only 128MB. When using Dynamips devices, use the same device model for all routers in your project; GNS3 can then share resources between them. Using several different router models can lead to resource consumption and poor performance. You can also use emulated devices, such as the Ethernet switch node rather than an EtherSwitch router, to conserve both memory and processor.

Optimize Idle-PC Values

To reduce system resource usage, fine-tune your Idle-PC values. Your current values may be fine when you're running a small number of IOS devices, but larger projects will benefit from more optimized values.

To find the best values for you, first put your computer in a mostly idle state: restart it and close all programs, including antivirus software. If you're using Windows, close as many applications from the system tray as you can. When you're ready, add a router to your workspace, start it, right-click the router, and choose **Idle-PC** to begin calculating Idle-PC values. During the process, carefully monitor your CPU after applying each new value, and record all the values. Look for the one that uses the least resources, and when you find it, apply it to the device.

Backing Up Your Projects

Backing up your GNS3 projects is important, especially as they grow more complex and take more time to create. No one likes to lose the work they've spent hours creating! You can either back up the entire GNS3 folder, back up your projects folder, or back up individual project folders.

Regularly backing up the entire GNS3 folder is the best way to ensure you always have a current copy of all projects and images, but it can be time-consuming and may require a fair amount of disk space.

If you're short on time or resources, at least back up individual projects from the projects folder. Make sure you still have a backup copy of your entire GNS3 folder and then update the full GNS3 backup by copying individual projects to the backup as needed. The disadvantage to this approach is that it relies on you remembering to copy new or updated projects every time you update your backup, and you may forget to back up an important project. I know from experience that discovering you've just lost all the work that you put into a complex project can be a sobering revelation.

I suggest a complete backup strategy, as well as backing up individual projects as you create them. You could create large projects in phases and test each component along the way and, once you have a group of components working properly, back up the project. Then, repeat this procedure until the project is fully configured and your network is functional. Employing GNS3 snapshots while creating complex projects can also be helpful: if you make a mistake, just revert to a working state by restoring a snapshot (refer to "Using the GNS3 Toolbar" on page 34). But no matter which backup strategy you choose, the simplest way to store your backup project files is by copying the entire project folder to a large thumb drive or external hard disk.

Welcome to the Jungle

When a problem is too great for you to figure out on your own, don't be afraid to ask for help. The GNS3 website (*http://www.gns3.com/*) provides a plethora of information and houses a dedicated forum, called the *GNS3 Jungle*. Here you can report problems, ask questions, and help other users with their questions. To access the GNS3 Jungle, go to the GNS3 site and select **Community**.

Before posting a question, search the site to see whether your question has already been asked and answered. The GNS3 Jungle has an extremely active member base, so questions generally receive quick responses. If you do post a question and it doesn't receive an answer as quickly as you'd like, please don't repost it or reply to your own post to bump it up the list. Posting the same question multiple times will only confuse the people trying to help. Usually when a question goes unanswered, it's because no one currently viewing the forum has the answer. Be patient, and someone should respond in due time.

When asking a question, I recommend providing the following information:

- GNS3 version
- Name and version of your operating system
- Platform specifics (32-bit or 64-bit, processor, and RAM)
- A clear description of the problem
- A screenshot of error messages (if applicable)
- A screenshot of preference settings (if applicable)
- Topology (if applicable)
- Device configurations (if applicable)

Detailed information helps your fellow GNS3 users determine your problem and return a solution more quickly.

Final Thoughts

Although GNS3 generally runs well, problems do crop up from time to time. In this appendix, you looked at some common problems and basic troubleshooting strategies for correcting those problems.

You learned that firewalls, antivirus software, and occasionally a TCP/IP-based application can wreak havoc on GNS3. When in doubt, disable your firewall, disable your antivirus software, and close any unnecessary programs before launching GNS3.

You also learned that often the fastest way to fix a broken project is to restore the project from a backup. You should always keep a current backup copy of the entire GNS3 folder and your GNS3 settings file. Restoring data from a backup is the surest way to get up and running after a disaster.

B

CISCO HARDWARE COMPATIBLE WITH GNS3

This appendix lists the Cisco hardware that's supported by Dynamips and GNS3. Dynamips only emulates Cisco routers that use MIPS architecture and does not support all Cisco models. After the list of supported routers, you'll find a list of recommended IOS image files that GNS3 can automatically apply the correct Idle-PC values to, without performing an Idle-PC calculation.

Supported Cisco Hardware

In GNS3, you can emulate Cisco routers from five different series (1700, 2600, 3600, 3700, and 7200), with varying degrees of feature support.

Table B-1: 1700 Series Routers

Model	Slots	WIC	Card Support
1720, 1721, 1750, and 1751	One (none available) CISCO1710-MB-1FE-1E in Slot 1 provides one Fast Ethernet: F0	None	None
1760	One (none available) C1700-MB-1ETH in Slot 1 provides one Fast Ethernet port: F0	Two	WIC-1T (1 serial port) WIC-2T (2 serial ports) WIC-1ENET (1 Ethernet port)

Table B-2: 2600 Series Routers

Model	NM Slots	WIC	Card Support
2610	One (one available) CISCO2600-MB-1E in Slot 1 provides one Ethernet port: F0/0	Two	NM-1FE-TX (1 Fast Ethernet port) NM-1E (1 Ethernet port) NM-4E (4 Ethernet ports) NM-16ESW (16 port switch) WIC-1T (1 serial port) WIC-2T (2 serial ports)
2611	Two (one available) CISCO2600-MB-2E in Slot 1 provides two Ethernet ports: F0/0 and F0/1	Two	NM-1FE-TX (1 Fast Ethernet port) NM-1E (1 Ethernet port) NM-4E (4 Ethernet ports) NM-16ESW (16 port switch) WIC-1T (1 serial port) WIC-2T (2 serial ports)
2620	Two (one available) CISCO2600-MB-1FE in Slot 1 provides one Fast Ethernet port: F0/0	Two	NM-1FE-TX (1 Fast Ethernet port) NM-1E (1 Ethernet port) NM-4E (4 Ethernet ports) NM-16ESW (16 port switch) WIC-1T (1 serial port) WIC-2T (2 serial ports)
2621	Two (one available) CISCO2600-MB-2FE in Slot 1 provides two Fast Ethernet ports: F0/0 and F0/1	Two	NM-1FE-TX (1 Fast Ethernet port) NM-1E (1 Ethernet port) NM-4E (4 Ethernet ports) NM-16ESW (16 port switch) WIC-1T (1 serial port) WIC-2T (2 serial ports)
2610XM	Two (one available) CISCO2600-MB-1FE in Slot 1 provides one Fast Ethernet port: F0/0	Two	NM-1FE-TX (1 Fast Ethernet port) NM-1E (1 Ethernet port) NM-4E (4 Ethernet ports) NM-16ESW (16 port switch) WIC-1T (1 serial port) WIC-2T (2 serial ports)
2611XM	Two (one available) CISCO2600-MB-2FE in Slot 1 provides two Fast Ethernet ports: F0/0 and F0/1	Two	NM-1FE-TX (1 Fast Ethernet port) NM-1E (1 Ethernet port) NM-4E (4 Ethernet ports) NM-16ESW (16 port switch) WIC-1T (1 serial port) WIC-2T (2 serial ports)

Model	NM Slots	WIC	Card Support
2620XM	Two (one available) CISCO2600-MB-1FE in Slot 1 provides one Fast Ethernet port: F0/0	Two	NM-1FE-TX (1 Fast Ethernet port) NM-1E (1 Ethernet port) NM-4E (4 Ethernet ports) NM-16ESW (16 port switch) WIC-1T (1 serial port) WIC-2T (2 serial ports)
2621XM	Two (one available) CISCO2600-MB-2FE in Slot 1 provides two Fast Ethernet ports: F0/0 and F0/1	Two	NM-1FE-TX (1 Fast Ethernet port) NM-1E (1 Ethernet port) NM-4E (4 Ethernet ports) NM-16ESW (16 port switch) WIC-1T (1 serial port) WIC-2T (2 serial ports)
2650XM	Two (one available) CISCO2600-MB-1FE in Slot 1 provides one Fast Ethernet port: F0/0	Two	NM-1FE-TX (1 Fast Ethernet port) NM-1E (1 Ethernet port) NM-4E (4 Ethernet ports) NM-16ESW (16 port switch) WIC-1T (1 serial port) WIC-2T (2 serial ports)
2651XM	Two (one available) GT96100-FE in Slot 1 provides one Fast Ethernet port: F0/0	Three	NM-1FE-TX (1 Fast Ethernet port) NM-1E (1 Ethernet port) NM-4E (4 Ethernet ports) NM-16ESW (16 port switch) WIC-1T (1 serial port) WIC-2T (2 serial ports)
2691	Two (one available) CISCO2600-MB-2FE in Slot 1 provides two Fast Ethernet ports: F0/0 and F0/1	Two	NM-1FE-TX (1 Fast Ethernet port) NM-1E (1 Ethernet port) NM-4E (4 Ethernet ports) NM-16ESW (16 port switch) WIC-1T (1 serial port) WIC-2T (2 serial ports)

Table B-3: 3600 Series Routers

Model	NM Slots	WIC	Card Support
3620	Two (one available) CISCO2600-MB-2FE in Slot 1 provides two Fast Ethernet ports: F0/0 and F0/1	None	NM-1FE-TX (1 Fast Ethernet port) NM-1E (1 Ethernet port) NM-4E (4 Ethernet ports) NM-16ESW (16 port switch) NM-4T (4 serial ports)
3640	Four	None	NM-1FE-TX (1 Fast Ethernet port) NM-1E (1 Ethernet port) NM-4E (4 Ethernet ports) NM-16ESW (16 port switch) NM-4T (4 serial ports)
3640	Four	None	NM-1FE-TX (1 Fast Ethernet port) NM-1E (1 Ethernet port) NM-4E (4 Ethernet ports) NM-16ESW (16 port switch) NM-4T (4 serial ports)

Table B-4: 3700 Series Routers

Model	NM Slots	WIC	Card Support
3725	Three (two available) GT96100-FE in Slot 1 provides one Fast Ethernet port: F0/0	Three	NM-1FE-TX (1 Fast Ethernet port) NM-4T (4 serial ports) NM-16ESW (16 port switch) WIC-1T (1 serial port) WIC-2T (2 serial ports)
3745	Three (two available) GT96100-FE in Slot 1 provides one Fast Ethernet port: F0/0	Three	NM-1FE-TX (1 Fast Ethernet port) NM-4T (4 serial ports) NM-16ESW (16 port switch) WIC-1T (1 serial port) WIC-2T (2 serial ports)

Table B-5: 7200 Series Routers

Model	Slots	Chassis	NPE	Card Support
7206	Six	STD VXR	NPE-100 NPE-150 NPE-175 NPE-200 NPE-225 NPE-300 NPE-400 NPE-G2	C7200-IO-FE (1 Fast Ethernet port) C7200-IO-2FE (2 Fast Ethernet ports) C7200-IO-GE-E (1 Gigabit Ethernet port) PA-FE-TX (1 Fast Ethernet port) PA-2FE-TX (2 Fast Ethernet ports) PA-4E (4 Ethernet ports) PA-8E (8 Ethernet ports) PA-4T+ (4 serial ports) PA-8T (8 serial ports) PA-A1 (1 ATM port) PA-POS-OC3 (1 POS port) PA-GE (1 Gigabit Ethernet port)

IOS Compatibility

The following routers are no longer getting IOS updates from Cisco. The IOS filenames listed here are the recommended versions for GNS3, though older versions should work fine.

Table B-6: c1700 Series Routers

Version	Filename	MD5 Checksum	Minimum RAM
12.4.25d Mainline	c1700-adventerprisek9-mz.124-25d.bin	3ed8d56a8757771105a56070e4147716	128MB
12.4.15T14 Technology Train	c1700-adventerprisek9-mz.124-15.T14.bin	351190de8764263e85a2b50718f394fd	160MB

Table B-7: c2600 Series Routers

Version	Filename	MD5 Checksum	Minimum RAM
12.4.25d Mainline	c2600-adventerprisek9 -mz.124-25d.bin	8eca1f6fe57dfb3c3 cf3568c0e475853	128MB
12.4.15T14 Technology Train	c2600-adventerprisek9 -mz.124-15.T14.bin	12b8548b23e2ec593 652ae9310ac797f	256MB

Table B-8: c2691 Series Routers

Version	Filename	MD5 Checksum	Minimum RAM
12.4.25d Mainline	c2691-adventerprisek9 -mz.124-25d.bin	a8e1f5821d874565 95488d6221ce42e5	192MB
12.4.15T14 Technology Train	c2691-adventerprisek9 -mz.124-15.T14.bin	91388104d7276ad 09204e36d2dfcf52d	256MB

Table B-9: c3620 Series Routers

Version	Filename	MD5 Checksum	Minimum RAM
12.2.26c	c3620-a3jk8s-mz.122 -26c.bin	dd34b958ad362ef54 ba48b187f4c97b4	64MB

Table B-10: c3640 Series Routers

Version	Filename	MD5 Checksum	Minimum RAM
12.4.25d Mainline	c3640-a3js-mz.124-25d .bin	db9f63ca1b46d18f b835496bfffe608a	128MB

Table B-11: c3660 Series Routers

Version	Filename	MD5 Checksum	Minimum RAM
12.4.25d Mainline	c3660-a3jk9s-mz.124 -25d.bin	4ac7e947f13c189d 746149dc74992890	192MB
12.4.15T14 Technology Train	c3660-a3jk9s-mz .124-15.T14.bin	39950b7a563aa08 e94a168260409f1e6	256MB

Table B-12: c3725 Series Routers

Version	Filename	MD5 Checksum	Minimum RAM
12.4.25d Mainline	c3725-adventerprisek9 -mz.124-25d.bin	ac3d313d3caff5be eee244b81d2c024c	128MB
12.4.15T14 Technology Train	c3725-adventerprisek9 -mz.124-15.T14.bin	42baf17af10d9a147 1bf542f0bfd07c7	256MB

Table B-13: c3745 Series Routers

Version	Filename	MD5 Checksum	Minimum RAM
12.4.25d Mainline	c3745-adventerprisek9 -mz.124-25d.bin	563797308a3036337 c3dee9b4ab54649	256MB
12.4.15T14 Technology Train	c3745-adventerprisek9 -mz.124-15.T14.bin	a696619869a972ec3a 27742d38031b6a	256MB

The Cisco c7200 series router continues to receive IOS updates from Cisco and supports version 15.*x* of IOS.

Table B-14: c7200 Series Routers

Version	Filename	MD5 Checksum	Minimum RAM
12.4.25g Mainline	c7200-a3jk9s-mz.124 -25g.bin	3a78cb61831b3ef1 530f7402f5986556	256MB
12.4.24T4 Technology Train	c7200-adventerprisek9 -mz.124-24.T5	3c4148f62acf56602 ce3b371ebae60c9	256MB
IOS 15.2.4	c7200-adventerprisek9 -mz.152-4.M7.bin		512MB

NM-16ESW AND IOU L2 LIMITATIONS

The GNS3 Dynamips NM-16ESW module operates identically to its real Cisco counterpart. Like that physical module, the Dynamips module does not support all the features of a Cisco Catalyst switch, meaning the only guaranteed way to get full Catalyst switch functionality is to integrate one or more real switches into your GNS3 projects. I list those unsupported features in this appendix, as well as features that IOU L2 images may not support.

If you want to use a particular Catalyst switch feature, check these lists first to see whether you need to use a physical switch.

Unsupported NM-16ESW Features

The NM-16ESW switch module does not support the following features:

- Access Switch Device Manager (SDM) Template
- ACL – Improved Merging Algorithm

- ARP Optimization
- BGP Increased Support of Numbered as-path Access Lists to 500
- BGP Restart Neighbor Session After max-prefix Limit Reached
- BGP Route-Map Continue Support for Outbound Policy
- Clear Counters Per Port
- DHCP Snooping
- DHCP Snooping Counters
- Diagnostics Options on Bootup
- ErrDisable Reactivation Per Port
- ErrDisable Timeout
- EtherChannel
- EtherChannel – Flexible PAgP
- EtherChannel Guard
- Fallback Bridging
- Flex Link Bi-directional Fast Convergence
- Flex Link VLAN Load-Balancing
- Flex Links Interface Preemption
- GOLD – Generic Online Diagnostics
- IEEE 802.1ab, Link Layer Discovery Protocol
- IEEE 802.1s – Multiple Spanning Tree (MST) Standard Compliance
- IEEE 802.1s VLAN Multiple Spanning Trees
- IEEE 802.1t
- IEEE 802.1W Spanning Tree Rapid Reconfiguration
- IEEE 802.1x Auth Fail Open
- IEEE 802.1x Auth Fail VLAN
- IEEE 802.1x VLAN Assignment
- IEEE 802.1x Wake on LAN Support
- IEEE 802.1x Authenticator
- IEEE 802.1x Multi-Domain Authentication
- IEEE 802.1x with Port Security
- IEEE 802.1x RADIUS Accounting
- IEEE 802.3ad Link Aggregation (LACP)
- IEEE 802.3af Power over Ethernet
- IGMP Fast Leave
- IGMP Version 1
- IGRP

- IP Phone Detection Enhancements
- IP Phone Enhancement – PHY Loop Detection
- IPSG (IP Source Guard)
- Jumbo Frames
- L2PT – Layer 2 Protocol Tunneling
- MAC Authentication Bypass
- MLD Snooping
- Multicast EtherChannel Load Balancing
- NAC – L2 IEEE 802.1x
- NAC – L2 IP
- NAC – L2 IP with Auth Fail Open
- Packet-Based Storm Control
- Per Port Per VLAN Policing
- Port Security
- Port Security on Private VLAN Ports
- Private VLANs
- QoS Policy Propagation via Border Gateway Protocol (QPPB)
- Rapid-Per-VLAN-Spanning Tree (Rapid-PVST)
- Reduced MAC Address Usage
- Remote SPAN (RSPAN)
- Smart Port
- Spanning Tree Protocol (STP) – Loop Guard
- Spanning Tree Protocol (STP) – PortFast BPDU Filtering
- Spanning Tree Protocol (STP) – PortFast Support for Trunks
- Spanning Tree Protocol (STP) – Root Guard
- Spanning Tree Protocol (STP) – Uplink Load Balancing
- SRR (Shaped Round Robin)
- Standby Supervisor Port Usage
- STP Syslog Messages
- Switching Database Manager (SDM)
- Trunk Failover
- Trusted Boundary (extended trust for CDP devices)
- Unicast MAC Filtering
- UniDirectional Link Detection (UDLD)
- VLAN Access Control List (VACL)
- VLAN Aware Port Security
- Weighted Tail Drop (WTD)

Unsupported Features in Cisco IOU L2 Images

IOU is said to support roughly 90 percent of the capabilities of an actual Cisco Catalyst switch. The following features are probably unsupported by IOU L2 images. However, because Cisco is responsible for updating IOU images, your mileage may vary.

- DHCP snooping
- ISL trunks
- L3 Etherchannel
- MLS QoS
- Port-security
- Private VLAN
- QinQ
- SPAN/RSPAN/ERSPAN
- UDLD
- Voice VLANs

GLOSSARY

The following is a glossary of acronyms used throughout the book.

APT (Advanced Package Tool) A command-line tool for handling packages on Debian-based Linux computers.

ARP (Address Resolution Protocol) A protocol used to map network layer addresses to link layer addresses. Often used for IP to MAC address resolution.

AS (autonomous system) A group of routers that share network prefixes under the administrative control of a single organization.

ASA (adaptive security appliance) A Cisco firewall device.

ASDM (Adaptive Security Device Manager) Cisco software used to manage and monitor Cisco security devices.

ASIC (application-specific integrated circuit) A specialized circuit that is often proprietary of a particular vendor.

ATM (Asynchronous Transfer Mode) A technology designed for the transfer of voice, video, and data through public and private networks. Largely replaced by MPLS.

BGP (Border Gateway Protocol) The routing protocol of the Internet. BGP uses autonomous systems to exchange route information.

BSD (Berkeley Software Distribution) A Unix operating system that was developed in Berkeley, California.

CCIE (Cisco Certified Internetwork Expert) The expert level of certification from Cisco Systems.

CCNA (Cisco Certified Network Associate) The associate level certification from Cisco Systems.

CCNP (Cisco Certified Network Professional) The professional level certification from Cisco Systems.

CCP (Cisco Configuration Professional) Software used to manage and monitor Cisco routers.

CDP (Cisco Discovery Protocol) A Cisco proprietary protocol used to collect hardware and configuration information from directly connected Cisco devices on a network.

CIDR (Classless Inter-Domain Routing) A shorthand method of assigning a network mask to an IP address. CIDR uses a slash, followed by the number of binary bits for the mask portion of an IP address; for example, 192.168.1.1 255.255.255.0 is written as 192.168.1.1 /24 in CIDR notation.

CPU (central processing unit) The circuitry in a computer that's responsible for executing code and controlling input/output operations.

DHCP (Dynamic Host Configuration Protocol) A protocol used for dynamically applying IP addresses and other network settings to a host.

DLCI (data link connection identifier) A link-local virtual circuit identifier used to assign frames to a PVC or SVC.

DNS (Domain Name System) A hierarchy of database servers that map Internet hostnames to IP addresses.

EIGRP (Enhanced Interior Gateway Routing Protocol) A Cisco proprietary advanced distance-vector routing protocol.

FTP (File Transfer Protocol) A protocol used to transfer files from one host to another using TCP/IP. Also the name of the program that allows a user to transfer files to and from a remote host.

GLBP (Gateway Load Balancing Protocol) A Cisco proprietary redundant router protocol that supports load-balancing.

HSRP (Hot Standby Routing Protocol) A Cisco proprietary redundant router protocol that provides automatic router failover at a default gateway.

IDS/IPS (Intrusion Detection System/Intrusion Prevention System) A device that monitors network activities for malicious code, usually working in conjunction with a firewall. Unwanted activities trigger alarms that are reported to a system administrator.

I/O (input/output) Used to describe any program, operation, or device that transfers data to or from a computer or device.

IOL (IOS on Linux) Software that runs on Linux and emulates the features of a Cisco IOS router or switch.

IOS (Internetwork Operating System) Cisco's primary router and switch operating system.

IOU (IOS on Unix) Software that runs on Linux/Unix and emulates the features of a Cisco IOS router or switch.

IP (Internet Protocol) The network layer protocol in the TCP/IP stack that provides routing and logical addressing.

IPv4 (Internet Protocol version 4) The fourth version of the IP. IPv4 uses a 32-bit address scheme.

IPv6 (Internet Protocol version 6) The sixth version of the IP. IPv6 uses a 128-bit address scheme.

ISL (Inter-Switch Link) A Cisco proprietary VLAN trunking protocol, replaced by 802.1Q on modern networks.

ISP (Internet service provider) A company that provides consumers and businesses with access to the Internet.

ISR (integrated service router) A Cisco router model used in small businesses or home offices, usually connected to the Internet using DSL or cable modems. ISR hardware is often designed using application-specific integrated circuits.

JNCIA (Juniper Networks Certified Associate) The Juniper entry-level associate certification for Junos OS.

LAN (local area network) A network that connects computers and peripherals within a small geographic area, such as a single building or a group of buildings.

LMI (logical management interface) A signaling standard used between routers and Frame Relay switches.

MAC (media access control) A unique identifier that's written into the firmware of a network Ethernet card. MAC addresses are used for communication on a physical network segment.

MPLS (Multiprotocol Label Switching) A packet-forwarding technology that uses labels to make data forwarding decisions. Replaces ATM and Frame Relay on modern networks.

MTU (maximum transmission unit) The maximum frame size of a protocol data unit. The Ethernet default frame size is 1500 bytes, but it can be reduced or increased depending on your Ethernet hardware and drivers.

NAT (network address translation) A method of using a single IP address on an edge router or firewall so that devices on the network behind the edge device can access networks (like the Internet) beyond the edge using a single IP address. NAT is responsible for rewriting datagram headers to keep track of packets between the edge device and the inside hosts.

NIO (Network Input/Output) Used to describe any program, operation, or device that transfers data to or from a computer or device over a network.

NPE (Network Processing Engine) A Cisco chassis card that provides additional functionality to some Cisco router models, such as the c7200.

NVRAM (non-volatile random access memory) A type of memory that retains its contents when power is turned off.

OS (operating system) Manages a computer's memory, processes, and all of its software and hardware.

OSPF (Open Shortest Path First) An interior gateway protocol that uses a link-state database and a shortest path first (SPF) algorithm to calculate the best routes to reach a network.

OVA (Open Virtual Appliance) A standard file format used for packaging and distributing virtual appliances that can be run using virtual machine software, such as VirtualBox and VMware.

POS (Packet over SONET) A communications protocol used for transmitting Point-to-Point Protocol (PPP) packets over SONET.

PVC (permanent virtual circuit) A permanent connection that's established between two or more nodes in a Frame Relay or ATM network.

QEMU (Quick Emulator) An open source machine emulator and virtualizer.

RAM (random access memory) A type of memory that does not retain its contents when power is turned off.

RIP (Routing Information Protocol) A distance vector protocol that primarily uses hop count as a metric for choosing the best route to remote networks. Often referred to as routing by rumor.

SSH (Secure Shell) Used for securely logging into a remote machine and executing commands on a remote machine.

SONET (Synchronous Optical Network) A protocol used to synchronously transfer data over fiber-optic networks.

SVC (switched virtual circuit) A dynamic connection that's established between two or more nodes in a Frame Relay or ATM network.

TAR (Tape Archive) files Creates and manipulates streaming archive files.

TCP (Transmission Control Protocol) The connection-oriented transport layer of the TCP/IP stack. TCP is responsible for creating reliable end-to-end connections.

TFTP (Trivial File Transfer Protocol) TFTP allows users to transfer files to and from a remote machine using no authentication or error correction.

UDP (User Datagram Protocol) A connectionless transport layer protocol that does not use handshaking. UDP exchanges datagrams without acknowledgments.

VIRL (Virtual Internet Routing Lab) Cisco's network simulation platform that includes virtual machines running Cisco's core network operating systems.

VLAN (virtual local area network) A mechanism for partitioning a layer-2 network into separate broadcast domains.

VM (virtual machine) A program that emulates specific hardware and allows you to install and run operating systems designed for that hardware.

VMDK (virtual machine disk) A virtual hard disk image file that is often used by virtual machine software, such as VMware, VirtualBox, and QEMU.

VPCS (Virtual PC Simulator) A simple program that simulates the basic networking features and commands of a PC.

VPN (virtual private network) A group of security protocols that allow two devices to share encrypted information over a public network (like the Internet).

VPNC (Virtual Private Network Connection) A software client for Cisco VPN3000 Concentrator, IOS devices, and PIX devices.

VRRP (Virtual Router Redundancy Protocol) An open standard redundant router protocol that provides automatic router failover at a default gateway.

WAN (wide area networks) A network that covers a wide geographic range, often made up of multiple networks connected using one or more VPNs.

WIC (WAN interface card) A Cisco proprietary interface card that often provides serial port interfaces to a router.

INDEX

Numbers and Symbols

A

B

C

D

E

F

G

H

I

J

K

L

M

N

O

P

Q

R

S

T

U

V

W

X

Z

The Book of GNS3 is set in New Baskerville, Futura, Dogma, and TheSansMono Condensed. The book was printed and bound by Lake Book Manufacturing in Melrose Park, Illinois. The paper is 60# Husky Opaque Offset, which is certified by the Sustainable Forestry Initiative (SFI).

The book uses a layflat binding, in which the pages are bound together with a cold-set, flexible glue, and the first and last pages of the resulting book block are attached to the cover. The cover is not actually glued to the book's spine, and when open, the book lies flat and the spine doesn't crack.

RESOURCES

Visit *http://nostarch.com/gns3/* for resources, errata, and more information.

More no-nonsense books from  **NO STARCH PRESS**

THE BOOK OF PF, 3RD EDITION
A No-Nonsense Guide to the OpenBSD Firewall
by PETER N.M. HANSTEEN
OCTOBER 2014, 248 PP., $34.95
ISBN 978-1-59327-589-1

PRACTICAL PACKET ANALYSIS, 2ND EDITION
Using Wireshark to Solve Real-World Network Problems
by CHRIS SANDERS
JULY 2011, 280 PP., $49.95
ISBN 978-1-59327-266-1

THE PRACTICE OF NETWORK SECURITY MONITORING
Understanding Incident Detection and Response
by RICHARD BEJTLICH
JULY 2013, 376 PP., $49.95
ISBN 978-1-59327-509-9

THE TCP/IP GUIDE
A Comprehensive, Illustrated Internet Protocols Reference
by CHARLES M. KOZIEROK
OCTOBER 2005, 1616 PP., $99.95
ISBN 978-159327-047-6
hardcover

THE LINUX COMMAND LINE
A Complete Introduction
by WILLIAM E. SHOTTS, JR.
JANUARY 2012, 480 PP., $39.95
ISBN 978-1-59327-389-7

BLACK HAT PYTHON
Python Programming for Hackers and Pentesters
by JUSTIN SEITZ
DCEMBER 2014, 192 PP., $34.95
ISBN 978-1-59327-590-7

PHONE:
800.420.7240 OR
415.863.9900

EMAIL:
SALES@NOSTARCH.COM

WEB:
WWW.NOSTARCH.COM